TRENDS IN WORLD SOCIAL DEVELOPMENT

TRENDS IN WORLD SOCIAL DEVELOPMENT

THE SOCIAL PROGRESS OF NATIONS, 1970–1987

Richard J. Estes

New York
Westport, Connecticut
London

Library of Congress Cataloging-in-Publication Data

Estes, Richard J.
    Trends in world social development : the social progress of
nations, 1970–1987 / Richard J. Estes.
        p. cm.
    Bibliography: p.
    ISBN 0–275–92613–3 (alk. paper)
    1. Social history—1970– 2. Progress. 3. Social indicators.
4. Social status—Developing countries.   I. Title.
HN17.5.E82   1988
303.4′4—dc19   87–36132

Library of Congress Catalog Card Number: 87–36132

ISBN: 0–275–92613–3

First published in 1988

Praeger Publishers, One Madison Avenue, New York, NY 10010
A division of Greenwood Press, Inc.

Printed in the United States of America

The paper used in this book complies with the
Permanent Paper Standard issued by the National
Information Standards Organization (Z39.48–1984).

10 9 8 7 6 5 4 3 2 1

For the Children of War
whose pain and suffering
touch all of our lives

CONTENTS

TABLES

INTRODUCTION

Many hundreds of millions of people in the poorer countries are preoccupied solely with survival and elementary needs. For them work is frequently not available or, when it is, pay is very low and conditions often barely tolerable. Homes are constructed of impermanent materials and have neither piped water nor sanitation. Electricity is a luxury. Health services are thinly spread and in rural areas only rarely within walking distance. Primary schools, where they exist, may be free and not too far away, but children are needed for work and cannot be easily spared for schooling. Permanent insecurity is the condition of the poor. There are no public systems of social security in the event of unemployment, sickness or death of a wage-earner in the family. Flood, drought or disease affecting people or livestock can destroy livelihoods without hope of compensation. . . .

The poorest of the poor in the world will remain for some time to come outside the reach of normal trade and communications. The combination of malnutrition, illiteracy, disease, high birth rates, underemployment and low income closes off the avenues of escape; and while other groups are increasingly vocal, the poor and illiterate are usually and conveniently silent. It is a condition of life so limited as to be, in the words of the President of the World Bank, 'below any rational definition of human decency.'

Independent Commission on International Development Issues,
North South: A Program for Survival, pp. 49–50

One of the great dilemmas confronting people everywhere concerns the gap in the social development that continues to exist between the richest and poorest nations. For centuries this gap has steadily widened, and in the process, has doomed new generations of people to levels of deprivation that cannot be imagined by people living in more affluent countries. These trends have continued despite historically unparalleled efforts on the part of the international community to help impoverished nations achieve a degree of social parity with economically advanced countries. The persistence of the gap also threatens the social and political security of rich and poor nations alike. Indeed, the disparities represented by this gap in development contribute significantly to the international tensions and regional conflicts that result each year in the deaths of hundreds of thousands of persons and threaten the security of people worldwide.

The research described in this volume was undertaken for the purpose of better understanding the myriad social, economic, and political factors that sustain social inequality. The approach adopted has drawn heavily on the use of international social indicators to document changes in the "level of living" of people inhabiting the world's most populous nations. The changing social status of developing and "least developing" countries, however, receives special attention throughout the book. More particularly, the volume examines the extent of international progress in both promoting *and achieving* a more secure "social safety net" for the world's rapidly increasing population.

Elements of the international social safety net scrutinized in this book include changes in the extent of national and international progress in providing improved health services, in ensuring increased access to at least basic education, in controlling the rate of population growth, in reducing levels of adult illiteracy, in increasing life expectancy, and in promoting increased national respect for and observance of the internationally guaranteed human rights and freedoms of individual citizens. The volume also examines the impact of racial, religious, ethnic, and linguistic differences on development trends within nations. It reports, too, on international progress in improving the legal status of women and children, in reducing the proportion of national wealth allocated to defense and related military purposes, as well as in establishing legally protected opportunities for individual citizens to participate regularly in the political decisions of their societies.

Each of these objectives of social development represents a separate strand of the international social safety net. Considered together they constitute the "social agenda" on which governments, specialists in development, international organizations, private citizens, and others have been working since at least the end of World War II. These strands also form a new international social order that must come into being if nations and people are to achieve social and economic parity.

The substance of this volume will be of interest to development specialists, scholars, researchers, officials in government ministries, other government leaders, students, as well as citizens who are concerned with the current world social situation. In a very real way, and in considerable detail, this volume documents international shifts in the capacity of nations to provide more adequately for the basic social and material needs of their populations.

The work is organized into six chapters. Chapter 1 contains a readable summary of the study's methodology.[1] The chapter also contains a listing of the 124 countries included in the analysis and explains the conceptual basis for classifying these countries into the study's four socioeconomic groupings. The chapter also states the principal operating assumptions that were used throughout all phases of the investigation. Interested readers are referred to Appendix B, which reports the sources, operational definitions, and inherent limitations of each of the study's 36 social indicators; the appendix also identifies those international organizations, institutions, and independent scholars from which comparative social welfare data were collected. Appendix C contains detailed information—including the statistical formulae and procedures—that were used to construct the study's ten subindexes. Factor analytic scores and a matrix of correlation coefficients for the study's indexes are reported in the appendix.

Chapters 2 and 3 report changes in global patterns of social provision for the 14-year period 1970–1983. Chapter 2 summarizes the changes for the world as a whole; Chapter 3 reports development trends for major regional groupings of nations. The majority of the tables presented in these two chapters report development trends for each of the study's four socioeconomic groupings, i.e., for the developed market economy nations (DMEs) of "the West," for the eastern trading area nations (ETAs) of Eastern Europe, for the developing nations (DCs) of Asia, Africa, and Latin America, and for the group of 25 least developing countries (LDCs) that have been singled out by the United Nations for special international development assistance. These chapters also report subindex score changes for the study's three baseline time periods, i.e., 1970, 1980, and 1983.

Chapter 4 reports changes over time in "adequacy of social provision" for each of the 124 nations included in the analysis. Index, subindex, and percentage change scores for selected countries, and for socioeconomic groupings are separately reported in this chapter. Chapter 4 also identifies those countries with the "most favorable" and "least favorable" index scores at the three time periods. Nations are also identified in which significant 14-year advances and deteriorations occurred in level of attained social development. World "social leaders" and "socially least developing" countries, again for the three time periods, are also identified.

Of special interest to many readers, Chapter 4 also contains comparative social rankings for individual countries in relation to earlier levels of development as well as in comparison with those attained by all other nations at the same time intervals. These comparisons have been reported extensively by international news media and have been the subject of considerable debate. Because of the extensive nature of the data, detailed index and subindex data for individual countries are reported separately in Appendix A. This appendix also contains 1983 national rankings for all 124 nations on each of the study's ten subindexes.

Essentially non-quantitative in nature, Chapters 5 and 6 focus on what I regard as the most serious continuing threats to future progress in global development: militarism, war, and the spread of nuclear weapons; uncontrolled population growth; world hunger, malnutrition, and famine; the international debt crisis; the relative neglect of the contribution of women in development; the crisis in financing welfare programs and services; and the global AIDS (Acquired Immune Deficiency Syndrome) epidemic. Alternative solutions to resolving each of these global social problems are discussed in Chapter 5.

Finally, the volume contains a selected bibliography of supplemental reading materials that relate to social development broadly. The bibliography also contains many readings concerning the three objectives of international development on which people everywhere in the world agree: war prevention, improved economic security, and enhanced international social justice.

NOTE

1. For a complete conceptual and methodological history of this research the reader is referred to Richard J. Estes, *The Social Progress of Nations* (New York: Praeger Publishers, 1984), especially Chapters 1 and 2.

ACKNOWLEDGMENTS

An international research project of the magnitude described in this volume requires the support and cooperation of many individuals and institutions. Since beginning this work in 1974 I have benefited considerably from the help of many persons. In this third report I want to especially thank Mary Boes, Amy Cumming, Eve Collelo, and Sally Walker for their research assistance. Without their painstaking attention to detail the data collection phase of the study could not have been completed on a timely basis. Gail Cairns of the Columbia University Development Law and Policy Program provided updated comparative data on the legal status of women around the world. Lois Copeland, Acting Director of the International Activities and Studies Staff of the Social Security Administration in Washington, made available prepublication information concerning changes in patterns of formal social security provision for more than a dozen countries.

Funding in partial support of this project was received from the Provost's Committee on Contacts with the People's Republic of China, the International Programs Office, the Public Policy Initiatives Fund, and the Research Foundation, all of the University of Pennsylvania. Thanks to Eliot Stellar, Barry Cooperman, Joyce Randolph, and Jeffrey Sheehan for their participation in these funding decisions and for the encouragement that their support provided. Michael J. Austin, Dean of the School of Social Work, is acknowledged for administrative support in providing the critically needed time and opportunity to complete this research.

Nelson Chow of the University of Hong Kong, John Dixon of the Management and Policies Study Center in Canberra, Australia, James

Midgley of Louisiana State University, Daniel Sanders of the University of Illinois at Urbana, and Arthur Schwartz of the University of Maryland are deeply thanked for their much appreciated counsel and encouragement during especially difficult stages of the research effort. Andrew Baggaley of the University of Pennsylvania and Jeffrey Green of Hay Associates in Philadelphia are thanked for their statistical consultations.

Field research in China would not have been possible without the help of Ma Jing Liang and Zhu Rong Lin of the Shanghai Division of the Center for Economical, Technical and Social Development of the State Council of the PRC. Pan Jieren and Wu Jia Zhen of the Management School of Shanghai Jiao Tong University are thanked for their many efforts on behalf of the project. Lu Chao-Quing, Deputy Director of the Shanghai Civil Affairs Bureau, and Professor "Irving" Y. Y. Lin of the Shanghai Academy of Social Sciences are acknowledged for introducing me to the philosophical underpinnings of social welfare in contemporary China. I thank these colleagues for their splendid cooperation with the project's multiple research objectives and for their tireless commitment to resolving cross-cultural difficulties that otherwise would have made completion of the China portion of the research impossible.

Daniel Wagner of the University of Pennsylvania and Philix Aragon of the U. S. Information Agency made possible my participation in field research and lectures in North Africa. Bent Skou and Hans Grunnet of the Royal Danish Foreign Ministry, Marjaliisa Kaupinnen of the National Social Welfare Board of Finland, and Harald Swedner of the University of Gothenburg in Sweden contributed substantially to my field research and professional contacts in Europe. I would like to thank Armaity Desai and K. S. Mandal of the Tata Institute of Social Sciences and Peter Lee of Tunghai University for their facilitation of my field work in India and Taiwan, respectively.

Bonnie Clause reviewed and edited substantial portions of several versions of the manuscript. As always, I am grateful to her for many valuable suggestions that helped to communicate accurately and simply the study's sometimes obtuse findings.

Finally, I want to acknowledge with deep appreciation my editors at Praeger, Alison Bricken and Lauren Pera. Their patience in awaiting the arrival of the final version of the manuscript and careful attention to editorial and production details made the whole task much easier.

TRENDS IN
WORLD SOCIAL
DEVELOPMENT

1

METHODOLOGY

The present study is the third in a series that seeks to measure changes *over time* in the ability of nations to provide for the basic social and material needs of their populations. The purpose of these studies is threefold: (1) to identify significant changes in "adequacy of social provision" occurring throughout the world; (2) using objective international social indicators, to assess national and international progress in providing more adequately for the basic social and material needs of the world's rapidly increasing population; and (3) to provide the basis for redirecting increasingly scarce international development assistance resources to those nations and world regions most in need of assistance.

The study utilizes a revised version of the author's "index of social progress" (ISP).[1] In its present form, as summarized in Table 1.1, the ISP83 consists of 36 social indicators divided into ten subindexes: education, health status, women's status, defense effort, economic, demographic, geographic, political participation, cultural diversity, and welfare effort. Each of the ISP indicators represents a major arena of social development activity and is considered a valid indicator of the status of human welfare nationally and internationally.[2] Appendix B contains detailed information concerning the operational definitions and data sources used for collecting nation-specific statistics for each of the ISP indicators.

The ISP83 differs from the original ISP in that the current index contains fewer items and one less subindex. The political stability subindex, for example, was dropped due to the unavailability of reliable information. The women's status subindex has been revised to reflect three of the most important priorities established by the United Nations for

Table 1.1
Index of Social Progress (ISP83) Indicators by Subindex (36 indicators, 10 subindexes)

I. EDUCATION SUBINDEX

   School Enrollment Ratio, First Level (+)

   Pupil-Teacher Ratio, First Level (-)

   Percent Adult Illiteracy (-)

   Percent GNP in Education (+)

II. HEALTH STATUS SUBINDEX

   Male Life Expectancy at 1 Year (+)

   Rate of Infant Mortality Per 1000 Liveborn (-)

   Population in Thousands Per Physician (-)

   Per Capita Daily Calorie Supply as % of Daily Requirement (+)

III. WOMEN STATUS SUBINDEX

   Percent Age Eligible Girls Attending First Level Schools (+)

   Percent Adult Female Illiteracy (-)

   Age Constitutional Document Affecting Legal Rights of Women (+)

VI. DEMOGRAPHY SUBINDEX

   Total Population (Millions) (-)

   Crude Birth Rate Per 1000 Population (-)

   Crude Death Rate Per 1000 Population (-)

   Rate of Population Increase (-)

   Percent of Population Under 15 Years (-)

VII. GEOGRAPHY SUBINDEX*

   Percent Arable Land Mass (+)

   Natural Disaster Vulnerability Index (-)

   Average Annual Deaths From Natural Disasters Per Million Pop. (-)

VIII. POLITICAL PARTICIPATION SUBINDEX

   Violations of Political Rights Index (-)

   Violations of Civil Liberties Index (-)

   Composite Violations of Human Freedoms Index (-)

2

IV. DEFENSE EFFORT SUBINDEX

Military Expenditures as Percent of GNP (-)

V. ECONOMIC SUBINDEX

Per Capita Gross National Product (+)

GNP Per Capita Annual Growth Rate (+)

Average Annual Rate of Inflation (-)

Per Capita Food Production Index (+)

External Public Debt as Percent of GNP (-)

IX. CULTURAL DIVERSITY SUBINDEX‡

Largest Percent Sharing Same Mother Tongue (+)

Largest Percent Sharing Same Basic Religious Beliefs (+)

Largest Percent Sharing Same or Similar Racial/Ethnic Origins (+)

X. WELFARE EFFORT SUBINDEX

Years Since First Law--Old Age, Invalidity, Death (+)

Years Since First Law--Sickness & Maternity (+)

Years Since First Law--Work Injury (+)

Years Since First Law--Unemployment (+)

Years Since First Law--Family Allowances (+)

‡These indicators are used as statistical constants for all years.

3

the International Decade on Women (1975–1985): reduced adult female illiteracy; increased access to primary education for girls; and "constitutional protection" for the legal rights of women, equivalent to that found for men.[3]

The ISP83 still does *not* reflect changes in some sectors of development, however, that specialists recognize to be equally valid indicators of adequate social provision (e.g., access to safe water, national criminality patterns, the incidence of personal violence, prevalence of mental illnesses, suicide and homicide rates, the maldistribution of wealth, and so on). Reliable comparative data for these indicators of "human welfare" either do not exist for all of the countries included in the present analysis, or reasonable approximations for them could not be inferred from available data. Consequently, the ISP, which seeks to reflect the broadest possible range of social development activity, will continue to be revised in future studies to include other relevant and desirable indicators as reliable data become available.

Further, the reader is cautioned against thinking of the ISP as a measure of "quality of life," that is, as a tool that attempts to assess personal happiness, satisfaction with life, or the degree of personal "fulfillment" experienced by individuals living in particular nations. Rather, the ISP measures the changing capacity of nations to provide for the basic social and material needs of their populations as a whole, not the ability of nations to secure varying levels of life satisfaction for individuals residing within their borders. Consequently, the ISP should be regarded as a quantitative measure of *national* human welfare, and is *not* to be construed as a tool that can be used to assess directly varying degrees of individual personal fulfillment.[4]

THE INDEX OF SOCIAL PROGRESS (ISP83)

Statistically weighted and unweighted versions of the Index of Social Progress are reported in all of the study's major tables. For example, unweighted index and subindex scores are presented in which each of the 36 indicators is assigned an equal statistical weight of 1. In effect, this statistical approach assumes that each of the ISP indicators is of equal importance to all other indicators in describing levels of national social provision at different times. The unweighted version of the index thus does not distinguish between the *perceived* importance of political or economic factors in one society relative to the *perceived* importance of food, literacy, demographic trends, and similar development issues, either in the same society or within other nations. Nor does the unweighted ISP suggest that one or another form of political, social, or economic organization is superior to all other approaches. Rather, presentation of unweighted index and subindex scores makes it possible for individual readers to assign their own value or priority systems to the various composite scores (i.e., the *perceived* importance of an adequate food supply is likely to be higher in nations with a food shortage, whereas issues of "personal freedom" are likely to be assigned significantly greater importance in nations where food is plentiful).[5]

Unweighted ISP and component subindex scores are reported in each of the major tables. The computational steps used to construct these scores are described fully in steps 1 through 5 of Appendix C. Summary index and subindex scores—including measures of central tendency and dispersion—are reported in Table C.6. Table C.7 contains a matrix of index and subindex correlation coefficients. Throughout the appendix, the derivation of subindex and index scores for the People's Republic of China (PRC), the world's largest developing country, is used to illustrate the study's computational procedures.

THE WEIGHTED INDEX OF SOCIAL PROGRESS (WISP)

The analysis also reports weighted scores for the Index of Social Progress. Referred to as WISP scores, these numbers reflect the *relative*, but differing, contribution of each of the 10 subindexes to composite ISP scores. In this way, WISP scores for individual nations reflect the great diversity of ways in which individual nations have been able to realize the social development successes (and failures) reflected on the ISP and its component indexes.

Briefly, WISP scores were constructed using a system of statistical weights derived through a varimax factor analysis of the 10 unweighted subindexes of the ISP.[6] As described in steps 6a through 6c of Appendix C, the resulting statistical weights were then applied to the standardized subindex scores for each nation; subsequently, the weighted subindex scores were totaled to form WISP scores. This process was repeated for each set of standardized subindex scores for the study's three time periods (i.e., 1970, 1980, and 1983).

In addition to providing a more precise estimate of national social development gains and failures over time, the use of WISP scores also results in the realignment in the comparative development rankings of countries that otherwise would not have occurred. Using only ISP scores, for example, the overall adequacy of social provision observed for the United States in 1983 was ranked only 27 out of 124 nations; using the WISP measure, the nation's comparative ranking was raiseed to 18. Conversely, the overall 1983 ranking of the Dominican Republic dropped from 36 on the ISP to 45 on the WISP. For the majority of nations, however, their comparative rankings on both indexes tended to remain more or less comparable.

COUNTRY SELECTION

The present study reports social development patterns for the majority of the world's 154 nations. To be included in the analysis the countries selected had to meet the following four criteria:

1. a 1980 population base of at least 1 million persons;
2. political sovereignty;
3. membership in the United Nations since at least 1980; and,
4. data missing for no more than four of the 36 indicators.

Countries with missing data for four or fewer of the ISP indicators were retained in the analysis only if reasonable estimates of the missing information could be derived either from local embassies or on the basis of patterns found in other nations of the region that shared more or less the same level of socioeconomic development. In situations where reasonable estimates of missing data could not be derived, nations were excluded from the analysis. Trust territories (such as the Pacific nations in Micronesia and Melanesia, even though in transition to independence), city-states (East and West Berlin), and politically dependent territories (e.g., Puerto Rico) were excluded from the analysis as well. Table 1.2 identifies the 124 nations selected for inclusion in the study. The table groups these nations by continent and geographic subgroupings and identifies those 17 nations for which only 1980 and 1983 comparative data could be obtained.

SOCIOECONOMIC DEVELOPMENT GROUPINGS

The present study utilizes the same system of socioeconomic groupings for countries as used in earlier reports.[7] In essence this approach, which mirrors that adopted by the United Nations' Economic and Social Council (ECOSOC),[8] groups nations on the basis of seven criteria:

1. Per capita gross domestic product (GDP)
2. Percentage population living in rural areas
3. Percentage adult illiteracy
4. Dominant type of economic system
5. Percentage GDP in manufacturing
6. Degree of centralized versus decentralized social and economic planning
7. Import and export patterns

Using these criteria, four socioeconomic development groupings emerge.

Developed Market Economy Nations

Developed market economy nations (DMEs) consist of Western-oriented democracies that are characterized by open-market economic systems. The majority of these nations are located in Europe and North America; however, the grouping also includes Japan and Israel as well as Australia and New Zealand. Average 1983 per capita GNP for DME nations exceeded U.S. $8,850.[9]

Eastern Trading Area

The Eastern trading area (ETA) consists of the Soviet Union and its Eastern European allies (with the exception of Yugoslavia, which is classified as a DME nation). The ETA grouping is basically a closed economic system, characterized by strong central planning and economic controls. Per capita GNP levels for ETA nations averaged $3,894 in 1983.

Developing Countries

Developing countries (DCs) consist of middle-income nations with a per capita gross national product (GNP) averaging $1,600 in 1983. The majority of these nations are located in Africa, Latin America, the Caribbean, and Asia. Approximately 70 percent of the populations of developing countries live in rural areas. Adult illiteracy in DCs averaged 34 percent in 1983.

Least Developing Countries

Often referred to as the "poorest of the poor" or as the "fourth world," the majority of least developing countries (LDCs) are located in Africa and Asia. The economies of these mostly young countries tend to be of a mixed nature, that is, they include elements of both open and centrally planned systems. Per capita GNP for the LDCs averaged $260 in 1983. Illiteracy in LDCs averaged in excess of 70 percent of the adult population aged 15 years or older in 1983. Countries designated by the United Nations as LDCs are targeted for priority international development assistance.[10]

Table 1.3 groups the 124 nations included in the present study by socioeconomic development grouping and by geographic location. As reported in the table, the study includes 24 developed market economy nations (DMEs), 8 eastern trading area nations (ETAs), 67 developing countries (DCs), and 25 least developing countries (LDCs).

Table 1.4 reports the population distribution for the four socioeconomic groupings. Of interest to most readers will be the fact that the

Table 1.2
Nations Grouped by Continent and Geographic Subregion ($n = 124$)

AFRICA (N=40)

Western Africa (N = 13)
- Benin‡
- Burkina-Faso†
- Ghana
- Guinea‡
- Ivory Coast
- Liberia
- Mali‡
- Mauritania
- Niger†
- Nigeria
- Senegal
- Sierra Leone‡
- Togo‡

Eastern Africa (N = 13)
- Burundi‡
- Ethiopia‡
- Kenya
- Madagascar
- Malawi‡
- ‡Mozambique
- ‡Mauritius
- Rwanda‡
- Somalia‡
- Uganda‡
- Tanzania‡
- Zambia
- Zimbabwe

NORTH AMERICA (N=2)
- Canada
- United States

LATIN AMERICA (N=22)

Tropical So. America (N=6)
- Bolivia
- Brazil
- Columbia
- Ecuador
- Peru
- Venezuela

Middle America (N=7)
- Costa Rica
- El Salvador
- Guatemala
- Honduras
- Mexico
- Nicaragua
- Panama

Temperate So. America (N=4)
- Argentina
- Chile
- Paraguay
- Uruguay

ASIA (N=32)

East Asia (N = 3)
- ‡Korea, Democratic (North)
- Korea, Republic (South)
- ‡Taiwan

Mainland East Asia (N = 3)
- ‡Hong Kong
- ‡China
- ‡Mongolia

Other East Asia (N = 1)
- Japan

Middle South Asia (N = 7)
- ‡Afghanistan‡
- ‡Bangladesh‡
- India
- Iran
- Nepal‡
- Pakistan
- Sri Lanka

Eastern South Asia (N = 9)
- Burma
- Kampuchea
- Indonesia
- ‡Lao, PDR‡
- Malaysia
- Philippines

EUROPE (N=24)

Western Europe (N = 6)
- Austria
- Belgium
- France
- Germany
- Netherlands
- Switzerland

Southern Europe (N = 6)
- Albania
- Greece
- Italy
- Portugal
- Spain
- Yugoslavia

Eastern Europe (N = 6)
- Bulgaria
- Czechoslovakia
- ‡Germany, Democratic
- Hungary
- Poland
- Romania

Northern Europe (N = 6)
- Denmark
- Finland
- Ireland
- Norway

Northern Africa (N = 6)
  Algeria
  Egypt
  Libya
  Morocco
  Sudan*
  Tunisia

Middle Africa (N = 6)
  #Angola
  Cameroon
  Central African Republic*
  #Congo
  Chad*
  Zaire

Southern Africa (N = 2)
  South Africa
  #Lesotho*

Caribbean (N = 5)
  Cuba
  Dominican Republic
  Haiti*
  Jamaica
  Trinidad and Tobago

UNION OF SOVIET
SOCIALIST REPUBLICS (N=1)

OCEANIA (N=3)
  Australia
  New Zealand
  #Papua-New Guinea

Singapore
Thailand
Vietnam

Western South Asia (N=9)
  Iraq
  Israel
  Jordan
  Lebanon
  #Saudia Arabia
  Syria
  Turkey
  #Yemen, Arab Rep.*
  Yemen, PDR*

Sweden
United Kingdom

* Indicates nations officially designated by the United Nations as "Least Developing Countries" (LDCs).
# Only 1980 and 1983 data are used for these countries; all others cover 14 year period 1970-1983.

Table 1.3
Country List by Continent and Economic Development Grouping ($n = 124$)

CONTINENT	DEVELOPED MARKET ECONOMIES (N = 24)	EASTERN TRADING AREA (N = 8)	DEVELOPING COUNTRIES EXCLUDING LEAST DEVELOPING COUNTRIES (N=67)	LEAST DEVELOPING COUNTRIES (N = 25)
AFRICA (N = 40)	South Africa		Algeria, Angola, Cameroon, Congo, Egypt, Ghana, Ivory Coast, Kenya, Liberia, Libya, Madagascar, Mauritania, Mauritius, Morocco, Mozambique, Nigeria, Senegal, Tunisia, Zambia, Zaire, Zimbabwe	Benin, Burkina-Faso, Burundi, Chad, Central African Republic, Ethiopia, Guinea, Lesotho, Malawi, Mali, Niger, Rwanda, Sierra Leone, Somalia, Sudan, Togo, Uganda, Tanzania
EUROPE (N = 25)	Austria, Belgium, Denmark, Finland, France, West Germany, Greece, Ireland, Italy, Netherlands, Norway, Portugal, Spain, Sweden, Switzerland, U.K., Yugoslavia	Albania, Bulgaria, Czechoslovakia, Germany, Dem., Hungary, Poland, Romania, U.S.S.R.		
NORTH AMERICA (N=2)	Canada, United States			

LATIN AMERICA (N = 17)

Argentina	Honduras	
Bolivia	Mexico	
Brazil	Nicaragua	
Chile	Panama	
Columbia	Paraguay	
Costa Rica	Peru	
Ecuador	Uruguay	
El Salvador	Venezuela	
Guatemala		

CARIBBEAN (N = 5)

Cuba	Jamaica	Haiti
Dominican Republic	Trinidad Tobago	

OCEANIA (N=3)

Australia	New Zealand	
Papua-New Guinea		

ASIA (N = 32)

Israel	Malaysia	Afghanistan
Japan	Mongolia	Bangladesh
Burma	Pakistan	Laos, PDR
China	Philippines	Nepal
Hong Kong	Saudi Arabi	Yemen, Arab Republic
India	Singapore	Yemen, PDR
Indonesia	Sri Lanka	
Iran	Syria	
Iraq	Taiwan	
Jordan	Thailand	
Kampuchea	Turkey	
Korea, Democratic (N)	Vietnam	
Korea, Republic (S)		
Lebanon		

11

Table 1.4
Population Size by Development Grouping and Year (in millions)

	(N)	% of Total	:		(N)	% of Total
Developed Market			:			
Economies	704.0	(24)	28.0⎤	:	806.0	(24)	17.30⎤
			⊢41.10	:			⊢25.60
Eastern Trading				:			
Area	329.0	(7)	13.10⎦	:	388.0	(8)	8.30⎦
				:			
Developing Countries	1379.0	(58)	54.80⎤	:	3146.8	(67)	67.70⎤
			⊢58.90	:			⊢74.40
Least Developing				:			
Countries	104.0	(18)	4.10⎦	:	310.0	(25)	6.70⎦
Study Total	2516.0	(107)	100.0	:	4650.8	(124)	100.0
World Total	3612.0			:	4716.4		
% World's Total in Study		69.70	:			98.60

vast majority of the world population (74.4 percent) resides in nations
that are officially classified as developing countries; only one in four of
the world population (25.6 percent) lives in the more economically advanced DME and ETA nations. In the context of the present study, the
nations selected for study include 98.6 percent of the 1983 total world
population, a considerably higher proportion than reported in earlier
studies of global social provision.

ISP VALIDITY AND FIELD TESTING

The reader is referred elsewhere for a full discussion of the extensive
international field tests that were conducted to establish ISP validity and
reliability.[11] A discussion of data collection and data quality control procedures employed throughout this series of studies can also be found
in the same sources.[12]

NOTES

1. Richard J. Estes, *The Social Progress of Nations* (New York: Praeger, 1984);

"World Social Progress: 1968–1978," *Social Development Issues,* 8(1984):54–63; "Toward a Quality of Life Index," in *The Third World: States of Mind and Being,* edited by James Norwine and Alfonso Gonzalez (London: George Allen & Unwin, 1987).

2. For a review of this literature see Richard J. Estes, "Education for Comparative Social Welfare Research," in *Education for International Social Welfare,* edited by Daniel S. Sanders (Honolulu: Joint Publication of the Council on Social Work Education and the University of Hawaii School of Social Work, 1983).

3. The author acknowledges with appreciation the international comparative data on the legal rights of women provided by Gail Cairns and her colleagues at the Development Law and Policy Program of Columbia University. Various versions of these data have been published by the International Planned Parenthood Federation (IPPF) and by the United Nations. See Gail Cairns et al., "Women: Progress Toward Equality" (London: IPFF, 1985). Also see the following publications of the UN's International Research and Training Institute for the Advancement of Women: *Improving Concepts and Methods for Statistics and Indicators on the Situation of Women* (New York: United Nations, 1984), sales no. E.84.XVII.3; *Compiling Social Indicators on the Situation of Women* (New York: United Nations, 1984), sales no. E.84.XVII.2.

4. However, comparative studies of the subjective aspects of personal "happiness" and "well-being" do exist. Readers who are interested in this subject are referred to Ruut Veenhoven, *Conditions of Happiness* (Hingham, MA: Kluwer Boston Academic Publishers, 1984).

5. Other recent international studies of comparative human welfare have employed the same general statistical procedures and assumptions. For examples, see Sharon L. Camp and J. Joseph Speidel, *The Human Suffering Index* (Washington, D.C.: Population Crisis Committee, 1987); Morris D. Morris, *Measuring the Conditions of the World's Poor* (New York: Pergamon, 1979).

6. For a discussion of the uses of factor analysis in constructing composite indexes such as the ISP see Kenneth D. Bailey, *Methods of Social Research* (New York: The Free Press, 1982), pp. 373–79; George H. Dunteman, *Introduction to Multivariate Analysis* (Beverly Hills, CA: Sage Publications, 1984), pp. 156–204; and I. Adelman and C. T. Morris, *Society, Politics, and Economic Development: A Quantitative Approach* (Baltimore, MD: Johns Hopkins University Press, 1967).

7. For a discussion of the conceptual and methodological issues considered prior to the adoption of the ECOSOC approach to socioeconomic development level classification see Estes, *The Social Progress of Nations,* pp. 36–40.

8. For a partial listing of countries by socioeconomic development grouping see United Nations, *World Economic Survey, 1976* (New York, 1977), sales no. E/5995/Rev.1, pp. 67–68. Five countries were added to the list of 31 "least developing countries" by the UN General Assembly in 1982—Djibouti, Equatorial Guinea, São Tome and Principe, Sierra Leone and Togo. For a complete listing of all 36 nations see William A. Landskron (ed.), *Annual Review of United Nations Affairs, 1982* (Dobbs Ferry, NY: Oceana Publications, 1983), p. 181.

9. Per capita GNP statistics reported here and in the following sections were obtained from data reported in this study. Specific dollar amounts and other relevant income data are reported in Table 2.1 of the next chapter.

10. For a discussion of this point see United Nations, *1978 Report on the World*

Social Situation (New York, 1979), sales no. E.79.IV.1 and E.79.IV.3. Also see David Morawetz, *Twenty-Five Years of Economic Development: 1950–1975* (Baltimore, MD: Johns Hopkins University Press, for the World Bank, 1977); and Rutherford M. Poats (chair), *Twenty-Five Years of Development Cooperation: A Review* (Paris: Organization for Economic Cooperation and Development, 1985).

11. Estes, *The Social Progress of Nations*, pp. 40–42.

12. Ibid., pp. 30–34.

GLOBAL TRENDS IN SOCIAL DEVELOPMENT

The next decade and a half—the last in this century—will be fateful for mankind. In this period crucial global issues will pass beyond the point of choice. Though many Americans and citizens of other developed nations do not yet realize it, an improvement in North–South relations is crucial to solution of a great number of these problems.[1]

Willy Brandt
Chairman,
Independent Commission on International Development Issues

Since the beginning of the second half of this century many nations have realized considerable progress in establishing more secure "social safety nets" for their populations. The purposes of these developments have been many, but central to them has been the desire to improve the material conditions under which people live. A second objective has been to reduce the risk of future wars by eliminating their social, political, and economic causes.

Recent international progress in achieving these objectives has been impressive. Even so, as the century draws to a close, and a new millennium is about to begin, enormous social inequalities continue to exist in many parts of the world. So widespread are these disparities that a substantial minority of the earth's population continues to live under conditions of unimaginable poverty, sickness, malnutrition, and ignorance. As recently as 1975, according to Brandt,[2]

- in the very poorest of countries, one of four children dies by its first birthday;

- in the very poorest countries, half of the inhabitants will have no chance to read in their lifetimes;

- in virtually half of the world, water supplies are uncertain, and every year in developing countries as many as 8 million children die from diarrhea caused by polluted water;

- over a million people are added to the world's population every five days, some nine-tenths of this in developing nations.

A great many of these "least developing" nations are besieged by internal conflicts and regional wars, some of which threaten to engulf even their more socially affluent neighbors as well.

This chapter reports changes that have occurred worldwide in adequacy of social provision for the 14-year period 1970 through 1983. The chapter is divided into three parts: (1) social changes are reported for particular sectors of social development activity (e.g., health, education, women's status, population control, etc.); (2) changes worldwide in adequacy of social provision as measured on the study's composite indexes are reported; and (3) the chapter reports on the extent of recent successes in narrowing the gap in social development between the world's richest and poorest nations. The chapter begins with a discussion of the major changes that have taken place in various sectors of social development activity worldwide.

SECTORS OF SOCIAL DEVELOPMENT ACTIVITY

As noted in the previous chapter, the Index of Social Progress (ISP) is made up of 36 social, economic, and political indicators that are grouped into 10 subindexes. The majority of these indicators have been used in other analyses of comparative social welfare. Other indicators, such as those contained on the geographic and political participation subindexes, have not been used routinely by other investigators to assess changes over time in the state of welfare worldwide. I have, however, used both the geographic and political participation subindexes in earlier reports of my research on adequacy of social provision and, once again, they are included in the present analysis.

In this section of the chapter I will summarize social development trends occurring worldwide on each of the study's 36 indicators. These findings, which are summarized in Table 2.1, are reported by subindex for both the world as whole and for each of the study's four socioeconomic development groupings. Social trends worldwide covering the 14-year period 1970–1983 are also presented.

Table 2.1
Mean Raw Scores and Percentage Change on the Index of Social Progress (ISP83) by Subindex and Development Grouping (*n = 124*)

Subindex and Indicators	Modal Data Year (N)	All (N=124) Mean (SD)	DME(N=24)	EE(N=8)	DC(N=67)	LDC(N=25)
I. EDUCATION SUBINDEX						
School Enrollment Ratio, First Level (+)						
	1970 (N=107)	83.1 (31.3)	104.1 (24)	102.3 (7)	87.1 (58)	34.3 (18)
	1980 (N=124)	88.5 (26.9)	103.3 (24)	99.3 (8)	93.7 (67)	57.0 (25)
	1983 (N=124)	89.2 (26.7)	103.5 (24)	99.0 (8)	94.7 (67)	57.6 (25)
	Change 70-80	6.0	-0.8	-2.9	7.6	66.2
	Change 70-83	7.0	-0.6	-3.2	8.7	67.9
Pupil-Teacher Ratio, First Level (-)						
	1970 (N=107)	34.9 (11.3)	25.4	21.4	38.0	42.9
	1980 (N=124)	33.7 (14.5)	20.9	19.8	35.9	44.5
	1983 (N=124)	33.1 (14.0)	20.4	19.5	34.9	44.6
	Change 70-80	-3.0	-17.7	-7.5	-5.5	3.7
	Change 70-83	-5.0	-20.0	-8.9	-8.2	4.0
Percent Adult Illiteracy (-)						
	1970 (N=107)	42.8 (33.6)	7.3	8.7	48.3	85.9
	1980 (N=124)	36.8 (30.1)	5.1	2.1	39.0	72.7
	1983 (N=124)	33.5 (28.5)	4.1	4.9	33.8	70.2
	Change 70-80	-14.0	-30.0	-75.9	-19.3	-15.4
	Change 70-83	-22.0	-43.8	-43.7	-30.0	-18.3
Percent GNP in Education (+)						
	1970 (N=107)	4.1 (1.6)	5.0	5.1	3.7	3.6
	1980 (N=124)	4.4 (1.9)	5.9	4.8	4.2	3.4
	1983 (N=124)	4.5 (1.8)	5.7	4.8	4.3	3.8
	Change 70-80	7.0	18.0	-5.9	13.5	5.6
	Change 70-83	10.0	14.0	-5.9	16.2	5.6
II. HEALTH STATUS SUBINDEX						
Male Life Expectancy at 1 Year (+)						
	1970 (N=107)	55.8 (11.8)	68.8	68.0	54.0	39.6
	1980 (N=124)	56.6 (10.8)	69.5	66.9	55.7	43.4
	1983 (N=124)	58.8 (10.8)	71.5	67.1	58.5	44.4
	Change 70-80	1.0	1.0	-1.6	3.1	9.6
	Change 70-83	5.0	3.9	-1.3	8.3	12.1
Rate of Infant Mortality Per 1000 Liveborn (-)						
	1970 (N=107)	73.8 (55.3)	27.7	41.6	78.7	131.9
	1980 (N=124)	77.1 (55.0)	16.7	24.6	79.0	147.1
	1983 (N=124)	71.6 (51.3)	15.0	22.1	72.5	139.7
	Change 70-80	4.0	-39.7	-40.9	0.4	11.5
	Change 70-83	-3.0	-45.8	-46.9	-7.9	5.9
Population in Thousands Per Physician (-)						
	1970 (N=107)	11.2 (17.8)	0.8	0.7	7.5	41.2
	1980 (N=124)	8.2 (11.8)	0.6	0.5	5.7	24.8
	1983 (N=124)	8.5 (13.0)	0.6	0.5	5.5	26.8
	Change 70-80	-27.0	-27.5	-22.9	-24.0	-39.8

17

Table 2.1 (cont.)

Subindex and Indicators	Modal Data Year (N)	All (N=124) Mean (SD)	DMK(N=24)	KK(N=8)	DC(N=67)	LDC(N=25)
	: Change 70-83 :	-24.0 :	-27.5	-28.6	-26.7	-35.0
Per Capita Daily Calorie Supply as Percent of Daily Requirement (+)	: :	:				
	: 1970 (N=107) :	NA :	NA	NA	NA	NA
	: 1980 (N=124) :	109.7 (19.9) :	132.1	133.4	106.4	89.5
	: 1983 (N=124) :	110.8 (19.8) :	132.0	134.6	108.1	90.2
	: Change 80-83 :	1.0 :	-0.1	0.9	1.6	0.8
III. WOMEN'S STATUS SUBINDEX	: :	:				
Percent Age Eligible Girls Attending First Level Schools (+)	: :	:				
	: 1970 (N=107) :	74.8 (35.1) :	102.4	101.3	75.8	24.3
	: 1980 (N=124) :	75.0 (27.5) :	96.1	97.9	79.0	36.8
	: 1983 (N=124) :	84.6 (28.4) :	100.8	99.3	89.8	50.6
	: Change 70-80 :	1.0 :	-6.2	-3.4	4.2	51.4
	: Change 70-83 :	13.0 :	-1.6	-2.0	18.5	108.2
Percent Adult Female Illiteracy (-)	: :	:				
	: 1970 (N=107) :	47.1 (37.5) :	5.3	5.8	55.6	91.5
	: 1980 (N=124) :	43.5 (33.8) :	6.5	9.3	47.1	80.5
	: 1983 (N=124) :	43.5 (33.8) :	6.5	9.3	47.1	80.5
	: Change 70-80 :	-8.0 :	22.6	60.3	-15.3	-12.0
	: Change 70-83 :	-8.0 :	22.6	60.3	-15.3	-12.0
Age of Constitutional Document Affecting Legal Rights of Women (+)	: :	:				
	: 1970 (N=107) :	NA :	NA	NA	NA	NA
	: 1980 (N=124) :	4.9 (8.1) :	7.3	7.4	4.7	2.6
	: 1983 (N=124) :	7.1 (8.7) :	9.4	10.4	6.9	4.3
	: Change 80-83 :	45.0 :	28.8	40.5	46.8	65.4
IV. DEFENSE EFFORT SUBINDEX	: :	:				
Military Expenditures as Percent of GNP (-)	: 1970 (N=107) :	3.6 (3.9) :	4.3	4.2	3.5	2.7
	: 1980 (N=124) :	5.0 (5.4) :	4.1	6.8	5.5	4.0
	: 1983 (N=124) :	5.5 (7.0) :	4.2	6.8	6.3	4.1
	: Change 70-80 :	39.0 :	-4.7	61.9	57.1	48.1
	: Change 70-83 :	53.0 :	-2.3	61.9	80.0	51.9
V. ECONOMIC SUBINDEX	: :	:				
Per Capita Gross National Product (in $) (:	: :	:				
	: 1970 (N=107) :	772 (910) :	1961.0	2100.0	334.5	76.8
	: 1980 (N=124) :	2827 (3832) :	8900.0	4120.0	1457.0	254.0
	: 1983 (N=124) :	2901 (3853) :	8876.0	3894.0	1629.0	260.0

18

Table 2.1 (cont.)

Subindex and Indicators	Modal Data Year (N)	All (N=124) Mean (SD)	DME(N=24)	EE(N=8)	DC(N=67)	LDC(N=25)
	: Change 70-80 :	266.0 :	353.9	96.2	335.6	230.7
	: Change 70-83 :	276.0 :	352.6	85.4	386.9	238.5
GNP Per Capita Annual Growth Rate (+)	: :	:				
	: 1970 (N=107) :	4.6 (4.1) :	4.7	8.3	4.3	3.8
	: 1980 (N=124) :	2.9 (2.3) :	3.6	5.0	3.0	1.6
	: 1983 (N=124) :	2.7 (3.9) :	2.8	4.0	3.0	1.4
	: Change 70-80 :	-37.0 :	-23.4	-39.8	-30.2	-57.9
	: Change 70-83 :	-41.0 :	-40.4	-51.8	-30.2	-63.2
Average Annual Rate of Inflation (-)	: :	:				
	: 1970 (N=107) :	6.8 (18.7) :	4.9	0.0	9.2	4.0
	: 1980 (N=124) :	14.9 (20.5) :	12.2	3.1	18.6	11.6
	: 1983 (N=124) :	16.2 (19.6) :	13.9	1.2	19.9	13.2
	: Change 70-80 :	119.0 :	149.0	310.0	102.2	190.0
	: Change 70-83 :	138.0 :	183.7	120.0	116.3	230.0
Per Capita Food Production Index (+)	: :	:				
	: 1970 (N=107) :	101.8 (12.8) :	108.4	114.6	100.4	92.8
	: 1980 (N=124) :	102.5 (17.9) :	111.5	122.8	100.3	93.2
	: 1983 (N=124) :	99.9 (14.9) :	106.0	107.8	97.8	97.2
	: Change 70-80 :	1.0 :	2.9	7.2	-0.1	0.4
	: Change 70-83 :	-2.0 :	-2.2	-5.9	-2.6	4.7
External Public Debt as Percent of GNP (-):	:	:				
	: 1970 (N=107) :	NA :	NA	NA	NA	NA
	: 1980 (N=124) :	21.4 (22.8) :	4.1	6.8	5.5	4.0
	: 1983 (N=124) :	32.7 (31.7) :	4.2	6.8	6.3	4.1
	: Change 80-83 :	53.0 :	2.4	0.0	14.5	2.5
	: :	:				
VI. DEMOGRAPHY SUBINDEX	: :	:				
	: :	:				
Total Population (Millions) (-)	: :	:				
	: 1970 (N=107) :	23.5 (062.0) :	29.3	47.0	23.8	5.8
	: 1980 (N=124) :	35.4 (110.0) :	32.9	47.2	43.9	11.1
	: 1983 (N=124) :	37.5 (116.4) :	33.6	48.5	47.0	12.4
	: Change 70-80 :	51.0 :	12.3	0.4	84.5	91.4
	: Change 70-83 :	60.0 :	14.7	3.2	97.5	113.8
Crude Birth Rate Per 1000 Population (-)	: :	:				
	: 1970 (N=107) :	36.4 (13.3) :	18.5	19.9	42.2	47.9
	: 1980 (N=124) :	33.6 (13.1) :	16.1	18.6	36.7	46.5
	: 1983 (N=124) :	33.0 (13.7) :	15.0	17.3	36.3	46.6
	: Change 70-80 :	-8.0 :	-13.0	-6.5	-13.0	-2.9
	: Change 70-83 :	-9.0 :	-18.9	-13.1	-14.0	-2.7
Crude Death Rate Per 1000 Population (-)	: :	:				
	: 1970 (N=107) :	14.5 (6.3) :	10.2	9.4	14.2	23.0
	: 1980 (N=124) :	12.8 (5.5) :	9.6	10.3	11.6	20.0
	: 1983 (N=124) :	12.1 (5.4) :	9.3	10.8	10.5	19.7
	: Change 70-80 :	-12.0 :	-5.9	9.6	-18.3	-13.0
	: Change 70-83 :	-17.0 :	-8.9	14.9	-26.1	-14.3

Table 2.1 (cont.)

Subindex and Indicators	Modal Data Year (N)	All (N=124) Mean (SD)	DME(N=24)	EE(N=8)	DC(N=67)	LDC(N=25)
Rate of Population Increase (-)						
	1970 (N=107) :	2.2 (0.90) :	1.1	0.9	2.7	2.4
	1980 (N=124) :	2.1 (1.07) :	0.9	0.9	2.6	2.5
	1983 (N=124) :	2.1 (1.12) :	0.7	0.7	2.5	2.6
	Change 70-80 :	-5.0 :	-21.8	-5.6	-3.7	4.2
	Change 70-83 :	-5.0 :	-32.7	-22.2	-7.4	8.3
Percent of Population Under 15 Years (-)						
	1970 (N=107) :	39.8 (0.1) :	26.7	26.1	43.7	43.8
	1980 (N=124) :	---- :	----	----	----	----
	1983 (N=124) :	37.0 (0.1) :	23.0	25.0	41.0	44.0
	Change 70-83 :	-7.0 :	-13.9	-4.2	-6.2	0.5
VII. GEOGRAPHY SUBINDEX‡						
Percent Arable Land Mass (+)						
	1970-1983 :	18.0 (15.0) :	21.6	37.9	15.2	16.0
Natural Disasters Vulnerability Index (-) :						
	1947-1979 :	9.0 (30.2) :	0.4	0.2	0.2	0.1
Average Annual Fatalities From Natural Disasters Per Million Population (-)						
	1947-1979 :	307.3 (611.6) :	62.6	31.1	397.4	388.9
VIII. POLITICAL PARTICIPATION SUBINDEX						
Violations of Political Rights Index (-) :	1970 (N=107) :	NA :	NA	NA	NA	NA
	1980 (N=124) :	4.5 (2.2) :	1.7	6.6	4.7	6.0
	1983 (N=124) :	4.4 (2.2) :	1.5	6.6	4.6	6.2
	Change 80-83 :	-2.0 :	-11.8	0.0	-2.1	3.3
Violations of Civil Liberties Index (-)						
	1970 (N=107) :	NA :	NA	NA	NA	NA
	1980 (N=124) :	4.4 (2.0) :	1.7	6.2	4.6	5.8
	1983 (N=124) :	4.5 (2.0) :	1.7	6.2	4.7	5.9
	Change 80-83 :	2.0 :	0.0	0.0	2.2	1.7
Composite Violations of Freedoms Index (-):	1970 (N=107) :	NA :	NA	NA	NA	NA
	1980 (N=124) :	2.1 (0.8) :	1.1	2.9	2.1	2.7
	1983 (N=124) :	2.1 (0.8) :	1.1	2.9	2.1	2.7
	Change 80-83 :	0.0 :	0.0	0.0	0.0	0.0
IX. CULTURAL DIVERSITY SUBINDEX‡						
Largest Percent Sharing Same Mother Tongue (+)						
	1970-1983 :	71.9 (25.2) :	86.8	82.8	70.4	58.0
Largest Percent Sharing Same						

Table 2.1 (cont.)

Subindex and Indicators	Modal Data Year (N)	All (N=124) Mean (SD)	DME(N=24)	EE(N=8)	DC(N=67)	LDC(N=25)
Basic Religious Beliefs (+)	1970-1983	81.3 (18.9)	89.5	75.4	82.4	72.1
Largest Percent Sharing Same or Similar Racial/Ethnic Group Origins (+)	1970-1983	72.0 (24.2)	83.9	84.3	70.9	59.6
X. WELFARE EFFORT SUBINDEX						
Years Since First Law--Old Age, Invalidity, and Death (+)						
	1970 (N=107)	29.0 (21.0)	55.0	51.0	20.0	12.0
	1980 (N=124)	30.1 (25.9)	59.5	61.6	23.3	10.0
	1983 (N=124)	32.7 (25.9)	62.5	64.6	26.0	11.8
	Change 70-80	4.0	8.2	20.8	16.5	-16.7
	Change 70-83	13.0	13.6	26.7	30.0	-1.7
Years Since First Law--Sickness and Maternity (+)						
	1970 (N=107)	30.0 (23.0)	53.0	61.0	21.0	13.0
	1980 (N=124)	30.9 (26.3)	57.8	72.1	23.3	12.8
	1983 (N=124)	33.4 (26.3)	60.0	75.1	25.8	14.6
	Change 70-80	3.0	9.1	18.2	10.9	-1.5
	Change 70-83	11.0	13.2	23.1	22.9	12.3
Years Since First Law--Work Injury (+)						
	1970 (N=107)	47.0 (20.0)	70.0	64.0	42.0	29.0
	1980 (N=124)	47.5 (25.6)	75.9	73.4	42.2	27.6
	1983 (N=124)	50.6 (25.6)	78.9	76.9	44.9	30.0
	Change 70-80	1.0	8.4	14.7	0.5	-4.8
	Change 70-83	8.0	12.7	20.2	6.9	3.4
Years Since First Law--Unemployment (+)						
	1970 (N=107)	13.0 (21.0)	46.0	13.0	4.0	1.0
	1980 (N=124)	13.1 (23.8)	52.4	13.1	4.0	0.0
	1983 (N=124)	14.1 (23.8)	55.4	14.3	4.6	0.0
	Change 70-80	1.0	13.9	0.8	0.0	-100.0
	Change 70-83	8.0	20.4	10.0	15.0	-100.0
Years Since First Law--Family Allowances (+)						
	1970 (N=107)	15.0 (15.0)	29.0	30.0	9.0	8.0
	1980 (N=124)	15.4 (18.5)	33.9	36.0	8.8	8.6
	1983 (N=124)	16.8 (18.5)	36.8	39.0	9.7	9.7
	Change 70-80	3.0	16.9	20.0	-2.2	7.5
	Change 70-83	12.0	26.9	30.0	7.8	21.3

*Subindex was used as a statistical constant in 1980 and 1983.

Signs indicate directionality of indicators, i.e., a positive sign (+) indicates that more of factor "X" is more desirable from a social development perspective than is less of factor "X"; similarly, a (-) sign indicates that less of factor "X" is more desirable from a social development perspective.

Education

The education subindex consists of four indicators: primary school enrollment ratio; primary school pupil–teacher ratio; percentage adult illiteracy; and the percentage of gross national product (GNP) allocated for education (including public and private expenditures for primary, secondary, and post-secondary education). These indicators are widely used in other comparative studies of education and, here, provide a reasonable basis for assessing national progress in ensuring the availability of *basic* education, at least at the primary school level.

Primary school enrollment levels increased steadily over the period 1970 to 1983. More specifically, a worldwide average increase of 7.0 percent occurred over the 14-year period. The most significant improvements in childhood access to basic education occurred in the LDCs, where the average ratio increased by 67.9 percent, the highest gain ever experienced during a comparatively brief time period. Steady, but not dramatic, improvements in the primary school enrollment patterns of children residing in the DCs was also found (+8.7 percent). Virtually all children in DME and ETA nations continue to have at least primary school educations available to them. Today, then, approximately 89.2 percent of all the world's children—but still only 57.6 percent of those living in LDCs—have at least some opportunity to participate in primary school education.

Primary school *pupil–teacher ratios* are also improving worldwide; the size of an average class is down by 5.0 percent, from 34.9 students per teacher in 1970 to an average of 33.1 students per teacher in 1983. The most notable gains, however, took place in the DME nations (−20.0 percent)[3] in which even 1970 DME pupil–teacher ratio levels (25.4) were significantly more favorable than those achieved by either the LDCs (44.6) or the DCs (34.9) by 1983. Children in ETA nations continue to enjoy the lowest pupil–teacher ratio worldwide (mean = 19.5).

Successes in the global campaign to reduce levels of *adult illiteracy* are beginning to be achieved. Certainly current social indicator readings reflect steady progress in bringing basic literacy skills to a larger number and percentage of the world's total population. Between 1970 and 1983, for example, the rate of adult illiteracy worldwide declined by an average of 22.0 percent. The most impressive decreases took place in the DME and ETA nations, however, which experienced average declines in adult illiteracy of −43.8 and −43.7 percent, respectively. Though continuing to improve steadily, solutions to adult illiteracy appear to be much more elusive in the DCs and the LDCs. Today, for example, more than 70.2 percent of the adult populations of the LDCs and 33.8 percent of those living in the DCs are still unable to read or write. The comparative slowness with which these data are changing makes it highly unlikely that the goal of a fully literate world will be achieved by the year 2000.

As reported in earlier studies, the net *percentage of gross national product* allocated to education—including both private and public sources— tends to vary enormously from country to country (world 1983 average = 4.5 percent). On average, DME and ETA nations spend more on education than do other groupings (5.7 and 4.8 percent, respectively), but the GNPs of the LDCs also reflect significant positive trends in national expenditures for education (+16.2 percent, to a 1983 high of 4.3 percent). Even so, the most significant worldwide average increases for education between 1970 and 1983 occurred in the DME (+14.0 percent) and DC nations (+16.2 percent). Increases in GNP allocated for education have been comparatively meager in the LDCs (+5.6 percent) and, in the case of ETA nations, a substantial net decline in overall expenditures occurred in 1983 over 1970 levels (−5.9 percent).

In terms of worldwide trends in education, then, a relatively favorable picture emerges for the period 1970 through 1983. More particularly, a higher proportion of the world's children now have access to at least some form of primary education than at any other time in history. The number of teachers available to educate these children has grown considerably over the period, with the result that the average class size has become smaller. Adult illiteracy is also on the decline, although the vast majority of persons living in the LDCs continue to lack basic reading and writing skills. National expenditures for education at all levels were significantly higher in 1983 than in 1970. The world's most socially impoverished nations, the LDCs, however, will need to make even more substantial investments in literacy education.

Health

Global health trends were measured through the use of four frequently used indicators of international health: infant mortality rate; population in thousands per physician; male life expectancy; and per capita caloric intake as a percentage of daily requirements. Male life expectancy, rather than a composite measure of male and female life expectancy, was selected for special attention because of the relative vulnerability of males everywhere to early death, including higher rates of infant mortality. Both population in thousands per physician and infant mortality rates reflect access to quality health care as well as changes that are occurring in the supply of trained medical personnel. The caloric intake measure serves as a valuable indicator of a nation's nutritional health.

Worldwide trends in *male life expectancy* indicate that males everywhere are beginning to survive beyond the first year of life in higher numbers;

on average, they are also beginning to live longer lives, although both the actual and percentage increase in life expectancy for males continues to be less favorable than that for females.[4] Average male life expectancy worldwide, for example, increased +5.0 percent in 1983 over 1970 levels to 58.8 years. Male life expectancy is most favorable in DME nations (average = 71.5 years) and at its lowest in the LDCs (average = 44.4 years). Life expectancy for males in ETA nations declined slightly in 1983 compared with 1970 levels, from 68.0 to 67.1 years.

More favorable trends in *infant mortality* also are generally occurring worldwide. On average, global infant mortality rates improved by an average of −3.0 percent in 1983 over 1970 levels, to a world rate of 71.6 per 1,000 liveborn. Declines were most striking in the DME and ETA nations, however, where 14-year declines averaged −45.8 percent and −46.9 percent, respectively. Only in the LDCs was the incidence of infant mortality found to be higher in 1983 than in 1970 (139.7 per 1,000 liveborn versus 131.9), an increase of nearly 6.0 percent over the period. A combination of famines, wars, and deteriorating economic and political conditions in the LDCs account for much of their increase in infant deaths.

Worldwide improvements in the supply of trained *medical personnel* also took place between 1970 and 1983. More specifically, the average number of persons in thousands per physician declined by 24.0 percent in 1983 and 1970 levels to a worldwide average 8,500 persons per physician. Worldwide patient–physician ratios continue to decline steadily, but even with significant improvements the least favorable ratios exist in the LDCs (average = 26,800:1) and the DCs (average = 5,500:1). Even so, the supply of trained physicians in the LDCs increased by 35.0 percent over 1970 levels.

Notwithstanding the devastating African famines of the late 1970s and early 1980s,[5] and even taking into account the near-term famines that have been projected for Africa and elsewhere,[6] the *minimum* nutritional needs of a larger proportion of the world's total population are beginning to be met, from a worldwide average of 109.7 percent of minimum caloric need in 1980 to a worldwide average in 1983 of 110.8 percent of minimum need. However, the average nutritional supply available in the LDCs continues to be well below that of other socioeconomic development groupings (LDC 1983 average = 90.2 percent of minimum need), and the food supplies in the LDCs are continuing to deteriorate. So precipitous are these declines that the UN Food and Argriculture Organization (FAO) has predicted an additional drop of more than 30 percent in per capita food production for food-deficit African nations through the year 2010. These trends are so ominous that the FAO concluded that if the downward trend is not arrested, "it would be exceedingly difficult to meet this gap through any combination of commercial imports and food aid. The result could be massive and chronic famine, with many coun-tries on the brink of survival."[7] Continuing widespread famines in Africa can be expected to harbor significant social consequences for other areas of the world as well. The present food-deficit situation in sub-Saharan Africa is all the more disconcerting given the extraordinary food surplus situation that currently exists in virtually every other region of the world, including many DCs and even some LDCs.[8]

Improvements in the world health profile, to a very large extent, reflect significant improvements resulting from international public health in-itiatives. The success of these global efforts is especially apparent in the areas of communicable disease control—with the exception of the spread of sexually transmitted diseases, including Acquired Immune Deficiency Syndrome (AIDS)[9]—mass immunization programs, innovations in pub-lic health education, the increased availability of prenatal and early in-fancy care programs, and in the steadily increasing supply of trained medical personnel. These social trends are all to the common good; their positive, and potentially long-lasting, effects can be expected to impact favorably on other sectors of national and international social develop-ment as well.

Natural and human-made disasters, political strife, regional wars, and even misapplied development strategies, though, are seriously interfer-ing with the availability of adequate food supplies in some areas of the world.[10] In combination with unrelenting population growth in the world's poorest nations, the devastating nature of this amalgam of nat-ural and human-made forces will very likely frustrate achievement of the goal of the World Health Organization of "health for all by the year 2000."

Women

"Women constitute 53 percent of the world's population, perform two-thirds of the work and earn one-tenth of the world's wages," according to Margaret Schuler, director of the Women, Law and Development Program of OEF International.[11] Even so, as Schuler and others have found, women have tended to benefit least from national and global efforts at social development.[12] In the present study, the changing status of women worldwide was measured through the use of three indicators: percentage of age-eligible girls attending primary schools; percentage adult female illiteracy; and the age of constitutional documents (includ-ing amendments) affecting the legal status of women.

A review of the data on the women's status subindex reported in Table 2.1 reveals a number of important trends relating to the changing status of women worldwide. First, a higher percentage of age-eligible *girls are attending primary schools* than ever before (average = 84.6 percent, an increase in 1983 of 13.0 percent over 1970 levels). This increase has been most significant in the LDC nations, where a doubling of school enrollment patterns for girls occurred between 1970 and 1983, from 24.3 percent of the age-eligible female population to 51.4 percent. Second, adult female illiteracy is on the decline worldwide, from 47.1 percent of all women in 1970 to 43.5 of all women in 1983. However, 80.5 percent of women in the LDCs and 47.1 percent of the women in DCs are not able to read or write—illiteracy rates that are substantially higher than those for males in these countries. As has been the case for nearly a century, *adult female illiteracy* remains very low in both DME and ETA nations (average = 6.5 and 9.3 percent, respectively).[13]

Third, *constitutional protections for women*—including constitutional protection for women of legal rights equivalent to those accorded men—are most pervasive in ETA and DME nations. However, recent extensions of constitutional protections to women have been occurring most rapidly in those nations in which gender differences have been the least equal for millennia, the world's developing and least developing nations. Throughout the world, however, the average age of *constitutional* documents relating to the rights of women are only a little more than seven years. Within the LDCs the average age of such documents is only 4.3 years.

One may infer from these trends that the recently concluded International Decade on Women did, indeed, realize significant progress in having a greater number of the world's nations declare in their official documents that women's legal rights are equivalent to those of men. Only in the decades ahead, however, will a fuller picture emerge concerning how enhanced constitutional protections for women translate into improved social conditions. This is a particularly important trend to follow inasmuch as an unprecedented number of women worldwide are working outside of the home, often for inadequate wages that are earned under the most deplorable of conditions.[14]

Defense

In this report, and in others that preceded it, sharp increases in national expenditures for defense and military purposes are treated as being in opposition to social development worldwide. The reasons for this are twofold. First, nearly all of the world's nations struggle continuously with the dilemma concerning what portions of their scarce national resources are to be committed to "guns" versus "butter" issues. That is to say, the policymakers of virtually all nations are continuously having to decide on the share of government expenditures to be allocated for what is loosely referred to as "national defense" and that to be allocated to advancement of socioeconomic development. Second, excessive expenditures for the military deprive nations of the resources that may be needed to reduce or eliminate the very problems for which such expenditures are being made in the first place (e.g., civil strife, regional conflict, discrimination of minorities, dwindling national resources, etc.).

Successful resolution of this age-old dilemma is especially critical inasmuch as international experience has shown repeatedly that excessive expenditures for military purpopses weaken, not strengthen, the social fabric of nations. The fact that real and sustained improvements in national social conditions may obviate the need for high levels of national expenditures for defense, let alone additional increases, too often seems to elude the public officials of many nations.

In this study a single indicator was used to assess changes over time in the defense activities of nations: the percentage of gross national product (GNP) allocated to military and defense spending.

The data reported in Table 2.1 make clear that the world is moving toward a more armed, less peaceful environment. This trend is particularly reflected in the worldwide 14-year average increase of 53 percent in GNP expenditures for defenses and military purposes (from 3.6 percent of average GNP in 1970 to 5.5 percent in 1983). And the rate of increase in military expenditures was highest among those nations least able to afford such expenditures, the DCs (+80.0 percent in 1983 over 1970 expenditures) and LDCs (+51.9 percent over 1970 levels)! Only among DME nations did 1983 group expenditures for defense decrease—though only slightly so—compared with average DME expenditures for defense in 1970 (4.2 versus 4.3 percent). Military expenditures within ETA nations rose by 61.9 percent (to a conservative figure of 6.8 percent of GNP) over the 14-year period of the study.

These trends must be regarded as especially worrisome given the social deterioration that is occurring in the majority of LDCs. The situation is compounded further by the high number of civil and regional wars being fought between developing countries. That the weaponry being purchased by DCs and LDCs originates in DME and ETA nations is also troublesome. In effect, through their arms and arms-related purchases the DCs and LDCs are buoying up the troubled economies of the DMEs and ETAs at the expense of adding to their own economic difficulties.

Not so obvious, but true nonetheless, is that many DC and LDC leaders, while acting on the belief that they are contributing to the solution of their own internal security problems, are actually adding to them through their enormous foreign indebtedness, social insecurity, and public distrust that is created through excessive expenditures for "defensive" purposes. Evidence in support of this conclusion is readily available.[15]

Economic Trends

World economic progress is measured through five indicators: per capita gross national product (measured in U.S. dollars); GNP per capita annual growth rate; inflation rates; per capita food production; and external public debt as a percentage of GNP. While these indicators are not an inclusive list of the rich array of economic indexes that might have been included in the Index of Social Progress, they represent a sufficiently broad range of economic activity of interest to development specialists.

Analysis of worldwide economic trends over the period 1970 to 1983 reveals a number of trends. First, levels of *per capita GNP*, as measured in U.S. dollars, have increased everywhere in the world. The largest 14-year increases occurred among the DCs (+386.9 percent), a level of growth that surpassed even that achieved by the DME nations (+352.5 percent). Even within the LDCs per capita GNP rose between 1970 and 1983 by 238.5 percent, a magnitude of increase higher than that thought probable at the outset of the decade. Per capita GNP levels in ETA nations remained comparatively stable, with a period overall net increase of only 85.4 percent.

To be meaningful, however, changes in per capita GNP levels must be contrasted with global inflationary trends occurring during the same time frame. The *inflation* data presented in Table 2.1 report a global inflation rate of +138.0 percent for the period, that is, an average world-wide annual increase approximating 10 percent over the 14 years. The highest increases in net inflation are found in the LDCs (+230.0 percent) and in the DMEs (+183.7 percent). By comparison, more modest inflationary increases were found in the ETAs (+120.0 percent) and the DCs (+116.3 percent). Note, however, that average annual rates of inflation doubled for the DCs between 1970 and 1983, but more than tripled for the DMEs (4.9 versus 13.9 percent) and LDCs (4.0 versus 13.2 percent) during the same time periods. Clearly, the net gains reflected on the per capita GNP indicator were substantially offset by dramatic increases in global inflation.

Not surprisingly, given the substantial negative trends worldwide in world per capita GNP and inflation averages, international *annual rates of per capita GNP growth* declined as well. Indeed, the average decline in economic expansion worldwide exceeded −41.0 percent. Even more to the point, the most significant net declines in economic growth took place in the LDCs (−63.2 percent), the ETAs (−51.8 percent), and the DMEs (−40.4 percent). Only the DCs experienced a rate of economic contraction lower than the world average (−30.2 percent).

Similarly, between 1970 and 1983 global *per capita food production* levels declined by 2.0 percent, with the most significant drops occurring in the

ETA nations (−5.9 percent). Only the LDCs managed to eke out a somewhat higher level of food productivity (+4.7 percent) but, given the intense population pressures being experienced by the LDCs, these net increases in food production during the period were insufficient to forestall the devastating famines that wracked sub-Saharan Africa beginning in the late 1970s. Modest declines in overall food production levels were also found for the DCs (−2.6 percent) and DME nations (−2.2 percent).

Viewed from a global perspective, the long-term economic picture does not look especially favorable. For obvious reasons, the highly complex economic disappointments just described are combining to produce potentially explosive situations in many areas of the world. The rapidly increasing debt crisis of the majority of Third World nations, coupled with their inability to service such debts under what most regard as highly unfavorable financial terms, is but one manifestation of the crisis.[16] Other symptoms include the widening trade imbalances that exist between major import and export nations,[17] the serious economic slumps that exist in many previously successful DCs,[18] and the rapidly emerging economic protectionist actions, including trade tariffs, undertaken by many nations. The reemergence worldwide of highly conservative attitudes toward virtually all areas of public responsibility is but yet another indication of the sense of apprehension with which many nations view their economic futures.[19]

Population Trends

Changes in world population are among the most significant trends scrutinized by development specialists. Concerns about the size of the global population stem not from the need to know the numbers of people who inhabit the planet but, more fundamentally, from the need to understand the long-established relationship between fertility and poverty, population size and premature mortality, and population size and assaults on the physical environment.[20] Rapid increases in population size also threaten the success of development efforts by imposing even greater demands on the comparatively modest social accomplishments that nations are able to achieve. So troublesome is the concern over unbridled population growth that, second only to the threat of global nuclear holocaust, the majority of development specialists regard population growth as the most significant threat to future world development.

In this study, global population trends are assessed through five indicators that have been widely used in similar studies: changes in total population size, changes in the crude birth rate, changes in the crude death rate, the rate of net population increase, and the proportion of age-dependent population under 15 years of age.

As reported in Table 2.1 *population size* is on the increase everywhere in the world. Indeed, the average population base of all 124 nations studied increased by an average of 60 percent over the 14-year time frame of the study, from a 1970 average of 23.5 million to 37.5 million in 1983. Population increases were most significant among the LDCs (+113.8 percent) and the DCs (+97.5 percent). By comparison, population size has tended to remain more or less constant in both ETA (+3.2 percent) and DME nations (+14.7 percent). In effect, global population increases continue to occur within the very nations that can least absorb such increases—the nations of the developing world.

Viewed from the perspective of the *rate of population increase*, a slightly more favorable pattern of increases in global population emerges. For example, the rate of population increase declined for the DMEs, ETAs, and the DCs over the 14 years of the study. For the DMEs and ETAs average declines are below population replacement levels such that the countries contained in these development groupings, on average, are beginning to experience some net losses in the overall size of their populations. Similarly, the rate of DC population increase has slowed from 2.7 percent in 1970 to 2.5 percent in 1983. Within the LDCs, however, both the size and rate of natural increase in population continue to grow virtually unchecked, with an average increase in the growth rate, from 2.4 percent in 1970 to 2.6 percent in 1983.

Global gains on the rate of population increase indicator mean that the number of years that are required to double the world's population has increased from an average of 31.5 years in 1970 to 33.0 years in 1983.[21] The slowing of the population doubling time (PDT) is most apparent in the DME and ETA nations, in which doubling time now averages 99 years. The PDT of the LDCs, however, now averages 26.7 years compared with a group average of 28.9 years in 1970; within the DCs the 1983 average population doubling time is 27.7 years, an increase of 2.1 years over the 1970 rate.

The current population dilemma is further compounded by an overall increase of 0.5 percent (to 44.0 per 100 persons) in the LDCs of the number of *age-dependent persons under 15 years*. Increases in this ratio mean that comparatively fewer adults are available—relative to the growing numbers of children in the population—who can contribute to the raising or otherwise provide for the basic needs of a larger number of age-dependent children. Increases in age-dependency ratios also correlated with rises in infant mortality rates, such as the increase reported earlier for the LDCs. The LDCs were the only development grouping for which net increases in infant mortality were found. Significant declines in the age-dependency ratio were found for DME, ETA, and the

DCs, however; these declines contributed to an overall reduction worldwide of 7.0 percent in age-dependency ratios.

The global population situation today, then, is somewhat improved over earlier expectations, especially in light of the reduced overall rates of population increase, zero population growth in some countries, more favorable crude birth and death rates, and the more generally positive age-dependency ratios for the DMEs, ETAs, and the majority of DCs. But the rates of population increase in the LDCs, including the acceleration of population doubling time, suggest that effective controls on global population growth are beyond our grasp. Indeed, net global population growth is continuing at an alarming rate. Even the most conservative of estimates projects that global population size will exceed 6.2 billion by the year 2000 and will continue to rise until the year 2080, by which time the global population will "level off" at 10 billion—this in a world that is unwilling to feed, house, and otherwise provide for the basic needs of a population half that size.[22] Even more to the point, approximately two-thirds of the world's current population of 5 billion lives in developing nations; by the year 2000 these countries will contain in excess of 75 percent of the total.

Environmental Issues and Development

A comparatively innovative subindex used in this study reports on the degree of geographic stability characteristic of nations. The subindex makes use of such diverse natural phenomena as the percentage of arable land available for agricultural purposes, the frequency of natural disasters, and the number of fatalities associated with those disasters. National data on individual indicators were obtained through an analysis of disaster phenomena that occurred over the 32-year period 1947–1979.[23] Scores on the geographic subindex are treated as statistical constants for each of the study's three time periods.

Though recognized as having a profound impact on the development efforts of many Third World nations (e.g., the contribution of droughts, floods, and related natural phenomena to famines),[24] the more far-reaching significance of geographic factors on social development patterns is only beginning to be understood.[25]

Two patterns emerge from analysis of the geographic data presented in Table 2.1. First, *arable land* is unevenly distributed among the four socioeconomic groupings. More specifically, the average proportion of arable land worldwide is 18.0 percent of the total land mass. But the percentage of arable land available to the so-called First World DME nations and the Second World ETA nations greatly exceeds that available to either the Third World DCs or the Fourth World LDCs (i.e., 21.6, 37.9, 15.2, and 16.0 percent, respectively). In effect, the most economically advanced sectors of the planet have available to them the highest proportion of arable land mass; these lands, of course, can be and are used for agricultural and related food production purposes. Conversely, the planet's poorest sectors, on average, have significantly lower ratios of arable land mass available.

Second, more "major" natural disasters occur in DME nations than anywhere else on the planet—the United States alone, for example, experiences fully one-third of all the world's "major" natural disasters.[26] Even so, the *number of lives lost* in natural disasters in developing countries far exceeds those lost in either DME or ETA nations.

More particularly, an average of 393.2 fatalities per million population occurred within DCs and LDCs during the 32-year period of natural disasters analyzed as part of this study, versus an average of 46.9 fatalities per million population for DME and ETA nations. In effect, natural disasters in developed nations tend to produce significant property damage, whereas the most significant losses to the world's impoverished countries are human lives. In the main, disparities in the impact of natural disasters on rich and poor countries are accounted for by the absence of effective civil defense infrastructures in developing nations (e.g., early warning systems, protective shelters, formalized disaster relief services, etc.). Ineffective, delayed, or misapplied disaster relief assistance in developing countries also often exacerbates the initial losses experienced by these nations.[27] The higher assessed property values of real estate in developed countries accounts for the greater economic losses from natural disasters reported by DME and ETA nations. The higher incidence of natural disasters observed for DME nations may also be a function of the more accurate observation and reporting systems employed by these countries. By contrast, for developing nations the fatalities resulting from natural disasters—for reasons of both political sensitivity and practical difficulties associated with such enumerations—are believed to be significantly underestimated.

Political Participation

The extent of government respect for the internationally declared civil, political, and legal rights of individual citizens is of major concern to specialists in social development.[28] Indeed, increasing the opportunities for individuals to pursue their personal and collective objectives within the context of a mutually agreed upon and respected social contract has been on the world's social agenda for at least 400 years.

In this analysis, three indicators of political participation are examined in the context of broader development patterns: the extent of government violations of *political rights* (i.e., those rights relating to participation directly or through freely elected representatives in the determination of law and its administration); the extent of government violations of *civil rights* (including rights relating to freedom of the media, religious freedom, freedom from torture, freedom from imprisonment without trial, freedom of residence, and so on); and scores on a composite measure of *violations of freedom* are reported.

Using a scale of 1 to 3, in which 1 indicates the highest level of freedom (i.e., "free") and 3 the lowest (i.e., "not free"), for the period 1980 to 1983 the most favorable levels of freedom were found in the DME nations (1983 average = 1.1). The lowest levels of civil and political freedom were found in the ETA nations (1983 average = 2.9) and the LDCs (1983 average = 2.7). Indeed, within the LDCs levels of freedom remained consistently low for both time periods studied, a pattern that existed even before 1980. Between 1980 and 1983 the DCs made some modest gains in ensuring more favorable levels of political and civil liberties within their nations but, as a group, their level of violations of freedom remains high (1983 average = 2.1).

These patterns are all the more disturbing given the accelerating militarization of the developing world, a trend that has been on the increase in these countries since beginning their post-colonial independence in the early 1960s. The New York-based Freedom House conservatively estimates that a minimum of 64.1 percent of the world's population live under conditions that are either "not free" (42.5 percent) or only "partly free" (21.6 percent).[29] Military or other autocratic controls on civil rights and personal freedoms are almost universal in the LDCs (94 percent) and exist in a majority of the DCs (67 percent). All eight of the ETA nations are judged to be heavily "influenced" by military authorities as well.

In another study of human rights violations worldwide, research sponsored by *The Economist* assigned human rights ratings of 1 (most violations) to 100 (least violations) for each of 121 countries.[30] The 1984 world average was 55. Only 19 nations, containing 11.1 percent of the world's population, received favorable ratings, equal to or higher than 90; by contrast, 63 nations, containing 53.4 percent of the world's population, received highly unfavorable human rights scores lower than 49. Thirty-five nations were given scores lower than 20.

Levels of civil rights, personal freedoms, and political participation throughout the world, then, continue to be in a precarious state. Violations of freedoms are the most pronounced in the world's poorest nations, but individual freedoms are nearly all but absent in the more affluent ETA nations as well. Improvements are occurring for some countries, especially those DCs that are "on the move" (e.g., Argentina, Bolivia, Brazil and Uruguay). Clearly, though, greater worldwide social progress in political rights cannot be made so long as the majority of the world's population lives under conditions of squalor and poverty.

Nor will social progress be achieved through the oppression of the very people on behalf of whose interests autocratic governments contend they are acting.

Cultural Diversity

Similarities in language, religious beliefs, and racial and ethnic heritage constitute critical elements in the social development process. Evidence even exists that cultural homogeneity is the single most important factor in explaining differing patterns and rates of development worldwide. Certainly, comparative studies have found that many of the world's most socially successful nations, *in the main*, are relatively small and culturally homogeneous nations in which the vast majority of the population share the same language, ethnic roots, and basic religious beliefs (e.g., Scandinavian societies). Conversely, the world's least socially successful countries, again *in the main*, tend to be larger and more culturally diverse nations in which are found large numbers of religious, ethnic, and linguistic minorities (e.g., the LDCs of Africa and Asia).

The reasons for such a direct relationship between cultural homogeneity, cultural diversity, and social development are several. First, relative cultural homogeneity accelerates the process whereby a nation achieves agreement concerning its shared identity, national purposes, and national social commitments. Cultural homogeneity, at least as viewed within the context of national social development, facilitates the process by which governments and citizens, working together, arrive at common national objectives. Relative cultural homogeneity also increases the potential for nations to achieve workable compromises. Thus, the development planning reality is that people who, in addition to sharing the same physical geography, also share a common cultural identity and history arrive at a more complete agreement concerning national development goals and strategies than do people in countries characterized by lesser degrees of cultural homogeneity.[31]

Second, governments of culturally pluralistic nations often are compelled to frame national development initiatives that attempt to respond simultaneously to the legitimate, if at times divergent, needs of the many subgroups that make up their societies. This results in development initiatives that are amorphous and difficult to achieve. It also tends to result in levels of development investment which, at best, respond only partially to the broad range of needs that exist for all the subgroups that make up the society.

Third, cultural diversity is known to be a prime ingredient in the social tensions that characterize all nations of the world, rich and poor alike. Often culturally induced tensions can serve a catalytic function in promoting positive changes in nations, especially in reducing social inequalities between minority and majority groups.[32] These tensions, however, can also impede social progress, especially when the special interests or needs of one group of a country are advanced at great social cost to other groups or subgroups (e.g., as is the case of the blacks of South Africa).[33]

In this study, degree of cultural diversity was measured through three indicators: percentage of population sharing the same mother tongue, percentage of the population sharing the same religious beliefs, and percentage of the population sharing the same ethnic or racial group origins. Countries with smaller percentages of their populations sharing cultural attributes measured along these dimensions are conceptualized as more culturally diverse than nations in which greater homogeneity exists.

The world's most culturally diverse nations, as reported in Table 2.1, are the LDCs. As a group, for example, the nations of the LDC grouping are populated by a great variety of cultural subgroups, each with their own religious, linguistic, and racial-ethnic traditions. So diverse are the cultural subgroups that make up the LDCs that, on average, only 58.0 percent of persons in the LDC share the same mother tongue; similarly, only 59.6 percent share the same or similar racial or ethnic group origins. Approximately 72.1 percent of the populations of the LDCs, however, share similar religious beliefs. These cultural patterns obviously add enormously to the obstacles that leaders in many of the LDCs experience in identifying and advancing discrete development objectives in their nations.

In contrast to cultural patterns found in the LDCs, the DMEs are characterized by a high level of cultural homogeneity; on average, 86.8 percent of persons in DME nations speak the same mother tongue, 89.5 percent share similar religious beliefs, and 83.9 percent share the same racial or ethnic group origins. Further, patterns of cultural diversity in the socially advanced ETA nations more nearly approximate those of DMEs. Cultural diversity in the DCs, on the other hand, is much more varied but clearly reflects more of a middle range.

Analysis of selected country-specific data reveals the pervasiveness of the many culturally based conflicts that exist throughout the world. For example, *religious discrimination* is especially prominent in the continuing struggles between the Christians, Druze, and Moslems of Lebanon; between the Hindus, Sikhs, and Moslems of India; and between the Catholics and Protestants of the northern counties of Ireland. Social conflicts based on *race* are especially visible in the struggles between the blacks, whites, and Hispanics of the United States and between the blacks, whites, and "colored" of South Africa. The centuries-long conflicts between the Singhalese and Tamils of Sri Lanka, and those that continue to exist between the ethnic Chinese, Malays, and Indians of Malaysia are known to be deeply rooted in *ethnic* differences. *Language* differences continue to be a major source of social political unrest between French- and English-speaking Canadians and between the Dutch-speaking Flemish and French-speaking Walloons of Belgium. Further, the intense *cultural* differences that exist between the Turks and Greeks of Cyprus and between the Jews and Palestinian Arabs of Israel also contribute to a culturally divided world.[34]

Clearly, the intention of the majority of these confrontations is to evoke a more satisfactory redressing of some long-standing minority–majority group grievance. In some situations improvements will no doubt occur over time; in other situations, however, the cultural differences appear to be of such a fundamental nature that nothing short of a complete social, economic, and political transformation will achieve the sought-after changes (e.g., South Africa). In the meantime it is almost certain that additional tens of thousands will die in the struggle to have their cultural differences recognized and valued.

Welfare Effort

Nations everywhere seek to minimize the negative impact on their citizens of certain social risks to which all of us are exposed (e.g., sickness, injury, disability, early death, solitary survivorship, retirement, etc.). Most countries have developed a rich network of formalized social welfare programs and services in response to these predictable human risks, while others, typically for financial or ideological reasons, depend more heavily on voluntary and other less formal approaches to social care. The majority of nations, of course, are characterized by a mix of public and private social welfare services, some of which are of a more formalized nature (e.g., national social insurance trusts, government-organized and administered health and education systems) and others that are of a more informal nature (e.g., self-help and mutual aid groups, the use of volunteers, individual dependence on other family members for essential care-giving functions).

The degree of national success in providing a secure "social safety net" for its citizens varies from society to society. In the main, though, the size of the holes in the social safety net woven by particular nations depends, among other factors, on the size of their populations, the age of their social welfare systems, and the range of fiscal and human resources that are available to support such systems.[35]

Table 2.2 summarizes historical developments in the emergence of various types of social security programs for 142 nations over the period 1940–1985.[36] As seen in these data, *old age, invalidity, survivorship, and work injury programs* are the most common forms of social protection worldwide. These programs were also among the earliest welfare pro-

Table 2.2
Social Security Programs throughout the World, 1940–1985 ($n = 142$)

Program Type	1940	1949	1958	1967	1977	1985
Number of Countries with any type of program	57	58	80	120	129	142
Old age, invalidity, survivors	33	44	58	92	114	132
Sickness and maternity	24	36	59	65	72	83
Work injury	57	57	77	117	129	136
Unemployment	21	22	26	34	38	40
Family allowance	7	27	38	62	65	64

Source: U.S. Department of Health and Human Services, 1986, p. xxiii.

grams developed by governments. The purpose of each program is to provide some level of income protection for workers who are unable to continue their employment for reasons that are beyond their control. *Sickness and maternity programs,* including the establishment of national health services and subsidized health care for especially vulnerable populations (e.g., the aged, veterans), are the second most dominant form of social welfare provision; the majority of government-administered health programs have been developed since World War II. *Unemployment and family allowance provisions* are among the least-institutionalized programs worldwide, owing, no doubt, to the need for many nations to avoid creating work disincentives and to place controls on unwanted population growth. Further, throughout the world, the majority of government welfare programs are financed through a combination of employment- and tax-based contributions from employers, workers and, often, from central governments.[37]

Table 2.1 reports on the changing capacity of nations to provide more formal programs of social care. A number of significant developmental grouping patterns relating to social welfare programs worldwide can be discerned from these data. First, the most "socially protected" nations are the DMEs and ETAs. These nations, as a group, have in place the world's most extensive network of comprehensive, government-administered social welfare services. These programs are well financed, cover all or nearly all of the populations of these countries and, on average, 1983 programs range in age from a low of 14.3 years for unemployment protection in ETA nations to a high of 78.9 years in DME nations for programs that provide financial support to injured workers. The average age of ETA and DME social security programs of all types exceeds 50 years (that is, they were initiated prior to World War II).

By comparison, formally organized welfare programs, though on the increase, are currently least established in the DCs and LDCs. Even where such programs do exist they tend to be in their earliest stages of development; that is, a comparatively small percentage of the population tends to be covered by programs and services which, typically, are characterized by a series of exclusions, deductibles, and other limitations on the benefits provided. Further, DC and LDC social programs tend to be financed by a combination of employer and employee contributions; the role of central governments in contributing to the financial support of public sector welfare programs, to the extent that such participation occurs, tends to be minimal and highly particularized.[38] As with the majority of economically advanced nations, many developing countries are seeking ways to reduce even further the role of their central governments in the financing of human service programs.[39]

The most recurrent gap in the social protections of DCs and LDCs is income protection during periods of unemployment, disability, old age, and sickness. For reasons of fertility control comparatively few DCs and LDCs have instituted family allowance schemes. Similiarly, unemployment trusts are virtually nonexistent in developing countries. An increasing number of DCs and the LDCs, however, have established programs that provide some level of support to workers who experience injuries while working; work injury provisions have been in place for an average of more than 30 years in the LDCs and 45 years in the DCs.

INDEXES OF SOCIAL PROGRESS

In addition to reporting global development changes on individual indicators, the study also utilizes a variety of composite measures of social progress. These include ten subindexes and two summary indexes: the Index of Social Progress (ISP83) and the Weighted Index of Social Progress (WISP).[40] All 12 measures of global social progress are identified in Table 2.3. The table reports summary statistics for each of the study's four socioeconomic development groupings. Indeed, Table 2.3 is the study's single most important table in that it contains summary data concerning the major development trends that occurred worldwide over the period 1970–1983. The trends reported are significant and provide previously unavailable evidence of worldwide changes in adequacy of social provision that took place between 1970 and 1983.

Social Progress and Socioeconomic Development Groupings

Significant variations exist in the levels of social provision found among the study's four socioeconomic development groupings. As reported in earlier versions of this research,[41] DME and ETA nations continue to be the most socially advanced nations on earth. More specifically, 1983 ISP scores averaged 172 for the DMEs and 142 for the ETAs; by contrast DCs and LDCs averaged ISP scores of only 91 and 43, respectively, for the same time period. Further, the most substantial 14-year ISP score increases occurred for the group of 25 DME nations (+ 5.5 percent). By comparison, between 1970 and 1983, ISP scores increased by 4.6 percent for DCs but declined by 10.1 percent and 4.4 percent, respectively, for the ETA and LDC groupings.

The same disparities in levels of social provision were found using both the ISP and WISP, although WISP scores reveal a slightly different pattern of net social gains and losses. WISP scores, for example, confirm a higher net social gain for the DCs in 1983 (+ 5.3 percent) over 1970 levels than that found for the DMEs (+ 3.9 percent); similarly, the ISP social losses reported for the LDCs disappear on the WISP, which reflects a group net change for the LDCs of zero.

These WISP findings suggest that more favorable patterns of social development are taking place worldwide in developing nations than those identified using only the ISP. This is no doubt the case, especially for the group of 67 DCs included in the study. The absence of further social deterioration in the LDCs, especially given their already disadvantaged development status, is certainly to be preferred to the more negative findings reported for the LDCs on the ISP. Even so, social disparities of a considerable magnitude continue to exist between the LDCs (1983 WISP average = 13) and all other development groupings. Further, these disparities are increasing rapidly, but especially between the LDCs and the DMEs, and even between the LDCs and other developing nations. Despite decades of concentrated international efforts aimed at their development, the reality is that the LDCs remain the most socially impoverished nations on earth.[42] It is within the borders of the LDCs that human suffering and deprivation are at their worst levels; and it is within the LDCs that comparatively little optimism exists concerning the near-term prospects for an improved future.

Table 2.3
Mean Scores and Percentage Changes on the Indexes of Social Progress by Subindex, Development Grouping, and Year (n = 124)

	INDEX OF SOCIAL PROGRESS (ISP83)	Education Subindex	Health Subindex	Women Subindex	Defense Subindex	Economic Subindex	Demographic Subindex	Geographic Subindex	Participation Subindex	Cultural Subindex	Welfare Subindex	WEIGHTED INDEX OF SOCIAL PROGRESS
DEVELOPED MARKET ECONOMY NATIONS (N=24)												
1970	163	18.0	18.0	19.0	8.0	15.0	19.0	12.0	17.0	15.0	22.0	77
1980	174	18.2	20.2	17.2	12.0	16.5	19.0	10.8	22.8	15.1	22.2	81
1983	172	17.9	19.9	16.4	12.0	15.8	18.9	10.8	23.0	15.1	22.1	80
% 1970-1980	6.7	1.1	12.2	-9.5	50.0	10.0	0.0	-10.0	34.1	0.7	0.9	5.2
% 1980-1983	-1.1	-1.6	-1.5	-4.7	0.0	-4.2	-0.5	0.0	0.9	0.0	-0.5	-1.2
% 1970-1983	5.5	-0.6	10.6	-13.7	50.0	5.3	-0.5	-10.0	35.3	0.7	0.5	3.9
EASTERN TRADING AREA (N=8)												
1970	158	19.0	17.0	18.0	9.0	19.0	19.0	15.0	11.0	12.0	19.0	74
1980	145	16.8	19.4	17.2	7.0	17.8	17.9	16.5	0.5	12.1	20.1	68
1983	142	16.2	18.9	16.4	8.0	15.6	17.6	16.5	0.6	12.1	20.1	66
% 1970-1980	-8.2	-11.6	14.1	-4.4	-22.2	-6.3	-5.8	10.0	-95.5	0.8	5.8	-8.1
% 1980-1983	-2.1	-3.6	-2.6	-4.7	14.3	-12.4	-1.7	0.0	20.0	0.0	0.0	-2.9
% 1970-1983	-10.1	-14.7	11.2	-8.9	-11.1	-17.9	-7.4	10.0	-94.5	0.8	5.8	-10.8

DEVELOPING COUNTRIES (N=67)

1970	87	9.0	10.0	9.0	10.0	8.0	7.0	8.0	9.0	10.0	6.0	38
1980	90	9.6	9.8	10.0	9.0	8.3	8.1	8.9	9.2	9.9	6.9	40
1983	91	9.9	10.1	10.2	9.0	8.4	8.4	8.9	9.2	9.9	6.9	40
% 1970-1980	3.4	6.7	-2.0	11.1	-10.0	3.8	15.7	11.3	2.2	-1.0	15.0	5.3
% 1980-1983	1.1	3.1	3.1	2.0	0.0	1.2	3.7	0.0	0.0	0.0	0.0	0.0
% 1970-1983	4.6	10.0	1.0	13.3	-10.0	5.0	20.0	11.3	2.2	-1.0	15.0	5.3

LEAST DEVELOPING COUNTRIES (N=25)

1970	45	1.0	-3.0	0.0	13.0	7.0	5.0	11.0	5.0	3.0	3.0	13
1980	43	1.0	-2.3	0.7	12.0	6.0	3.8	10.2	2.9	4.9	3.5	13
1983	43	0.8	-2.7	1.3	12.0	7.0	3.4	10.2	2.7	4.9	3.5	13
% 1970-1980	-4.4	0.0	-23.3	70.0	-7.7	-14.3	-24.0	-7.3	-42.0	63.3	16.7	0.0
% 1980-1983	0.0	-20.0	17.4	85.7	0.0	16.7	-10.5	0.0	-6.9	0.0	0.0	0.0
% 1970-1983	-4.4	-20.0	-10.0	130.0	-7.7	0.0	-32.0	-7.3	-46.0	63.3	16.7	0.0

ALL COUNTRIES (N=124)

1970	100	10.0	10.0	10.0	10.0	10.0	10.0	10.0	10.0	10.0	10.0	45
1980	100	10.0	10.0	10.0	10.0	10.0	10.0	10.0	10.0	10.0	10.0	44
1983	100	10.0	10.0	10.0	10.0	10.0	10.0	10.0	10.0	10.0	10.0	44

Notes: Numbers do not always add up evenly because of index and subindex rounding.

WISP scores for all years were computed using the same factor loading weights.
See Appendix C for details concerning the construction of these scores.

Subindex Changes by Development Grouping

Social development is rarely, if ever, a linear process. By this I mean that the achievement of national development objectives almost never occurs through the orderly progression of societies from one discrete level or plateau to another. Nor is the social development of nations characterized by uniform progress in all social sectors; ample evidence to the contrary exists worldwide to confirm the comparatively asymmetrical, even "untidy" nature of social development.[43]

In the present study, development grouping subindex scores typify the irregular nature of development for nations individually and in the aggregate. These data also offer important clues for probable future development trends for the several development groupings.

Within the DME nations, for example, the most significant subindex improvements took place on the defense effort (+50.0 percent), political participation (+35.3 percent), health (+10.6 percent), and economic (+5.3 percent) subindexes.[44] DME subindex gains are substantial and contribute appreciably to their continuing international social leadership position. Improvements in each of these sectors reflect sustained social investments on the part of governments in the overall human welfare of their citizens; they also document improvements in the continuously evolving social contract that exists between governments and their citizens and, more fundamentally, between citizens.

But DME nations also experienced net social losses on several of the ISP's subindexes. These losses are concentrated on the women's status (−13.7 percent) and geographic (−10.0 percent) subindexes which, because of their magnitude, should also be regarded as significant.[45] Further, given the additive nature of the ISP and WISP, the combination of subindex gains and losses has the effect of offsetting gains in one area (or areas) of the indexes with losses in others. This process results in composite ISP and WISP scores that tend to be more stable than subindex scores. Four DME subindexes remained statistically constant between 1970 and 1983: education (−0.6 percent), demographic (−0.5 percent), cultural diversity (+0.7 percent), and welfare effort (+0.5 percent). Subindex fluctuations of such a relatively small magnitude contributed comparatively little to changes in overall index scores.

Within the DCs significant improvements in level of social provision were found on five of the ISP's ten subindexes: demographic (+20.0 percent), welfare (+15.0 percent), women's status (+13.3 percent), geographic (11.3 percent), and education (+10.0 percent). Significant DC subindex losses were recorded only on the defense effort subindex (−10.0 percent), a loss stemming from higher average national expenditures for defense and military purposes. Increases in group defense expenditures, as will be discussed more fully in the next section of this chapter, frequently are made at the expense of national investments in social programs (especially those designed to reduce illiteracy, promote improved health services, and reduce dependency on foreign imports). The health, political participation, and cultural diversity subindexes remained more or less stable within the DC grouping between 1970 and 1983.

The dramatic decline in ETA ratings on both the ISP (−10.1 percent) and WISP (−10.8 percent) reflects significant losses on six of the ISP's ten subindexes: political participation (−94.5 percent); economic (−17.9 percent); education (−14.7 percent); defense effort (−11.1 percent); women's status (−8.9 percent); and demographic (−7.4 percent). These losses are extraordinary and will prove difficult for the ETA nations to restore easily; they also reflect a steady deterioration in ETA levels of social provision spanning the entire period of the study. Only on the health (+11.2 percent), geographic (+10.0 percent), and welfare effort (5.8 percent) subindexes were improvements noted for the ETAs; further, ETA composite index losses would have been even more extreme were it not for the modest improvements on these subindexes.

Within the LDCs losses on both the ISP and WISP reflect a further erosion in the resources available to them. More particularly, between 1970 and 1983 net social losses for the LDCs occurred on six of the ISP's ten subindexes. The losses were most significant on the political participation (−46.0 percent), demographic (−32.0 percent), and education (−20.0) subindexes, but losses were also considerable on the health (−10.0 percent), defense effort (−7.7 percent), and geographic (−7.3 percent) subindexes. Increased militarism and internal political oppression—coupled with *decreased* government expenditures for health, education, fertility control and related programs—are only suggestive of the high level of "mal-development" that characterizes current social trends occurring in the LDCs.

On a more positive note, significant improvements in the areas of women's status (+130.0 percent), cultural diversity (+63.3 percent), and welfare effort (+16.7 percent) are beginning to take place in the LDCs. Many of these improvements resulted, in part, from the decade-long push worldwide to improve the social, economic, and legal well-being of women in the LDCs.[46] Even so, the profound losses found to be taking place in the majority of the LDC social sectors suggests that even the gains found in women's status and welfare effort may not be long-lasting.

THE SOCIAL DEVELOPMENT GAP

One of the central purposes of this research has been to use more objective criteria to assess the extent of global progress in narrowing the gap in social development that has long existed between the world's richest and poorest nations.[47] Achieving relative social parity between the nations of the world is seen as an essential ingredient, not only to provide a more secure social safety net for people living in less developed countries, but also and even more fundamentally, to reduce the risk of international wars by eliminating their causes. A narrowing of the global social development gap is also understood to be a critical first step for promoting equality and social justice worldwide.[48]

Measuring the Development Gap

For purposes of this study, a gap in socioeconomic development is said to exist when significant disparities are found in the social accomplishments of one development grouping of nations (e.g., along regional, economic, or political criteria) relative to the social accomplishments achieved by other development groupings. Necessarily, comparisons of the social development accomplishments of nations must be made on the basis of the same criteria undertaken at more or less the same moments in time.

In this study, development group scores on the ISP and WISP, as well as for their component subindexes, are used to determine the magnitude of development gaps between the study's four socioeconomic development groupings. More specifically, the social accomplishments of ETA nations, the DCs, and the LDCs are contrasted with those found for the 25 DME nations, that is, those countries that have consistently been found to be the world's social leaders.[49]

The methodology employed in this analysis provides assessments of both *absolute* and *relative* changes in adequacy of social provision for all four socioeconomic development groupings. By this I mean that the actual (i.e., the absolute) social gains and losses of each development grouping are contrasted with their own social gains and losses during earlier periods of development (e.g., group changes *over time* in infant mortality rates, patterns of adult illiteracy, and degrees of political oppression). In addition, though, the social gains and losses of each development grouping are compared with those of all other development groupings, again for the same time period (e.g., changes in infant mortality trends occurring within ETA nations compared with those taking place in the DCs, the LDCs, and the DMEs). This latter analysis provides an unequivocal picture of the social trends in each development grouping *relative* to trends occurring in all other groupings. The development gap, to the extent that one is found to exist, can be discerned in the inability of individual development groupings to improve their social trends *relative* to more positive changes that are observed for other development groupings, but especially in contrast to patterns of social provision found to exist in the DMEs.

The results of this analysis are summarized in Table 2.4. The table reports changes in assessed levels of social provision for ETA nations, the DCs, and the LDCs in absolute terms and as a *percentage* of the composite scores computed for DME nations. Development group index and subindex change scores are reported separately for each of the study's three time periods, 1970, 1980, and 1983.

Dimensions of the Gap in Social Development

Has the global gap in socioeconomic levels between the world's richest and poorest nations begun to narrow? In a word, no! Indeed, the data reported in Table 2.4 confirm that disparities in social provision between the world's poorest and most socially advanced nations are greater now than they were in 1970.

And still worse, the 14-year net declines in overall levels of social provision reported for the ETA nations (-14.4 percent), the DCs (-0.5 percent), and the LDCs (-2.6 percent) vis-à-vis the net social *gains* attained by the DMEs ($+5.5$ percent) occurred in both absolute and relative terms. Not only did the DMEs realize significant progress in advancing their level of social provision over the 14-year time period, but they managed to do so during periods when other nations were unable to maintain even the more modest levels of social provision they had achieved during earlier decades of development! Worldwide development trends of such a highly positive and a highly negative nature result in a considerable widening of the development gap between nations. Further, such a significant widening of the gap within a comparatively brief time period makes it even less likely that less socially developed nations will be able to achieve social parity with the DME nations.

Even more to the point, net social losses within the ETAs occurred on five of the ISP subindexes. The most substantial of these losses—especially when compared with DME net gains on same subindexes—were concentrated on the political participation (-62.1 percent), defense effort (-45.8 percent), economic (-27.9 percent), education (-15.1 percent), and demographic (-6.9 percent) subindexes. Similarly, the most substantial social losses observed for both the DCs and the LDCs, again compared with DME net gains on the same subindexes, occurred on the defense effort (-50.0 and -62.5 percent, respectively) and political participation (-12.9 and -17.7 percent, respectively) subindexes. For the DCs and the LDCs more moderate losses were found on other subindexes as well.

Advances in adequacy of social provision within the DMEs, then, are

Table 2.4
Eastern Trading Area (ETAs), Developing Countries (DCs), and Least Developing Countries (LDCs) Subindexes and Index of Social Progress (ISP) Scores as a Percentage of Developed Market Economy (DMEs) Scores, 1970–1983 ($n = 124$)

	DMEs	Percentage Change	ETAs	ETAs As A Percentage of DMEs	DCs	DCs As A Percentage of DMEs	LDCs	LDCs As A Percentage of DMEs
EDUCATION SUBINDEX								
1970	18.0		19.0	105.6	9.0	50.0	1.0	5.6
1980	18.2		16.8	92.3	9.6	52.7	1.0	5.5
1983	17.9		16.2	90.5	9.9	55.3	0.8	4.5
Net Change, 1970-83	-0.1	-0.6	-2.8	-15.1	0.9	5.3	-0.2	-1.1
HEALTH SUBINDEX								
1970	18.0		17.0	94.4	10.0	55.6	-3.0	-16.7
1980	20.2		19.4	96.0	9.8	48.5	-2.3	-11.4
1983	19.9		18.9	95.0	10.1	50.8	-2.7	-13.6
Net Change, 1970-83	1.9	10.6	1.9	0.5	0.1	-4.8	0.3	3.1
WOMEN SUBINDEX								
1970	19.0		18.0	94.7	9.0	47.4	0.0	0.0
1980	17.2		17.2	100.0	10.0	58.1	0.7	4.1
1983	16.4		16.4	100.0	10.2	62.2	1.3	7.9
Net Change, 1970-83	-2.6	-13.7	-1.6	5.3	1.2	14.8	1.3	7.9
DEFENSE SUBINDEX								
1970	8.0		9.0	112.5	10.0	125.0	13.0	162.5
1980	12.0		7.0	58.3	9.0	75.0	12.0	100.0
1983	12.0		8.0	66.7	9.0	75.0	12.0	100.0
Net Change, 1970-83	4.0	50.0	-1.0	-45.8	-1	-50.0	-1	-62.5
ECONOMIC SUBINDEX								
1970	15.0		19.0	126.7	8.0	53.3	7.0	46.7
1980	16.5		17.8	107.9	8.3	50.3	6.0	36.4
1983	15.8		15.6	98.7	8.4	53.2	7.0	44.3
Net Change, 1970-83	0.8	5.3	-3.4	-27.9	0.4	-0.2	0	-2.4
DEMOGRAPHIC SUBINDEX								
1970	19.0		19.0	100.0	7.0	36.8	5.0	26.3
1980	19.0		17.9	94.2	8.1	42.6	3.8	20.0
1983	18.9		17.6	93.1	8.4	44.4	3.4	18.0
Net Change, 1970-83	-0.1	-0.5	-1.4	-6.9	1.4	7.6	-1.6	-8.3
GEOGRAPHIC SUBINDEX								
1970	12.0		15.0	125.0	8.0	66.7	11.0	91.7
1980	10.8		16.5	152.8	8.9	82.4	10.2	94.4
1983	10.8		16.5	152.8	8.9	82.4	10.2	94.4
Net Change, 1970-83	-1.2	-10.0	1.5	27.8	0.9	15.7	-0.8	2.8
PARTICIPATION SUBINDEX								
1970	17.0		11.0	64.7	9.0	52.9	5.0	29.4
1980	22.8		0.5	2.2	9.2	40.4	2.9	12.7
1983	23.0		0.6	2.6	9.2	40.0	2.7	11.7
Net Change, 1970-83	6.0	35.3	-10.4	-62.1	0.2	-12.9	-2.3	-17.7
CULTURAL DIVERSITY SUBINDEX								
1970	15.0		12.0	80.0	10.0	66.7	3.0	20.0
1980	15.1		12.1	80.1	9.9	65.6	4.9	32.5

Table 2.4 (cont.)

	DMEs	Percentage Change		ETAs	ETAs As A Percentage of DMEs		DCs	DCs As A Percentage of DMEs		LDCs	LDCs As A Percentage of DMEs
1983	15.1		!	12.1	80.1 !		9.9	65.6 !		4.9	32.5
Net Change, 1970-83	0.1	0.7 !		0.1	0.1 !		-0.1	-1.1 !		1.9	12.5
WELFARE EFFORT SUBINDEX			!		!			!			
1970	22.0		!	19.0	86.4 !		6.0	27.3 !		3.0	13.6
1980	22.2		!	20.1	90.5 !		6.9	31.1 !		3.5	15.8
1983	22.1		!	20.1	91.0 !		6.9	31.2 !		3.5	15.8
Net Change, 1970-83	0.1	0.5 !		1.1	4.6 !		0.9	3.9 !		0.5	2.2
INDEX OF SOCIAL PROGRESS (ISP)			!		!			!			
1970	163		!	158	96.9 !		87	53.4 !		45	27.6
1980	174		!	145	83.3 !		90	51.7 !		43	24.7
1983	172		!	142	82.6 !		91	52.9 !		43	25.0
Net Change, 1970-83	9	5.5 !		-16	-14.4 !		4	-0.5 !		-2	-2.6
WEIGHTED INDEX OF SOCIAL PROGRESS (WISP)			!		!			!			
1970	77		!	74	96.1 !		38	49.4 !		13	16.9
1980	81		!	68	84.0 !		40	49.4 !		13	16.0
1983	80		!	66	82.5 !		40	50.0 !		13	16.3
Net Change, 1970-83	3	3.9 !		-8	-13.6 !		2	0.6 !		0	-0.6

the result of real and continuing improvements in the majority of social sectors within these countries. They are also the result of increased individual and personal freedoms within the majority of DME nations which, at least in 1983 compared with 1970, also managed to decrease their percentage of GNP allocated for defense spending. Net social losses for the ETA nations, the DCs, and the LDCs, by contrast, resulted from unparalleled "peace time" increases in central government expenditures for military and defense purposes. They are also the result of the political repression that is reported to be on the increase in the ETAs, DCs, and the LDCs.[50] The reality is that LDC central government expenditures for *social* development, in the main, have not kept pace with their comparative willingness, even apparent eagerness, to invest in military armaments and internal "security" measures. The net impact of such sharp rises in military spending is to unravel further the already fragile social fabric of these nations. In the process, the ETAs, DCs, and LDCs are contributing to increased world social *vulnerability*, not to the heightened sense of social security that many leaders associate with defense spending.

The socially destabilizing nature of sharp increases in global defense spending is reflected not only in the hidden costs of the arms race, which are known to be substantial,[51] but also in their direct economic and social consequences. In her 1985 annual report on *World Military and Social Expenditures*, for example, Ruth L. Sivard identifies some of the more apparent social development contradictions associated with worldwide militarism:

- In the Third World military spending has increased fivefold since 1960 and the number of countries ruled by military governments has grown from 22 to 57.
- The United States and the Soviet Union, first in military power, rank 14 and 51 among all nations in their infant mortality rates.
- The budget of the U.S. Air Force is larger than the total educational budget for 1.2 billion children in Africa, Latin America, and Asia, excluding Japan.
- The Soviet Union in one year spends more on military defense than the governments of all the developing countries spend for education and health care for 3.6 billion people.
- There is one soldier per 43 people in the world, one physician per 1,030 people.
- The developed countries on average spend 5.4 percent of their GNP for military purposes, 0.3 percent for development assistance to poorer countries.
- It costs $590,000 a day to operate one aircraft carrier, and every day in Africa alone 14,000 children die of hunger or hunger-related causes.[52]

The fiction of strenghtened global security arising from increased defense spending is made all the more transparent when one recognizes that the suppliers and financiers of the international arms race, according to the U.S. Congressional Service, are the ETA and DME nations, but especially the United States, the Soviet Union and their respective military allies.[53]

The uncomplicated reality is that the social advances achieved by some DME nations betweeen 1970 and 1983 were paid for, at least to some extent, by the arms and arms-related purchases of the DCs and the LDCs from the world's already richest and most socially advanced nations. In effect the DCs and the LDCs, to their long-term peril, are subsidizing the social advances of other nations while incurring social losses for themselves. In the process, of course, the development gap between the DCs, LDCs and both the DMEs and the ETA nations continues to widen.

Reflecting on what can only be regarded as a rather "peculiar" pattern of global relationships that results from the international transfer of arms, UN Secretary-General Javier Perez de Cuellar commented in 1984 that "the arms trade impoverishes the receiver and debases the supplier." He went on to say that "there is a striking resemblance to the drug trade." The Catholic bishops of France, in a favorably received pastoral letter, noted that "every citizen pays the price of nuclear armaments—first with taxes, then as potential victim."[54] The prestigious American Public Health Association, in a carefully constructed 1985 resolution, denounced the U.S. role in the financing of global militarism as a threat even to individual and world health.[55] The destabilizing impact of global "empire building" on the part of the Soviet Union and its East European allies also has been well documented.[56]

Overall, then, the social development trends reported in this chapter indicate that improvements in worldwide patterns of social provision are uneven at best. The most substantial changes occurred in the world's already economically advanced nations, but especially in the DMEs. The LDCs continue to be the nations with the least favorable development profiles. Indeed, the gap in social development between richest and poorest nations was found to have widened considerably over the 14-year period of the study. Further, negative trends in social development were observed for the majority of ETA nations as well.

The study's most positive findings are those development trends occurring in the DCs. Significant gains were observed for the majority of the DCs on many of the ISP indexes. These gains reflect marked improvements in the changing economic and political climates in many of the DCs. However, rapid increases in DC defense and military spending are worrisome. The large number of continuing civil and regional wars taking place within and between DCs also is ominous,[57] as is the push on the part of many DCs to become independent nuclear powers.[58]

Chapter 3 reports development trends in relation to the world's continents and major geographic regions and subregions.

NOTES

1. Willy Brandt, "The North–South Challenge," *World Press Review* (June 1984), p. 21.

2. Ibid., p. 21.

3. Note that on approximately half of the ISP indicators lower values reflect *higher* levels of net social progress (e.g., lower pupil–teacher ratios, lower infant mortality rate, decreased crude birth and death rates, etc.). The desired directionality of all 36 indicators is given in Table 1.1.

4. United Nations, *Demographic Yearbook, 1986* (New York, 1987).

5. See the Hunger Project, *Ending Hunger: An Idea Whose Time Has Come* (New York: Praeger, 1985); Richard J. Estes, "Beyond Famine Relief: The Continuing Crisis in Development," *International Journal of Contemporary Sociology* (Summer 1987).

6. International Food Policy Research Institute, *Food Needs of Developing Countries: Projections of Production and Consumption to 1990* (Washington, D.C., 1977); Sandra Hadler et al., *Developing Country Food Grain Projections for 1985* (Washington, D.C.: The World Bank, 1976), Staff Working Paper No. 247; Thomas Netter, "Food Outlook Poor in 6 African Nations," *New York Times*, April 21, 1986, p. A3.

7. As quoted by Blaine Harden, "Severe Famine Forecast in Africa's Future," *Washington Post*, September 7, 1986, pp. A21, A24.

8. Keith Schneider, "Scientific Advances Lead to Era of Food Surplus Around the World," *New York Times*, September 9, 1986, pp. C1, C10; Philip Abelson, "World Food," *Science* (April 3, 1987), p. 9.

9. Blaine Harden, "AIDS Seen as Threat to Africa's Future," *Washington Post*, May 31, 1987, pp. A1, A18.

10. John W. Mellor and Sarah Gavian, "Famine: Causes, Prevention, and Relief," *Science* (January 30, 1987), pp. 539–45; Foreign Affairs Committee, House of Commons, *Famine in Africa* (London: Her Majesty's Stationery Office, 1985).

11. As cited by Dorothy Gilliam in "Third World Strategies," *Washington Post*, April 6, 1987, p. D3. For Schuler's complete report see Margaret Schuler, *Empowerment and the Law: Strategies of Third World Women* (Washington, D.C.: OEF International, 1986).

12. As examples see Mary Ruggie, *The State and Working Women: A Comparative Study of Britain and Sweden* (Princeton, NJ: Princeton University Press, 1984); Victor R. Fuchs, "Sex Differences in Economic Well-Being," *Science* 232 (1986), pp. 459–64; *Rights of Women: A Workbook of International Conventions Relating to Women's Issues and Concerns* (Santo Domingo, Dominican Republic: International Women's Tribune, 1983).

13. In some cases, as in the United States, official estimates of illiteracy include persons who are not literate in the *official* language of the country but who may be highly literate in other languages, such as recently arrived immigrants, foreign workers, "ghetto-ized" racial and ethnic minority groups, and so on.

14. Data concerning the changing status of women worldwide are reported regularly by the United Nations International Research and Training Institute (INSTRAW) from its headquarters in the Dominican Republic.

15. See Kenneth Fidel (ed.), *Militarism in Developing Nations* (New Brunswick, NJ: Transaction Books, 1975); S. MacFarlane, *Superpower Rivalry and Third World Radicalism* (Baltimore, MD: Johns Hopkins University Press, 1985).

16. Cameron Duodu, "The IMF's African Nightmare," *South* (July 1985), pp. 31–38; D. Delamaide, *Debt Shock: The Full Story of the World Debt Crisis* (New York: Doubleday, 1985); P. Claudon, *World Debt Crisis* (New York: Ballinger, 1985). A succinct discussion of the major events that have contributed to the Third World debt "crisis" can be found in Rudiger Dornbusch and Stanley Fischer, "Third World Debt," *Science* 234 (1986):836–41. Also see P. Krugman, "International Debt Strategies in an Uncertain World," in *International Debt and the Developing Countries*, edited by G. Smith and J. Cuddington (Washington, D.C. World Bank, 1985), pp. 79–100.

17. For detailed discussions and trend data concerning these patterns see the World Bank's *World Development Report* series.

18. In addition to the United Nation's *National Accounts* series, see *South* magazine's annual "Socio-Economic Digest of the Third World."

19. Martin Rein and Lee Rainwater, *Public/Private Interplay in Social Protection: A Comparative Study* (Armonk, NY: M. E. Sharpe, 1986); Organization of Economic Cooperation and Development, *The Welfare State in Crisis: An Account of the Conference on Social Policies in the 1980s* (Paris, 1981); Organization for Economic Cooperation and Development, *Social Expenditures, 1960–1990: Problems of Growth and Control* (Paris, 1985).

20. The body of literature on these relationships is extensive. For an overview

of the issues see Paul Ehrlich and Anne Ehrlich, *Ecoscience: Population, Resources, and Environment* (San Francisco, CA: W. H. Freeman, 1972); also Lester R. Brown, "Stopping Population Growth," in *State of the World, 1985* (New York: W. W. Norton, 1985).

21. Population doubling time is computed by dividing 69.31 by the annual population growth rate; thus, the time required to double the 1983 population of the LDCs is 26.6 years—that is, 69.31/2.6 percent = 26.65 years (see Ehrlich and Ehrlich 1972 for a fuller discussion of the origins of this formula).

22. United Nations, *The State of the World's Population* (New York, 1987). The World Bank, however, estimates that the 10 billion population size may be reached as early as 2050.

23. For a description of the general approach used to measure the frequency of natural disasters see Joanna Regulska, *Global Trends in Natural Disasters* (Denver, CO: Natural Hazards Research Institute, University of Colorado, 1980). In the present study, final tabulations of natural disaster data were completed by John L. Reed, "A Comparative Analysis of Natural Disasters," Master of Social Work Thesis, University of Pennsylvania School of Social Work, 1981.

24. Frederick C. Cuny, *Disasters and Development* (Oxford: Oxford University Press, 1983); "Natural Disasters: The Human Connection," Cox Newspaper Special Report, 1986.

25. For a valuable new resource on the subject see World Resources Institute, *World Resources, 1987* (New York: Basic Books, 1987). The series of *State of the World* reports issued by Lester R. Brown and his colleagues at the Worldwatch Institute also are valuable sources of information on this subject. The complexities of managing the growing incidence of "man-made" disasters are discussed in Charles Perrow, *Normal Accidents: Living with High-Risk Technologies* (New York: Basic Books, 1984).

26. Citing an official report from the U.S. National Oceanic and Atmospheric Administration, *USA Today* reported that U.S. natural disasters in 1983 alone were responsible for more than 700 deaths and $27 billion in property damage (August 8, 1984, p. 8A).

27. Erik Eckholm, "Fatal Disasters on the Rise: Increased Peril Attributed to Unwise Land Use and Poverty," *New York Times*, July 31, 1984, pp. C2–C3; also Anders Wijkman and Lloyd Timberlake, *Natural Disasters: Acts of God or Acts of Man?* (Washington, D.C.: Earthscan, 1984).

28. These rights (and responsibilities) have been codified in the United Nations Universal Declaration of Human Rights. For a listing of all international conventions pertaining to human rights worldwide see United Nations, *Human Rights: A Compilation of International Instruments* (New York, 1978), sales no. E.78.XIV.2.

29. Raymond Gastil (ed.), *Freedom in the World: Political Rights and Civil Liberties, 1983–1984* (Westport, CT: Greenwood Press, 1984).

30. Charles Humana (ed.), *The Human Rights Guide* (New York: Facts on File, 1986).

31. For an example of the complex interplay of these forces at work see Robert Erikson et al. (eds.), *The Scandinavian Model: Welfare States and Welfare Research* (Armonk, NY: M. E. Sharpe, 1987).

32. William Barclay et al., *Racial Conflict, Discrimination, and Power: Historical and Contemporary Studies* (New York: AMS Press, 1976).

33. Richard T. Schaefer, *Racial and Ethnic Groups*, 2d edn. (Boston, MA: Little, Brown, 1984), Chapter 16, pp. 453–86.

34. For a more detailed listing of current ethnic conflicts worldwide see Don Podesta, "Ethnic Conflicts: Toll Mounts," *Washington Post*, May 26, 1987, pp. A1, A17.

35. For several very useful discussions of the dynamics of welfare development see Harold L. Wilensky, *The Welfare State and Equality* (Berkeley, CA: University of California Press, 1975); Gaston Rimlinger, *Welfare Policy and Industrialization in Europe, America, and Russia* (New York: John Wiley, 1971); John Dixon, *Social Security Traditions and Their Global Applications* (Belconnen, Australia: International Fellowship for Social and Economic Development, 1986).

36. Summary information concerning the social security programs of individual countries can be found in U.S. Department of Health and Human Services, *Social Security Programs Throughout the World, 1985* (Washington, D.C.: Social Security Administration, 1986), Office of Research, Statistics, and International Policy, report no. 60.

37. Detailed information concerning international social security financing patterns can be found in International Labour Office, *The Cost of Social Security*, 11th edn. (Geneva, 1985).

38. Emmanuel Jimenez, *Pricing Policy in the Social Sectors: Cost Recovery for Education and Health in Developing Countries* (Baltimore, MD: Johns Hopkins University Press, for the World Bank, 1987).

39. World Bank, *Financing Health Services in Developing Countries: An Agenda for Reform* (Washington, D.C., 1987).

40. The statistical procedures used to construct these indexes are described in Appendix C. Readers familiar with earlier versions of the ISP are cautioned against confusing those versions of the index with the ISP83. The ISP83 is constructed from 36 social, economic, and political indicators, for example, whereas earlier versions were formed out of 44. The Weighted Index of Social Progress (WISP) is new to this study.

41. See Richard J. Estes, *The Social Progress of Nations* (New York: Praeger, 1984).

42. The precise amount of financial and technical assistance that flows between nations is unknown. For an estimate of the levels of official development assistance from OECD and OPEC nations to the world's low- and middle-income countries see World Bank, *World Development Report, 1986* (Washington, 1986), Tables 20 and 21, pp. 220–23.

43. References that include discussions of these points are Jay W. Forrester, *World Dynamics*, 2d edn. (Cambridge, MA: Wright-Allen Press, 1973); Edgar Owens and Robert Shaw, *Development Reconsidered: Bridging the Gap Between Government and People* (Lexington, MA: Lexington Books, 1974); Edward G. Stockwell and Karen A. Laidlow, *Third World Development: Problems and Prospects* (Chicago, IL: Nelson-Hall, 1981); Margaret Hardiman and James Midgley, *The Social Dimensions of Development: Social Policy and Planning in the Third World* (Chichester: John Wiley and Sons, 1982).

44. For analytical purposes, *subindex* changes of less than 5.0 percent are not regarded as either statistically or substantively significant changes.

45. Losses on both of these subindexes may be more apparent than real, however, especially given the very basic indicators contained in the women's subindex and the concentration of such a large proportion of the world's "major" natural disasters in only one DME nation, the United States.

46. See *Women: A World Report* (Oxford: Oxford University Press, 1985).

47. A variety of analyses of the international social, economic, and political forces that sustain this gap are available. As examples see Barbara Ward et al. (eds.), *The Widening Gap: Development in the 70s* (New York: Columbia University Press, 1971); Jan Tinbergen, *Reshaping the International Order: A Report to the Club of Rome* (New York: E. P. Dutton, 1976).

48. Eloquent statements of the need for dramatic new initiatives directed at closing the "North–South" gap can be found in Independent Commission on International Development Issues (Willy Brandt, Chair), *North–South: A Program for Survival* (Cambridge, MA: MIT Press, 1980); Altaf Gauhar, *The Rich and the Poor: Development, Negotiations and Cooperation* (Boulder, CO: Westview, 1985).

49. United Nations Children's Fund, *The State of the World's Children, 1987* (New York: Oxford University Press, for UNICEF, 1987); Charles Humana, *World Human Rights Guide* (New York: Facts on File, 1986); Sharon L. Camp and J. Joseph Speidel, *The International Human Suffering Index* (Washington, D.C.: Population Crisis Committee); World Bank, *World Development Report, 1987* (Washington, D.C.: Oxford University Press, for the World Bank, 1987); among others.

50. United Nations, Yearbook of Human Rights (New York, 1987); Raymond Gastil, *Freedom In the World, 1986* (New York: Freedom House, 1986); Charles Humana, *World Human Rights Guide* (New York: Facts on File, 1986).

51. Altaf Gauhar et al., "The Hidden Costs of the Arms Race," *South* (July 1982): 7–14; United Nations, *Economic and Social Consequences of the Arms Race and of Military Expenditures: Updated Report of the Secretary-General* (New York, 1978), sales no. E.78.IX.1.

52. Ruth L. Sivard, *World Military and Social Expenditures, 1985* (Washington, D.C.: World Priorities, 1985), p. 5.

53. Robert A. Kittle and Robert F. Black, "U.S. Again World's No. 1 Arms Merchant," *U.S. News and World Report*, May 28, 1984, p. 59; Stockholm International Peace Research Institute, *World Armaments and Disarmament, 1986* (Stockholm, 1986); Ruth L. Sivard, *World Military and Social Expenditures, 1985*; U.S. Arms Control and Disarmament Agency, *World Military Expenditures and Arms Transfers, 1971–1980* (Washington, D.C.: 1983).

54. As cited by Sivard, *World Military and Social Expenditures*, pp. 14, 16.

55. American Public Health Association, "The Health Effects of U.S. Militarism," *The Nation's Health* (September 1985): 23–25.

56. John Van Oudenaren, *The Soviet Union and Eastern Europe: Options for the 1980s and Beyond* (Santa Monica, CA: Rand Corporation, 1984); Charles Wolf, Jr., "The Costs of the Soviet Empire," *Science*, November 29, 1985, pp. 997–1002.

57. A partial listing of these wars can be found in Estes, *The Social Progress of Nations*, pp. 138–40. Also see Center for Defense Information, *The World At War*

(Washington, D.C., 1983); Sivard, *World Military and Social Expenditures*, pp. 10–11.

58. For a partial listing of the nations included in the "global nuclear network" see "The Nuclear Race: Who Wants the Bomb," *South* (September 1985): 14–21.

REGIONAL TRENDS IN SOCIAL DEVELOPMENT

This chapter reports trends in social development for the world's major regional and subregional groupings. The geographic location of each of the 124 nations included in this study is identified in Chapter 1. For example, Table 1.3 lists nations by major continental and regional groupings; the table also classifies countries, within world regions, by the study's four socioeconomic development groupings. Table 1.2 identifies the subregional location of each country; this table also identifies and reports the geographic location of 17 nations added to the analysis in 1980.[1]

GEOGRAPHIC LOCALE AND SOCIAL DEVELOPMENT

The geographic distribution of nations (Tables 1.2 and 1.3) reveals the relationship between their location and their comparative level of social development. First, all of the most socially advanced nations—the developed market economy nations (DMEs) and Eastern trading area nations (ETAs)—are located either in Europe ($n = 25$), in North America ($n = 2$), or in Oceania ($n = 2$). Israel and Japan are the only two Asian nations grouped with the DMEs and, within Africa, only South Africa is classified as a DME nation. None of the European nations, which include some moderate-income countries (e.g., Greece and Portugal), are classified as either DCs or LDCs. Australia and New Zealand, two of the three Oceania nations included in the study, are unquestionably DME nations, but the majority of countries located in Oceania are comparatively small island nations that are more properly classified as either DCs or LDCs (e.g., Tonga, Samoa, Kiribati, Truk, etc.). Because of the unavailability of comparable data none of these smaller nations are included in the analysis; Papua New Guinea, however, is included for 1980 and 1983 and is grouped with the DCs.

Conversely, with the exception of Israel and Japan, no African, Latin American, Caribbean, or Asian nation is categorized either as a DME (i.e., a "First World") or as an ETA (i.e., a "Second World") nation. Rather, 91 of 94 of the nations located in these subregions are classified either as DCs (i.e., "Third World" nations) or as LDCs (i.e., "Fourth World" nations).[2] These countries, as of 1983, contained 74.4 percent of the world's total population (Table 1.4). By the middle of the next century their numbers are expected to increase to 86 percent of the world's total population of 10 billion persons;[3] the vast majority of the inhabitants of these nations are expected to live in comparative poverty and social deprivation.

REGIONAL GROUPINGS AND "ADEQUACY OF SOCIAL PROVISION"

Table 3.1 reports ISP findings for the eight regional groupings: Africa, North America, Latin America (which includes the Caribbean), South Asia, East Asia, Oceania, the Soviet Union, and Europe. The table includes all ISP, WISP, and subindex data for each region during the three time intervals. The percent change in scores between time intervals is reported in the table for 1970–1983 and 1980–1983.

Table 3.1 confirms that enormous variation exists in the levels of social provision found in each regional grouping. The regions with the highest levels of social provision, as measured by 1983 ISP scores, are Europe (average = 171.7), Oceania (average = 168.3) and North America (average = 156.9). The lowest levels of social provision exist in Africa (average = 56.3) and South Asia (average = 78.8). By comparison, average ISP scores for Latin America (average = 113.5), East Asia (average = 104.6), and the Soviet Union (average = 95.8) place these regions in a middle range with respect to overall adequacy of social provision.

The profound discrepancies in social provision that characterize the regional groupings is striking. Table 3.2, for example, reports subindex score averages in 1983 for Europe (the continent with the highest social provision rating) contrasted with those of Africa (the continent with the lowest social provision rating). The differences in levels of social provision that emerge from this comparison are stark indeed. On virtually every subindex Europe and Africa are at opposite ends of the social provision continuum in terms of their capacity to provide for the basic social needs of their populations. Only on the defense effort subindex do the average scores of the two regional groupings converge (11.6 and

12.3 for Africa and Europe, respectively). In effect, the 40 impoverished nations of Africa, on average, allocate approximately the same proportion of their GNP to defense spending as do the 25 more affluent nations of Europe (i.e., the convergence between the two subindex averages is 94.3 percent). By comparison central government expenditures for health, education, welfare, fertility control, and so on are far lower in Africa than in Europe.

The significance of the sharply different levels of social provision found in Africa and Europe—indeed those which characterize all of the nations of the "North" (i.e., the DMEs and ETAs) vis-à-vis those of the "South" (i.e., the DCs and LDCs)—is reflected in the Brandt Commission's poignant description of life in the South.[4]

Many hundreds of millions of people in the poorer countries are preoccupied solely with survival and elementary needs. For them work is frequently not available or, when it is, pay is very low and conditions often barely tolerable. Homes are constructed of impermanent materials and have neither piped water nor sanitation. Electricity is a luxury. Health services are thinly spread and in rural areas only rarely within walking distance. Primary schools, where they exist, may be free and not too far away, but children are needed for work and cannot be easily spared for schooling. Permanent insecurity is the condition of the poor. There are no public systems of social security in the event of unemployment, sickness or death of a wage-earner in the family. Flood, drought or disease affecting people or livestock can destroy livelihoods without hope of compensation. . . .

The poorest of the poor in the world will remain for some time to come outside the reach of normal trade and communications. The combination of malnutrition, illiteracy, disease, high birth rates, underemployment and low income closes off the avenues of escape; and while other groups are increasingly vocal, the poor and illiterate are usually and conveniently silent. It is a condition of life so limited as to be, in the words of the President of the World Bank, "below any rational definition of human decency."[5]

President Julius Nyerere of Tanzania, one of the Third World's most vocal spokespersons, commented on the disparities that exist in social development worldwide, noting that

Seventy percent of the world's population—the Third World—commands together no more than 12 percent of the gross world product. Eighty percent of the world's trade and investment, 93 percent of its industry, and almost 100 percent of its research is controlled by the industrial rich.[6]

The data reported in Tables 3.1 and 3.2 confirm the existence of a North–South division between social "have" and "have not" nations. These disparities stem, at least in part, simply from the physical location of nations on the planet.[7] The differences in levels of social provision

Table 3.1
Mean Scores and Percentage Change on the Indexes of Social Progress by Continent
(n = 107, n = 124)

WORLD REGIONS AND SUBREGIONS	INDEX OF SOCIAL PROGRESS (ISP)	Educa-tion	Health	Women	Defense	Economic	Demo-graphic	Geo-graphic	Partici-pation	Cultural	Welfare	WEIGHTED INDEX OF SOCIAL PROGRESS
AFRICA												
1970 (N=35)	57.0	3.4	0.7	2.3	12.6	8.2	5.0	11.4	6.0	2.7	4.7	19.8
1980B (N=40)	55.4	4.2	1.6	3.3	11.5	5.7	4.2	10.9	4.7	3.5	5.7	19.9
1983A (N=35)	55.1	3.8	1.5	2.8	12.1	6.0	3.8	10.7	4.7	3.5	6.3	19.5
1983B (N=40)	56.3	4.3	1.9	3.5	11.6	5.9	4.3	10.9	5.5	3.5	5.8	20.4
% 1980B-1983B (N=40)	1.6	2.4	18.7	6.1	0.9	3.5	2.4	0.0	17.0	0.0	1.8	2.5
% 1970-1983A (N=35)	-3.3	11.8	114.3	21.7	-4.0	-26.8	-24.0	-6.1	-21.7	29.6	34.0	-1.5
NORTH AMERICA												
1970 (N=2)	140.5	22.5	19.5	19.5	5.0	21.0	15.5	-7.0	19.5	9.5	15.5	73.9
1980 (N=2)	156.3	20.4	20.6	17.6	12.4	17.6	17.8	-2.5	25.5	11.1	15.7	77.3
1983 (N=2)	156.9	21.1	20.5	16.7	11.5	19.9	17.3	-2.5	25.4	11.1	15.8	77.7
% 1980-1983 (N=2)	0.4	3.4	-0.5	-5.1	-7.3	13.1	-2.8	0.0	-0.4	0.0	0.6	0.5
% 1970-1983 (N=2)	11.7	-6.2	5.1	-14.4	130.0	-5.2	11.6	-64.3	30.3	16.8	1.9	5.1
LATIN AMERICA												
1970 (N=21)	112.2	11.7	13.5	13.1	14.4	8.0	8.5	7.2	11.4	15.9	8.5	49.8
1980B (N=22)	113.8	11.7	12.6	12.4	14.9	7.0	10.8	7.9	13.0	13.2	10.2	50.4
1983A (N=21)	112.9	11.4	12.0	13.2	14.0	5.9	10.5	7.7	14.4	13.5	10.4	50.2
1983B (N=22)	113.5	11.7	12.3	13.3	13.8	6.2	10.9	7.9	13.8	13.2	10.3	50.6
% 1980B-1983B (N=22)	-0.3	0.0	-2.4	7.3	-7.4	-11.4	0.9	0.0	6.2	0.0	1.0	0.4
% 1970-1983A (N=21)	0.6	-2.6	-11.1	0.8	-2.8	-26.3	23.5	6.9	26.3	-15.1	22.4	0.8

SOUTH ASIA

1970 (N=20)	71.4	8.2	10.3	7.0	0.7	7.2	7.0	8.8	8.0	9.4	4.7	33.2
1980B (N=25)	77.3	8.2	7.5	8.9	4.0	10.1	7.2	9.3	7.5	10.6	4.0	34.4
1983A (N=20)	88.2	9.4	9.9	10.6	4.9	12.1	8.5	10.0	8.1	9.8	4.9	39.8
1983B (N=25)	78.8	8.3	7.7	8.9	4.4	11.6	7.3	9.3	6.7	10.6	4.0	35.0
% 1980-1983 (N=25)	1.9	1.2	2.7	0.0	10.0	14.9	1.4	0.0	-10.7	0.0	0.0	1.7
% 1970-1983 (N=20)	23.5	14.6	-3.9	51.4	600.0	68.1	21.4	13.6	1.2	4.3	4.3	19.9

EAST ASIA

1970 (N=3)	129.0	12.5	18.0	15.0	13.0	14.5	14.0	2.0	2.1	17.5	7.0	60.8
1980B (N=7)	104.4	11.4	16.9	17.4	-0.7	13.1	12.6	3.6	8.2	17.0	4.7	53.0
1983A (N=3)	120.2	13.7	16.8	16.1	10.5	15.1	11.0	-0.7	11.3	17.9	8.6	58.2
1983B (N=7)	104.6	11.1	16.8	16.5	0.7	13.6	12.7	3.6	7.8	17.0	4.7	52.6
% 1980B-1983B (N=7)	0.2	-2.6	-0.6	-5.2	-200.0	3.8	0.8	0.0	-4.9	0.0	0.0	-0.8
% 1970-1983A (N=3)	-6.8	9.6	-6.7	7.3	-19.2	4.1	-21.4	-135.0	438.1	2.3	22.9	-4.3

OCEANIA (Excluding PNG)

1970 (N=2)	174.0	17.0	19.0	27.0	12.0	13.5	17.0	14.5	16.0	13.5	24.5	81.0
1980 (N=2)	171.3	18.6	19.1	15.5	15.4	15.8	18.2	8.0	25.5	16.5	23.1	81.6
1983 (N=2)	168.3	17.8	19.6	15.0	14.3	16.2	19.0	8.0	25.4	16.5	23.0	81.2
% 1980-1983 (N=2)	-1.8	-4.3	2.6	-3.2	-7.1	2.5	4.4	0.0	-0.4	0.0	-0.4	-0.5
% 1970-1983 (N=2)	-3.3	4.7	3.2	-44.4	19.2	20.0	11.8	-44.8	58.8	22.2	-6.1	0.2

Table 3.1 (cont.)

WORLD REGIONS AND SUBREGIONS	INDEX OF SOCIAL PROGRESS (ISP)	Educa-tion	Health	Women	Defense	Economic	Demo-graphic	Geo-graphic	Partici-pation	Cultural	Welfare	WEIGHTED INDEX OF SOCIAL PROGRESS
U.S.S.R.												
1970 (N=1)	134.0	24.0	18.0	22.0	2.0	19.0	10.0		16.0	-4.0	17.0	66.9
1980 (N=1)	100.8	21.3	18.5	17.1	-6.8	18.1	11.8	6.9	1.3	-5.6	18.3	55.6
1983 (N=1)	95.8	20.5	18.0	16.3	-2.3	13.2	11.0	6.9	-0.2	-5.6	18.2	51.8
% 1980-1983 (N=1)	-5.0	-3.8	-2.7	-4.7	-66.2	-27.1	-6.8	0.0	-115.4	0.0	-0.5	-6.8
% 1970-1983 (N=1)	-28.5	-14.6	0.0	-25.9	-215.0	-30.5	10.0	-31.0	-101.3	40.0	7.1	-22.6
EUROPE												
1970 (N=23)	168.7	18.0	18.5	18.4	10.5	15.4	20.5	14.0	14.9	15.8	22.7	78.6
1980B (N=24)	174.1	17.8	20.4	16.7	12.1	17.4	19.8	14.6	16.5	15.7	23.1	80.4
1983A (N=23)	172.4	17.5	20.0	16.1	12.4	16.2	19.5	14.5	17.5	15.7	22.9	79.3
1983B (N=24)	171.7	17.4	20.0	16.1	12.3	16.2	19.6	14.6	16.7	15.7	23.0	79.1
% 1980B-1983B (N=24)	-1.4	-2.2	-2.0	-3.6	1.7	-6.9	-1.0	0.0	1.2	0.0	-0.4	-1.6
% 1970-1983 (N=23)	2.2	-2.8	8.1	-12.5	18.1	5.2	-4.9	3.6	17.4	-0.6	0.9	0.9
All Countries, Continents and Regions												
1970 (N=107)	100.0	10.0	10.0	10.0	10.0	10.0	10.0	10.0	10.0	10.0	10.0	44.5
1980B (N=124)	100.0	10.0	10.0	10.0	10.0	10.0	10.0	10.0	10.0	10.0	10.0	44.1
1983A (N=107)	100.0	10.0	10.0	10.0	10.0	10.0	10.0	10.0	10.0	10.0	10.0	44.1
1983B (N=124)	100.0	10.0	10.0	10.0	10.0	10.0	10.0	10.0	10.0	10.0	10.0	44.1

Table 3.1 (cont.)

Methodological Note: Inasmuch as a larger number of nations were included in the study in both 1980 and 1984 (n = 124) than in 1970 (n = 107), the tables contained in this chapter report data differently than elsewhere in the volume. More specifically, average Index of Social Progress (ISP), Weighted Index of Social Progress (WISP), and subindex scores are reported in three ways for each of the study's eight continental and 22 regional groupings.

First, average index scores are reported in the tables for each continent and region separately, for 1970 (labeled "1970"), 1980 (labeled "1980B"), and 1983 (labeled either "1983A" when the original listing and number of countries included in the regional grouping did not change between 1970 and 1983, or "1983B" when the number or listing of countries varied between the two time intervals). For nine regional groupings both "1983A" and "1983B" scores are reported inasmuch as additional nations were included in the analyses of these regions beginning in 1980, that is, the number of West African countries included in the study remained constant for all three time intervals, whereas two East Africa nations (Mozambique and Mauritius) were added to the analyses for 1980 and 1983. For the West African region, therefore, only 1983A scores are reported, whereas both 1983A and 1983B scores are reported for the East African region.

Second, percentage changes in index and subindex scores over time are reported separately for the 107 nations that were included in the study for the full 14-year time period. These change scores are labeled in the tables as "% 1970-1983A." Third, the tables also reflect changes in adequacy of social provision for all 124 nations for the four-year period 1980-1983. These shorter-term changes are labeled in the tables as either "% 1980B-1983B" for groupings for which additional countries were added in 1980 or "% 1980B-1983A" where the grouping contained the same nations for all three time intervals. Thus, the averages reported in this chapter's major tables are group averages based on the actual number of countries included in each grouping during the respective time period.

61

Table 3.2
Mean Scores and Percentage Change on the Indexes of Social Progress for Europe and Africa, 1983

CONTINENTS	INDEX OF SOCIAL PROGRESS (ISP)	Educa-tion	Health	Women	Defense	Economic	Demo-graphic	Geo-graphic	Partici-pation	Cultural	Welfare	WEIGHTED INDEX OF SOCIAL PROGRESS
Europe (N=24)	171.7	17.4	20.0	16.1	12.3	16.2	19.6	14.6	16.7	15.7	23.0	79.1
Africa (N=40)	56.3	4.3	1.9	3.5	11.6	5.9	4.3	10.9	5.5	3.5	5.8	20.4
African Scores as Percentage of European Scores	32.8	24.7	9.5	21.7	94.3	36.4	21.9	74.7	32.9	22.3	25.2	25.8

Table 3.3
Mean Index of Social Progress Scores and Percentage Change 1970–1983,
1980–1983 ($n = 107$, $n = 124$)

1970 (N=107)	1983 (N=107)	Percentage Change 1970-1983 (N=107)	CONTINENT	1980 (N=124)	1983 (N=124)	Percentage Change 1980-1983 (N=124)
57.0	55.1	-3.3	AFRICA	55.4	56.3	1.6
140.5	156.9	11.7	NORTH AMERICA	156.3	156.9	0.4
112.2	112.9	0.6	LATIN AMERICA	113.8	113.5	-0.3
71.4	88.2	23.5	SOUTH ASIA	77.3	78.8	1.9
129.0	120.2	-6.8	EAST ASIA	104.4	104.6	0.2
174.0	168.3	-3.3	OCEANIA	171.3	168.3	-1.8
134.0	95.8	-28.5	U.S.S.R.	100.8	95.8	-5.0
168.7	172.4	2.2	EUROPE	174.1	171.7	-1.4

between various groupings of nations by continent are real, and they are substantial. But is this gap in development increasing, or do trends in world social development suggest that a higher level of parity is beginning to occur between the richest and poorest areas?

REGIONAL CHANGES IN ISP PROFILES

The question concerning the changing nature of the gap in social development between the world's regional groupings is answered in Table 3.1. Average ISP scores are summarized in Table 3.3, which reports ISP scores for each region for the period 1970 to 1983 ($n = 107$) and for 1980 to 1983 ($n = 124$). Percentage changes in these scores between the various time periods are also reported in Table 3.3.

Several trends concerning the changing social capacity of the world's regional groupings are noteworthy:

1. Social development is not a stagnant process. Rather, substantial changes in levels of social development worldwide are continually taking place and these changes are reflected in group ISP scores.

2. Not all of the changes in social development taking place are of a

positive nature; instead, between 1970 and 1983 ISP scores declined by more than 5 percent for two regional groupings (Soviet Union and East Asia) and for one grouping between 1980 and 1983 (again, the Soviet Union). Smaller net losses were also found for Africa (−3.3 percent) and Oceania (−3.3 percent) during the 1970–1983 period and, between 1980 and 1983, for Latin America (−0.3 percent), and Europe (−1.4 percent).

3. Net declines in overall social capacity are occurring within some of the world's most socially advanced nations, that is, within selected DME and ETA nations located in Europe (e.g., Sweden, the United Kingdom, Albania, Poland, etc.), and the Soviet Union. Some of the changes found are very small indeed (e.g., −1.5 percent for Sweden) but, as in the case of the Soviet Union (−28.4 percent), some index declines are substantial.

4. ISP social gains amounting to +23.5 percent were registered for the predominately DC nations of South Asia between 1970 and 1983. Average ISP scores for North America increased by +11.7 percent during the same time period.

Worldwide changes in social provision, therefore, are occurring. The magnitude of these changes is especially significant for several regions. For the nations of South Asia and North America these changes are of a highly positive nature and reflect their improved capacity to provide for the basic needs of their populations. Net losses on the ISP were observed for the Soviet Union (−28.4 percent) and the nations of East Asia (−6.8 percent). These highly unfavorable ISP changes reflect diminished social capacity for the nations located in these regions.

The gap in social development, therefore, depending on the regional grouping, can be found to be either narrowing or widening. It is narrowing for those groupings for which positive social changes are registered, but widening for those regions that lost social ground between 1970 and 1983. The negative trends are especially alarming for the Soviet Union, the ETA nations of Eastern Europe and, to a lesser extent, for the DCs of East Asia.

REGIONAL AND SUBREGIONAL ANALYSES

Changes in patterns of social provision are reported in this section of the chapter for the majority of the world's major subregional groupings.

Africa

Forty African nations are included in this study (Table 1.2). These countries are distributed between five subregional groupings: West Africa ($n=$ 13), East Africa ($n=$ 13), North Africa ($n=$ 6); Middle Africa ($n=$ 6); and Southern Africa ($n=$ 2). Each of these subregions has its own political history and each, of course, is characterized by a somewhat different pattern of social development.

As identified in Tables 3.1 and 3.3, Africa is the least socially and economically developed of the continents. It is also Africa that has the highest rates of population growth and the largest number of countries with political dictatorships, and it is the continent on which human rights violations are the most widespread. Life expectancy in Africa is well below 50 years, and rates of infant mortality are in excess of 125 children per 1,000 live-born. Africa is also the "poorest of the poor" continents, including, as it does, 18 of the 25 LDCs in this study. Fourteen of these are divided equally between East and West Africa, two are located in Middle Africa, and one is located in each of the remaining two subregions.[8] Further, the chronicity of the social problems confronting Africa is reflected in the fact that the ISP scores of three African subregions declined significantly between 1970 and 1983: Southern Africa (-21.3 percent), West Africa (-9.8 percent), and East Africa (-9.1 percent). Average ISP scores for the continent as a whole dropped by 3.3 percent during the 14-year period.

But Africa is also the continent where the world's youngest nations are found. Formerly under colonial domination, lasting in some cases for centuries, the vast majority of these nations are newly autonomous, having achieved independence only in the early 1960s, a few even as late as the early 1970s.[9] Comparatively few of these youthful nations had available to them, at least at the time of independence, either indigenous leaders or the social and political infrastructures that are required to shape newly unified territories into fully integrated nations. Similarly, comparatively few of these countries possessed the fiscal, industrial, and other economic infrastructures that are required to finance industrial development. Not surprisingly, the majority of black African nations, but especially those south of the Sahara Desert, continue to struggle to find the ways for responding to the myriad social, political, economic, and other needs of their rapidly increasing populations (the average population doubling time is less than 35 years).[10] For most of these subregions social development has been uneven at best; for many a continuous downward spiral appears to be the norm.[11]

West Africa

West Africa is one of Africa's two least developed subregions. The subregion consists of 13 nations, seven of which are LDCs (Benin, Burkina-Faso, Guinea, Mali, Niger, Sierra Leone, and Togo). ISP scores for the subregion averaged 51.2 in 1970; however, between 1970 and 1983

Table 3.4
Scores and Percentage Change on the Indexes of Social Progress by
Subregion and Year ($n = 107$, $n = 124$)

WORLD REGIONS AND SUBREGIONS	INDEX OF SOCIAL PROGRESS! (ISP)	Educa-tion	Health	Women	Defense	Economic	Demo-graphic	Geo-graphic	Partici-pation	Cultural	Welfare	WEIGHTED INDEX OF SOCIAL PROGRESS
AFRICA												
Western												
1970 (N=13)	51.2	1.3	-0.8	1.6	13.8	7.7	5.1	11.8	5.3	1.2	4.2	16.2
1980B (N=13)	46.8	2.4	-0.6	0.0	14.0	3.9	3.0	9.9	7.1	0.3	6.9	14.7
1983A (N=13)	46.2	1.7	-0.8	-0.2	14.1	5.2	2.9	9.9	6.1	0.3	7.0	14.3
% 1980B-1983A (N=13)	-1.3	-29.2	33.3	NA	0.7	33.3	-3.3	0.0	-14.1	0.0	1.4	-2.7
% 1970-1983A (N=13)	-9.8	30.8	0.0	-112.5	2.2	-32.5	-43.1	-16.1	15.1	-75.0	66.7	-11.7
Eastern												
1970 (N=11)	56.0	3.2	1.2	1.4	15.0	7.7	4.1	12.6	6.9	1.8	2.1	18.0
1980B (N=13)	51.7	3.7	0.6	5.0	9.9	6.2	3.5	12.5	3.2	3.9	3.2	17.9
1983A (N=11)	50.9	4.4	0.1	5.1	10.9	5.8	2.4	12.0	3.2	3.8	3.2	17.4
1983B (N=13)	56.2	5.0	1.0	5.8	11.5	5.7	3.5	12.5	4.1	3.9	3.1	19.8
% 1980B-1983B (N=13)	8.7	35.1	66.7	16.0	16.2	-8.1	0.0	0.0	28.1	0.0	-3.1	10.6
% 1970-1983A (N=11)	-9.1	37.5	-91.7	264.3	-27.3	-24.7	-41.5	-4.8	-53.6	111.1	52.4	-3.3
Northern												
1970 (N=6)	71.8	8.7	5.5	1.7	6.0	10.3	5.3	8.3	4.5	14.0	7.5	30.5
1980B (N=6)	85.3	8.5	9.0	4.2	8.2	9.2	5.9	10.7	6.7	15.0	7.7	36.0
1983A (N=6)	83.7	8.5	9.2	4.4	8.0	7.8	5.8	10.7	6.5	15.0	7.9	35.4
% 1980B-1983A (N=6)	-1.9	0.0	2.2	4.8	-2.4	-15.2	-1.7	0.0	-3.0	0.0	2.6	-1.7
% 1970-1983A (N=6)	16.6	-2.3	67.3	158.8	33.3	-24.3	9.4	28.9	44.4	7.1	5.3	16.1
Middle												
1970 (N=4)	40.5	1.5	-5.2	3.7	11.5	7.0	5.7	9.8	6.0	-5.0	5.5	12.6
1980B (N=6)	38.4	3.5	-0.7	3.3	11.6	3.1	5.3	9.8	-0.2	-3.8	6.5	12.9
1983A (N=4)	42.8	1.8	-1.4	2.3	15.0	5.2	5.6	9.8	0.7	-4.2	8.0	13.5
1983B (N=6)	39.2	3.3	0.6	3.0	9.5	4.8	5.3	9.8	0.2	-3.8	6.6	14.0
% 1980B-1983B (N=6)	2.1	-5.7	-185.7	-9.1	-18.1	54.8	0.0	0.0	-200.0	0.0	1.5	8.5
% 1970-1983A (N=4)	5.7	20.0	-73.1	-37.8	30.4	-25.7	-1.8	0.0	-88.3	-16.0	45.5	7.1
Southern												
1970 (N=1)	120.0	10.0	8.0	21.0	14.0	13.0	8.0	19.0	13.0	-5.0	19.0	50.7
1980B (N=2)	96.6	7.7	8.0	10.6	14.9	11.3	8.2	11.6	7.8	9.2	7.1	39.8
1983A (N=1)	94.4	5.2	11.8	8.2	11.7	10.7	9.5	11.7	7.0	3.0	15.7	40.7
1983B (N=2)	91.1	6.7	7.4	11.6	12.1	9.5	8.3	11.6	7.9	9.2	6.9	38.0
% 1980B-1983B (N=2)	-5.7	-13.0	-7.5	9.4	-18.8	-15.9	1.2	0.0	1.3	0.0	-2.8	-4.5
% 1970-1983A (N=1)	-21.3	-48.0	47.5	-61.0	-16.4	-17.7	18.8	-38.4	-46.2	-160.0	-17.4	-19.7

Table 3.4 (cont.)

WORLD REGIONS AND SUBREGIONS	INDEX OF SOCIAL PROGRESS (ISP)	Education	Health	Women	Defense	Economic	Demographic	Geographic	Participation	Cultural	Welfare	WEIGHTED INDEX OF SOCIAL PROGRESS
LATIN AMERICA												
Tropical												
1970 (N=6)	105.7	11.8	12.8	13.0	14.0	7.0	6.5	5.8	9.8	14.2	10.7	47.3
1980B (N=6)	115.3	12.6	10.5	12.4	15.2	9.0	8.8	6.2	17.6	11.4	11.4	50.9
1983A (N=6)	114.3	12.6	9.8	13.8	14.8	6.1	9.1	6.2	19.1	11.4	11.5	50.7
% 1980B-1983A (N=6)	-0.9	0.0	-6.7	11.3	-2.6	-32.2	3.4	0.0	8.5	0.0	0.9	-0.4
% 1970-1983A (N=6)	8.1	6.8	-23.4	6.2	5.7	-12.9	40.0	6.9	94.9	-19.7	7.5	7.2
Middle												
1970 (N=7)	104.1	10.4	13.1	11.7	15.6	9.4	5.7	3.4	13.4	16.0	5.3	46.0
1980B (N=7)	102.8	10.5	11.7	9.5	15.1	7.6	8.3	5.0	13.1	14.3	7.8	45.1
1983A (N=7)	99.5	10.4	12.0	10.4	13.0	5.7	8.4	5.0	12.4	14.3	7.9	44.5
% 1980B-1983A (N=7)	-3.2	-1.0	2.6	9.5	-13.9	-25.0	1.2	0.0	-5.3	0.0	1.3	-1.3
% 1970-1983A (N=7)	-4.4	0.0	-8.4	-11.1	-16.7	-39.4	47.4	47.1	-7.5	-10.6	49.1	-3.3
Temperate												
1970 (N=4)	132.8	14.0	15.0	15.5	14.3	4.7	14.3	12.3	11.5	16.0	15.0	59.5
1980B (N=4)	124.5	13.4	16.0	16.6	13.9	2.0	15.1	9.1	5.0	15.5	17.9	57.6
1983A (N=4)	129.6	14.0	15.5	17.5	13.4	3.4	15.1	9.1	8.3	15.5	18.0	60.0
% 1980B-1983A (N=4)	4.1	4.5	-3.1	5.4	-3.6	70.0	0.0	0.0	66.0	0.0	0.6	4.2
% 1970-1983A (N=4)	-2.4	0.0	3.3	12.9	-6.3	-27.7	5.6	-26.0	-27.8	-3.1	20.0	0.8
Caribbean												
1970 (N=4)	114.8	11.4	13.2	13.4	13.4	9.6	10.4	10.0	10.4	17.6	5.4	50.3
1980B (N=5)	118.9	10.9	13.8	13.3	15.2	7.9	13.0	13.0	13.6	12.1	6.1	51.4
1983A (N=4)	117.5	8.6	11.6	12.9	15.2	8.2	11.9	13.1	17.0	13.5	5.5	49.6
1983B (N=5)	119.2	10.8	13.2	13.6	13.9	9.2	13.3	13.0	13.9	12.1	6.2	51.8
% 1980B-1983B (N=5)	0.3	-0.9	-4.3	2.3	-8.6	16.5	2.3	0.0	2.2	0.0	1.6	0.8
% 1970-1983A (N=4)	2.4	-24.6	-12.1	-3.7	13.4	-14.6	14.4	31.0	63.5	-23.3	1.9	-1.4
SOUTH ASIA												
Middle-South												
1970 (N=5)	67.8	3.4	7.0	4.2	12.4	9.0	3.4	6.6	10.8	5.6	5.4	27.0
1980B (N=7)	65.0	4.1	2.9	2.6	12.5	7.8	4.4	5.4	10.7	9.3	5.2	25.2
1983A (N=7)	79.1	4.8	6.5	3.6	13.1	12.5	5.3	6.7	11.7	8.0	6.9	32
1983B (N=7)	66.2	2.8	4.0	1.8	13.0	11.4	4.1	5.4	9.1	9.3	5.2	25.6
% 1980B-1983B (N=7)	1.8	-31.7	37.9	-30.8	4.0	46.2	-6.8	0.0	-15.0	0.0	0.0	1.6
% 1970-1983A (N=5)	16.7	41.2	-7.1	-14.3	5.6	38.9	55.9	1.5	8.3	42.9	27.8	18.5
Southeastern												
1970 (N=8)	72.1	8.9	10.0	10.6	5.2	2.7	8.6	7.6	6.9	6.8	4.7	33.5
1980B (N=9)	86.7	8.4	8.9	11.3	12.3	10.5	9.9	10.3	5.2	6.7	3.1	37.1
1983A (N=8)	92.6	8.9	9.6	11.6	12.1	12.4	10.5	10.3	6.3	7.3	3.5	40
1983B (N=9)	86.9	8.9	7.2	10.9	12.1	12.4	10.0	10.3	5.5	6.7	2.9	36.9
% 1980B-1983B (N=9)	0.2	6.0	-19.1	-3.5	-1.6	18.1	1.0	0.0	5.8	0.0	-6.5	-0.5
% 1970-1983A (N=9)	28.4	0.0	-4.0	9.4	132.7	359.3	22.1	35.5	-8.7	7.4	-25.5	19.4
Southwestern												
1970 (N=7)	73.3	10.9	12.9	5.0	-12.7	11.1	7.9	11.6	7.3	15.3	4.1	37.4

Table 3.4 (cont.)

WORLD REGIONS AND SUBREGIONS	INDEX OF SOCIAL PROGRESS (ISP)	Educa-tion	Health	Women	Defense	Economic	Demo-graphic	Geo-graphic	Partici-pation	Cultural	Welfare	WEIGHTED INDEX OF SOCIAL PROGRESS
1980B (N=9) !	77.7 !	11.9	9.6	11.5	-10.8	11.6	6.7	11.3	7.3	15.3	4.1 !	38.9
1983A (N=7) !	89.6 !	13.2	12.7	14.5	-9.4	11.6	8.6	12.0	7.4	14.0	5.0 !	45.1
1983B (N=9) !	80.3 !	4.1	11.2	12.4	-10.0	11.0	7.1	11.3	6.1	15.3	4.1 !	40.4
% 1980B-1983B (N=9) !	3.3 !	-65.5	16.7	7.8	-7.4	-5.2	6.0	0.0	-16.4	0.0	0.0 !	3.9
% 1970-1983A (N=7) !	22.2 !	21.1	-1.6	190.0	-26.0	4.5	8.9	3.4	1.4	-8.5	22.0 !	20.6
EAST ASIA !	!										!	
!	!										!	
Mainland East !	!										!	
1970 (N=0) !	NA !	NA	NA	NA	NA	NA	NA	NA	NA	NA	NA !	NA
1980B (N=3) !	89.9 !	11.4	15.5	11.8	6.0	10.6	9.2	2.1	5.4	15.4	2.5 !	43.9
1983A (N=3) !	93.8 !	11.1	15.8	10.8	8.4	13.1	9.6	2.1	5.0	15.4	2.5 !	44.9
% 1980B-1983A (N=3) !	4.3 !	-2.6	1.9	-8.5	40.0	23.6	4.3	0.0	-7.4	0.0	0.0 !	2.3
% 1970-1983A (N=0) !	NA !	NA	NA	NA	NA	NA	NA	NA	NA	NA	NA !	NA
!	!										!	
Other East !	!										!	
1970 (N=1) !	103.0 !	9.0	17.0	15.0	9.0	12.0	10.0	2.0	14.0	14.0	1.0 !	49.0
1980B (N=3) !	94.2 !	9.4	17.3	19.3	-13.6	13.8	14.0	7.5	5.7	17.7	3.2 !	51.1
1983A (N=1) !	112.1 !	11.5	16.5	12.5	9.5	12.7	15.6	4.6	7.0	18.3	3.9 !	53.1
1983B (N=3) !	92.2 !	9.0	16.8	18.6	-12.2	13.0	13.9	7.5	4.7	17.7	3.1 !	49.6
% 1980B-1983B (N=3) !	-2.1 !	-4.3	-2.9	-3.6	-10.3	-5.8	-0.7	0.0	-17.5	0.0	-3.1 !	-2.9
% 1970-1983A (N=1) !	8.8 !	27.8	-2.9	-16.7	5.6	5.8	56.0	130.0	-50.0	30.7	290.0 !	8.4
!	!										!	
Japan !	!										!	
1970 (N=1) !	155.0 !	16.0	19.0	15.0	17.0	17.0	18.0	2.0	17.0	21.0	13.0 !	72.6
1980B (N=1) !	178.3 !	18.0	20.0	28.8	18.0	19.0	19.0	-3.0	24.0	20.0	16.0 !	86.5
1983A (N=1) !	174.3 !	17.0	20.0	27.1	16.0	17.0	19.0	-3.0	25.0	20.0	16.0 !	84.7
% 1980B-1983A (N=1) !	-2.2 !	-5.6	0.0	-5.9	-11.1	-10.5	0.0	0.0	4.2	0.0	0.0 !	-2.1
% 1970-1983A (N=1) !	12.5 !	6.3	5.3	80.7	-5.9	0.0	5.6	-250.0	47.1	-4.8	23.1 !	16.7
EUROPE !	!										!	
!	!										!	
Western !	!										!	
1970 (N=6) !	176.5 !	19.0	19.2	18.0	11.7	15.3	20.2	14.2	18.7	14.0	26.3 !	82.1
1980B (N=6) !	191.5 !	19.8	21.3	17.4	14.1	19.4	21.1	12.7	25.0	14.3	26.4 !	88.8
1983A (N=6) !	188.4 !	19.6	20.8	16.8	13.7	18.8	20.8	12.7	24.8	14.3	26.2 !	87.3
% 1980B-1983A (N=6) !	-1.6 !	-1.0	-2.8	-3.4	-2.8	-3.1	-1.4	0.0	-0.8	0.0	-0.8 !	-1.7
% 1970-1983A (N=6) !	6.7 !	3.2	7.8	-6.7	17.1	22.9	3.0	-10.6	32.6	2.1	-0.4 !	6.3
!	!										!	
Southern !	!										!	
1970 (N=6) !	146.2 !	13.5	17.5	14.5	8.7	13.3	19.0	14.5	11.0	16.0	18.2 !	67.4
1980B (N=6) !	158.8 !	15.0	19.6	15.9	11.3	14.1	18.4	15.0	15.1	15.4	18.9 !	72.7
1983A (N=6) !	158.6 !	14.6	19.7	15.7	12.3	12.3	18.6	15.0	16.1	15.4	19.0 !	72.3
% 1980B-1983A (N=6) !	-0.1 !	-2.7	0.5	-1.3	8.8	-12.8	1.1	0.0	6.6	0.0	0.5 !	-0.6
% 1970-1983A (N=6) !	8.5 !	8.1	12.6	8.3	41.4	-7.5	-2.1	3.4	46.4	-3.7	4.4 !	7.3
!	!										!	
Eastern !	!										!	
1970 (N=5) !	166.6 !	18.4	17.8	18.2	9.6	19.2	21.6	16.0	10.0	14.6	21.2 !	77.5
1980B (N=6) !	157.0 !	16.1	20.3	18.1	9.2	18.4	19.3	18.5	0.7	14.7	21.8 !	72.7
1983A (N=5) !	152.6 !	16.1	19.1	17.5	9.6	15.9	18.6	18.7	1.7	14.3	21.1 !	70.2

Table 3.4 (cont.)

WORLD REGIONS AND SUBREGIONS	INDEX OF SOCIAL PROGRESS (ISP)	Education	Health	Women	Defense	Economic	Demographic	Geographic	Participation	Cultural	Welfare	WEIGHTED INDEX OF SOCIAL PROGRESS
1983B (N=6)	153.1	15.9	19.4	17.3	9.4	16.3	18.9	18.5	1.1	14.7	21.6	70.6
% 1980B-1983B (N=6)	-2.5	-1.2	-4.4	-4.4	2.2	-11.4	-2.1	0.0	57.1	0.0	-0.9	-2.9
% 1970-1983A (N=5)	-8.4	-12.5	7.3	-3.8	0.0	-17.2	-13.9	16.9	-83.0	-2.1	-0.5	-9.4
Northern												
1970 (N=6)	185.3	21.0	19.3	23.0	12.0	14.3	21.5	11.7	19.2	18.5	24.8	87.4
1980B (N=6)	189.2	20.2	20.4	15.5	14.0	17.5	20.3	12.4	25.0	18.5	25.4	87.3
1983A (N=6)	186.8	19.6	20.3	14.6	13.6	17.6	20.0	12.4	24.9	18.5	25.2	86.1
% 1980B-1983A (N=6)	-1.3	-3.0	-0.5	-5.8	-2.9	0.6	-1.5	0.0	-0.4	0.0	-0.8	-1.4
% 1970-1983A (N=6)	0.8	-6.7	5.2	-36.5	13.3	23.1	-7.0	6.0	29.7	0.0	1.6	-1.5
All Subregions												
1970 (N=107)	100.0	10.0	10.0	10.0	10.0	10.0	10.0	10.0	10.0	10.0	10.0	44.5
1980B (N=124)	100.0	10.0	10.0	10.0	10.0	10.0	10.0	10.0	10.0	10.0	10.0	44.1
1983A (N=107)	100.0	10.0	10.0	10.0	10.0	10.0	10.0	10.0	10.0	10.0	10.0	44.1
1983B (N=124)	100.0	10.0	10.0	10.0	10.0	10.0	10.0	10.0	10.0	10.0	10.0	44.1

Note: See Table 3.1 note.

average ISP scores dropped by 9.8 percent to 46.2, the second lowest ISP average in the world (1983 rank = 21 out of 22 subregions).

The most significant period declines in West Africa occurred in the women's status (−112.5 percent), cultural diversity (−75.0 percent), demographic (−43.1 percent), and economic (−32.5 percent) subindexes. These declines should be regarded as especially significant given the very inadequate levels of social provision that already existed in West Africa in 1970. Net social declines were especially steep for Guinea (−50.0 percent), Sierra Leone (−49.4 percent), Mauritania (−39.7), Senegal (−28.9 percent), and Mali (−26.7 percent). Index losses were also found for Ghana and the Ivory Coast. In all, ISP scores declined by more than 5 percent over the 14-year period for eight of the 13 West African nations.

Positive social trends in West Africa include substantial improvements on the welfare effort (+66.7 percent) and education (+30.8 percent) subindexes. ISP scores for Nigeria improved by 278.9 percent, and those of Togo, Niger, and Benin increased by 28.9, 20.6, and 16.3 percent, respectively. These are impressive gains indeed, especially those for Nigeria. Overall, though, social development trends in West Africa are moving in a generally negative direction. Present trends indicate that the high levels of human deprivation that have long characterized the nations of this subregion are on the increase.

Table 3.5
Regional Index of Social Progress (ISP83) Scores, Percentage Change, and Ranks for 1970 and 1983 (n = 22 Regions)

SUBREGIONS	ISP 1970	Rank ISP 1970	ISP 1983	Rank ISP 1983	AMT ISP Change	Rank % CHANGE
West Europe	176.5	2	188.4	1	6.7	10
North Europe	185.3	1	186.8	2	0.8	13
Other East Asia (Japan)	155.0	5	174.3	3	12.5	5
Oceania	174.0	3	168.3	4	-3.3	15
Southern Europe	146.2	6	158.6	5	8.5	8
North America	140.5	7	156.9	6	11.7	6
East Europe (N=5)	166.6	4	152.6	7	-8.4	17
Temperate Latin America	132.8	9	129.6	8	-2.4	14
Caribbean (N=4)	114.8	11	117.5	9	2.4	12
Tropical Latin America	105.7	12	114.3	10	8.1	9
East Asia (South Korea)	103.0	14	112.1	11	8.8	7
Middle Latin America	104.1	13	99.5	12	-4.4	16
Soviet Union	134.0	8	95.8	13	-28.5	21
Southern Africa (N=1)	120.0	10	94.4	14	-21.3	20
Mainland East Asia	NA	NA	93.8	15	NA	NA
East South Asia (N=8)	72.1	16	92.6	16	28.4	1
West South Asia (N=7)	73.3	15	89.6	17	22.2	2
North Africa	71.8	17	83.7	18	16.6	4
Middle South Asia (N=5)	67.8	18	79.1	19	16.7	3
East Africa (N=11)	56.0	19	50.9	20	-9.1	18
West Africa	51.2	20	46.2	21	-9.8	19
Middle Africa (N=4)	40.5	21	42.8	22	5.7	11

Notes:

1. The number of countries included in some regions varied from 1970 to 1983; parentheses indicate the number of countries included for both time periods.

2. Detailed subindex scores by region are reported in Table 4.1.

East Africa

East Africa, like West Africa, consists of 13 nations, seven of which are officially designated LDCs (Tanzania, Uganda, Ethiopia, Rwanda,

Burundi, Malawi, and Somalia). The recent famines of Africa brought international attention to the desperate circumstances within which the majority of people in this subregion live and have lived for centuries. Like West Africa, East Africa is desperately poor and has been the locus of numerous civil wars and regional conflicts. Currently, the majority of the population of the subregion live under varying forms of military dictatorships and political oppression.

ISP scores for East Africa averaged 56.0 in 1970; by 1983 average index scores dropped to 50.9, a net loss of 9.1 percent over the 14-year period. Social losses occurred in the subregion despite enormous levels of international financial and technical assistance. They occurred, too, despite a broad range of economic and related support from a broad range of multinational and private development assistance organizations. Today, East Africa ranks as the third poorest subregion (20th out of 22 subregions), the same position that it occupied in 1970 (Table 3.5).

The most significant losses in East Africa occurred on the health (− 91.7 percent), political participation (− 53.6 percent), demographic (− 41.5 percent), and defense effort (− 27.3 percent) subindexes. The most substantial social losses were sustained by Ethiopia (− 91.4 percent), Somalia (− 52.5 percent), and Zambia (− 29.2 percent). ISP scores for Malawi also declined significantly, by 19.0 percent, from 42 in 1970 to 34 in 1983.

Appreciable gains occurred within East Africa in the women's status (+ 264.3 percent), cultural diversity (+ 111.1 percent), welfare effort (+ 52.4 percent), and education (+ 37.5 percent) subindexes. ISP scores for Tanzania and Burundi increased by 29.3 percent and 28.6 percent, respectively. In all, positive net changes between 1970 and 1983 occurred in six East African nations.

Despite some impressive gains by selected nations of the subregion, East Africa remains one of the most socially and politically volatile areas on the planet. Basic human needs are largely unmet, with the result that high rates of infant mortality, premature adult mortality, illiteracy, and political oppression are commonplace. The social situation in East Africa continues to be desperate, with still more natural disasters projected for the decade just ahead.

North Africa

Social development trends in North Africa are far more favorable than those found elsewhere in Africa. Indeed, ISP scores increased by an average of 16.6 percent between 1970 and 1983, with significant gains reported on eight of the ten ISP subindexes. The most significant gains occurred in the women's status (+ 158.8 percent), health (+ 67.3 percent), political participation (+ 44.4 percent), defense effort (+ 33.3 percent), and geographic (+ 28.9 percent) subindexes.

Net social gains were found for all six nations that make up the subregion. Those with the most substantial gains were Libya (+48.9 percent), Egypt (+27.1 percent), and Morocco (+19.2 percent). ISP scores for the Sudan and Tunisia increased by +8.3 percent and +8.3 percent, respectively. Social gains for Algeria (+3.5 percent) were less impressive than those of other nations in the subregion but, nonetheless, do reflect favorably on the social improvements that are occurring in Algeria as well.

North Africa, which ranks 18th out of 22 subregions, is clearly on the move. Substantial gains in the capacity of North African nations to provide for the basic needs of their populations are increasing and are steady.

Middle Africa

Middle Africa is made up of six nations, two of which, Chad and the Central African Republic, are LDCs. Middle Africa ranks as the poorest subregion in the world. The center of considerable political instability, frequent serious natural disasters, and fragile social and economic systems, the nations of Middle Africa have barely been able to cope with the onslaught of problems confronting them. Nonetheless, modest gains in ISP levels occurred for the subregion between 1970 and 1983 (+5.7 percent).

Net gains, generally of a more moderate nature than the subregion's social losses, were found on the welfare effort (+45.5 percent), defense effort (+30.4 percent), and education (+20.0 percent) subindexes. The most significant losses in subregional social provision were found on the political participation (−88.3 percent), health (−73.1 percent), women's status (−37.8 percent), economic (−25.7 percent) subindexes. Social losses over the 14-year period were most significant for the famine-stricken nation of Chad (−48.0 percent) which, apart from its recurrent natural disasters, is besieged by a long-standing civil war. The nations with the most positive ISP gains were Zaire (+32.6 percent) and the Central African Republic (+29.4 percent).

All in all, Middle Africa continues to struggle with a broad range of social problems that are typical of newly emerging nations. The subregion lacks a firm economic base, most of the nations are land-locked and poor in natural resources, and many are in various states of armed siege either within their own borders or with neighboring states, or both. The prospects for Middle Africa, given the enormity of the subregion's social problems, continues to remain bleak. Certainly, further significant improvements cannot be expected until such time as armed conflicts within the subregion are brought to an end.

Southern Africa

Social development trends in Southern Africa are all bleak. This situation arises from the desperate social, economic, and political situation under which the majority of the inhabitants of Southern Africa live. ISP scores for the two nations of this subregion, South Africa and Lesotho, declined by 21.3 percent between 1970 and 1983 and are continuing to drop. As discussed more fully in Chapter 4, this pattern results directly from the system of racial apartheid and other forms of social oppression that exist in South Africa. Social developments in Lesotho, given its physical and political engulfment by South Africa, are virtually at a standstill.

Eight of the ISP subindexes declined for the Southern African subregion between 1970 and 1983; the highest net declines occurred on the cultural diversity (−160.0 percent), women's status (−61.0 percent), education (−48.0 percent), and political participation (−46.2 percent) subindexes. Between 1970 and 1983 Southern Africa dropped from tenth place in the subregional ranks to fourteenth position. Given South Africa's unwillingness to provide for the basic needs of its majority black population, it is highly probable that future drops in subregional rankings will occur.

The data on Africa make clear that the social situation on the continent continues to be the worst in the world. For some subregions modest gains have been recorded, but no subregion has really "leaped forward" during the 14-year time period covered by this study. On the contrary, a steady state of sorts exists for most of Africa's subregions; some modest improvements are occurring, especially in North Africa, but not enough to appreciably reduce the profound levels of poverty that have existed on the continent for decades. An unfortunate interplay of civil wars, regional conflicts, natural disasters, ethnic intolerance, and meager economic resources have all combined with historically low levels of African social provision to impede developments in Africa.[12] Relative to other regions, the prospects for more accelerated development do not appear to be optimistic for Africa, at least not for the near term.

North America

The North American region consists of only two nations, the United States and Canada. Both nations were included in the study for all three time intervals.

One of the world's most economically prosperous regions, the two nations of North America are characterized by considerably different approaches to providing for the basic needs of their populations. The social situation in the United States is far less predictable than that of Canada, with the result that ISP scores for the United States tend to fluctuate to a much greater extent. Nonetheless, between 1970 and 1983 subregional ISP levels increased by an average of 11.7 percent, with the largest net percentage increase occurring in the United States (+16.9 percent).

The most impressive regionwide gains were registered for the defense effort (+130.0 percent), political participation (+30.3 percent), and cultural diversity (+16.8 percent) subindexes. Net social losses were found on the geographic (−64.3 percent), women's status (−14.4 percent), and education (−6.2 percent) subindexes. The net losses on the geographic subindex reflect the fact that one-third of all the world's major natural disasters occur within the United States (which includes Alaska and Hawaii). Regional losses on the women's status subindex reflect the absence of constitutional guarantees concerning the rights of women compared to those of men. Regional losses on the women's status subindex are magnified by the relative gains achieved in this sector by many of the world's less economically developed nations during the International Decade of Women.

Overall, the North American region ranks 6 out of 22 subregions, a rise worldwide of one rank between 1970 and 1983. Given its relative economic prosperity, combined with high levels of political stability, the region's development prospects for the near term appear to be favorable.

Latin America

Latin America consists of 22 nations distributed among four subregional groupings: Tropical Latin America ($n=$ 6); Middle Latin America ($n=$ 7); Temperate Latin America ($n=$ 4); and the Caribbean ($n=$ 5). Latin America is enormously diverse politically, economically, and socially; it is also culturally varied despite the presence of a predominately Roman Catholic population.[13] Politically, the nations of Latin America range from highly stable to highly unstable; many are governed by military dictatorships.[14] In recent years human rights violations in Latin America have been so pervasive that the continent has been the focus of considerable attention from international human rights organizations. Assaults on internationally guaranteed human rights continue to be widespread among the nations of Latin America, although the restoration of personal freedoms in some countries is beginning to occur.[15]

Among Latin America's major economic problems is its extraordinarily high level of foreign indebtedness.[16] To date, efforts at coping with Latin America's debt crisis have not proven successful; to a very great extent, the chronicity of these economic woes is contributing to a further political destabilization of the continent. Latin America's economic difficulties have engulfed other areas of the world as well, including the largest of the world's international financial institutions.[17]

Tropical Latin America

Tropical Latin America is the third most developed of Latin America's four subregions. Between 1970 and 1983 average ISP scores for the subregion's six nations increased by 8.1 percent, from 105.7 to 114.3. Net gains on the ISP increased the subregion's world ranking from 12th place in 1970 to 10th place in 1983 (Table 3.5). The most significant social gains in Tropical Latin America occurred in the political participation (+94.9 percent) and demographic (+40.0 percent) subindexes. Significant gains were also found for the welfare effort, education, women's status, defense effort, and geographic subindexes. Subregional social losses occurred primarily in the health (−23.4 percent), cultural diversity (−19.7 percent), and economic (−12.9 percent) subindexes. In all, seven of the ISP subindexes for Tropical Latin America increased by more than 5 percent over the 14-year period.

Net social gains were found for all six Tropical Latin American nations. The most substantial social gains, however, were achieved by Ecuador (+13.0 percent), Colombia (+11.9 percent) and Venezuela (+12.0 percent).

Very much at the mid-point in terms of world ISP levels, prospects for Tropical Latin America's future development indicate that the subregion can be expected to continue to make social gains. Certainly the subregion's beginning success in controlling population growth, a persistent problem, as well as subregional improvements in education and welfare services, all suggest that further social improvements can be expected.

Middle Latin America

Made up of seven nations, Middle Latin America is the area's largest subregion. ISP levels for the subregion declined by an average of 4.4 percent from a subregional average of 104.1 in 1970 to 99.5 in 1983. The subregion's steepest social losses were recorded for Nicaragua (−22.2 percent), El Salvador (−15.7 percent), and Guatemala (−7.8 percent). A 14-year decline of 4.2 percent also occurred in Mexico.

For the subregion as a whole, social losses were most significant on the economic (−39.4 percent), women's status (−11.1 percent), cultural diversity (−10.6 percent), and health (−8.4 percent) subindexes. These losses were not offset by impressive subregional gains on the demographic, geographic, and welfare effort subindexes.

Despite overall net losses within the subregion, the social ranking of

Middle Latin America increased from thirteenth position worldwide in 1970 to twelfth position in 1983. Current social developments in the subregion appear to be at a standstill, however. Given current trends, the absence of further improvements is likely to continue for the near term, or until such time as the subregion's several civil wars and conflicts are brought to an end.[18]

Temperate Latin America

Temperate Latin America is the continent's most socially developed subregion. This is the case despite the fact that ISP levels dropped for the subregion by an average of −2.4 percent between 1970 and 1983. Net 14-year ISP declines were recorded for three of the subregion's four nations: Chile (−10.4 percent), Uruguay (−3.4 percent), and Argentina (−2.9 percent). ISP levels for Paraguay increased by 8.8 percent over the period.

The subregion's most significant social losses occurred in the political participation (−27.8 percent), economic (−27.7 percent), and geographic (−26.0 percent) subindexes. Net social gains were found for the subregion, however, on the welfare effort (+20.0 percent) and women's status (+12.9 percent) subindexes. The subregional ranking worldwide increased by one position, from ninth place in 1970 to eighth place in 1983.

Caribbean

The Caribbean subregion includes four nations, including Latin America's only LDC, Haiti. Ranked ninth out of 22 world subregions in terms of overall level of social provision, net social gains amounting to 2.4 percent were reported for the Caribbean between 1970 and 1983. The most significant gains occurred on the political participation (+63.5 percent), geographic (+31.0 percent), demographic (+14.4 percent), and defense effort (+13.4 percent) subindexes. Significant net social losses occurred on five of the subregion's ISP subindexes.

Especially impressive ISP gains were achieved by the Dominican Republic (+17.9 percent) and Trinidad/Tobago (+9.8 percent).[19] The social situation in Haiti continued to deteriorate over the study's time frame with a 14-year net loss of −6.9 percent. Haiti's social losses were especially steep on the education, political participation, and women's status subindexes (Table A.1). ISP losses amounting to 9.4 percent were recorded for Cuba.

As with other subregions in Latin America, social development in the Caribbean is at a virtual standstill.[20] Indeed, further reversals can be expected if present social patterns persist. The present negative situation in the Caribbean is due largely to the subregion's continuing political and economic uncertainties.

South Asia

Social progress in South Asia has been more substantial than anywhere else in the world. ISP levels for the 25 nations that make up the area, for example, increased by an average of 23.5 percent between 1970 and 1983. Gains were most significant for the nine nations of East South Asia (+28.4 percent), but were also substantial for West South Asia (+22.2 percent) and Middle South Asia (+16.7 percent). For South Asia as a whole, improvements on the defense effort subindex (+600.0 percent) were especially dramatic, owing in large measure to sharp reductions in military spending on the part of Vietnam, Kampuchea, and Burma. Widely based economic improvements (+68.1 percent) and advances in the legal status of women (+51.4 percent) also contributed to the high levels of social progress found for South Asia between 1970 and 1983, although absolute ISP scores for the area remain well below the world average of 100.0, at 78.8 in 1983. Relative to other world subregions, South Asia ranks 17th worldwide in terms of levels of social provision.

Middle South Asia

Middle South Asia is made up of seven nations, including Afghanistan, Bangladesh, India, Iran, Nepal, Pakistan, and Sri Lanka. Afghanistan, Bangladesh, and Nepal are officially designated LDCs. ISP levels for this subregion averaged 79.1 in 1983, a net increase of 16.7 percent over 1970 scores. One of the most populous subregions, Middle South Asia is also one of the poorest. Infant mortality rates are extraordinarily high and overall life expectancy averages well under 50 years. The majority of nations in the subregion are under military rule; others are experiencing considerable political instability resulting from minority–majority conflicts, or are in open conflict with the neighboring states.[21]

Scores on eight of the ISP subindexes increased for the subregion between 1970 and 1983. The largest increases occurred in the demographic (+55.9 percent), cultural diversity (+42.9 percent), education (+41.2 percent), and economic (+38.9 percent) subindexes. These positive changes all reflect favorably on the accomplishments of central governments and international development assistance organizations working together in promoting development objectives within the subregion. Given the subregion's substantial accomplishments, the net losses that occurred in the women's status (−14.3 percent) and health (−7.1 percent) subindexes should be regarded as moderate.

As a subregion, the social situation in Middle South Asia is steadily improving. The pace of these improvements is slow relative to the enormous social and economic needs of the subregion, however. Greater political stability, further reductions in defense spending, and increases in welfare programs and services should help to solidify the accomplishments that are presently taking place. Certainly, international assistance will continue to be needed to both stabilize and increase further the accomplishments that have already been achieved.

Southeast Asia

The locus of numerous civil and subregional wars for more than half a century, the social situation in Southeast Asia is beginning to improve. These improvements are significant and indicate that major national and international commitments are succeeding in furthering the subregion's social development.

One of the two largest subregions of Asia, Southeast Asia consists of Indonesia, Kampuchea, Thailand, the Philippines, Vietnam, Singapore, Laos, Malaysia, and Burma. Laos is the subregion's only officially designated LDC, but at least one other nation, Kampuchea, is sufficiently impoverished as to warrant consideration for classification as a LDC.

Average ISP scores for the nations of Southeast Asia increased by 28.4 percent between 1970 and 1984 to 92.6 in 1983. This increase constituted the largest percentage of social gains for any single subregion during the 1970–1983 period. Even so, Southeast Asia retained its overall social rank of 16th place for both 1970 and 1983 relative to other world subregions. The subregion's most substantial gains are found in the economic (+359.3 percent), defense effort (+132.7 percent), geographic (+35.5 percent), and demographic (+22.1 percent) subindexes. Subregional losses were found in the welfare effort (−25.5 percent) and political participation (−8.7 percent) subindexes, however.

Net social gains for Indonesia (+288.5 percent), Vietnam (+104.9 percent), Malaysia (+27.5 percent), and Singapore (+20.0 percent) were especially significant; conversely, significant social losses over the 14-year period were found in Kampuchea (−14.6 percent) and Burma (−7.7 percent), nations that could little afford further social deterioration.

The pattern of net gains and losses on the ISP indicates more substantial investments on the part of Southeast Asian nations in population control, economic development, and reduced military spending. The 14-year net losses in the welfare effort subindex, however, are indicative of the uneven nature of social development in Southeast Asia; the subregion's net losses in the political participation (−8.7 percent) subindex also reflect less than a full commitment on the part of these nations to popular participation in the area's complex political processes.[22] One can infer from these data that the nations of Southeast Asia are in somewhat of a social "take-off" pattern, but have not yet committed themselves fully to either national or subregional development objectives. Nonetheless, current social trends are generally positive in a subregion that for more than 40 years has engaged in brutal civil and regional wars.

Southwest Asia

The Southwest Asian subregion consists of Lebanon, Turkey, Saudi Arabia, PDR (South) Yemen, Arab (North) Yemen, Iraq, Israel, Jordan, and Syria. The subregion's two LDCs are North and South Yemen, nations that have been involved in open conflicts with one another for several decades.

Average ISP scores for Southwest Asia increased by 22.2 percent between 1970 and 1983 to 89.6. The subregion ranks as the 17th poorest of the 22 subregions worldwide. The most significant period gains on the ISP were found in the women's status (+190.0 percent), welfare effort (+22.0 percent), and education (+21.1 percent) subindexes. Significant losses occurred on the subregion's defense effort (−26.0 percent) subindex, however. ISP scores for Jordan (+131.7 percent) rose sharply over the period, and those of Syria (+32.9 percent) and Israel (+32.1) also improved markedly. The subregion's most significant social declines occurred in Iraq (−21.0 percent), which lost social ground on five of the ISP subindexes, including a precipitous drop of 395.5 percent on the defense effort subindex.

Though beset by subregional political problems of an enormous magnitude, including open hostilities between neighboring states, the Southwest Asian subregion is, nonetheless, making substantial progress toward providing more adequately for the basic needs of its population. The subregion's social gains have been steady and reflect the emergence of an increasingly secure social safety net. The major obstacles for further development stem from the subregion's extraordinarily complex political problems, including those that exist between Israel and its Arab neighbors, between Iran and Iraq, between the two Yemens, and between Syria and other nations both within and outside of the subregion.

East Asia

East Asia consists of seven nations distributed in three subregions: Mainland East Asia (Hong Kong, China, and Mongolia), East Asia (North and South Korea and Taiwan), and Japan. The area includes one of the most socially advanced nations, Japan, and one of the most rapidly developing subregions, Mainland East Asia.

Japan, because of its unique geographic location, is treated apart from the rest of East Asia. Japan enjoys the most favorable ISP score of any Asian nation, indeed one that is considerably higher than that of many nations in the West. Japan's 1983 ISP score, for example, was 174, 12.3 percent higher than in 1970. Improvements in Japanese social provision are fairly uniform across all ISP scores with the exception of the geographic subindex which, because of Japan's vulnerability to natural disasters, is very high. Overall, though, all of the subindexes for Japan reflect major 14-year improvements.

Similarly, the situation for South Korea reflects a strong and pervasive pattern of steady improvements in adequacy of social provision since 1970. South Korea's ISP score, for example, increased by 8.7 percent over 1970 levels to 112 in 1983, well above the world's average.

Four-year social development trends for Mainland East Asia (China, Hong Kong, and Mongolia) are all suggestive of strongly positive trends taking place within this subregion. Subregional ISP scores increased by an average of 4.3 percent between 1980 and 1983, for example, with the most significant increases found on the defense effort (+40.0 percent) and economic (+23.6 percent) subindexes. Net losses for the period were found in the women's status (−8.5 percent) and political participation (−7.4 percent) subindexes.

In terms of adequacy of social provision, Japan ranks third highest worldwide, East Asia ranks eleventh, and Mainland East Asia currently occupies fifteenth place. Indications are that significant improvements in these latter two subregions will continue to occur and that, in time, additional improvements can be expected.

Europe

Europe has long served as the standard against which social progress in other areas of the world has been judged. For nearly two centuries Europeans have sought to establish a broad range of social programs that are designed to provide a degree of financial protection against the social risks to which people everywhere are exposed, such as sickness, disability, old age, premature death, solitary survivorship, and so on.[23] And they have been enormously successful in realizing this objective. Today, Europe continues to lead the world in both the comprehensiveness and quality of its social safety net. It reaches not only the poor of Europe, of which there are still many, but the affluent as well.[24]

The 24 European nations included in this study are distributed among four subregions: Western Europe (*n* = 6); Southern Europe (*n* = 6), Eastern Europe (*n* = 6), and Northern Europe (*n* = 6). On a regionwide basis, European ISP scores increased by an average of 2.2 percent between 1970 and 1983, from an index average of 168.7 to 171.7 in 1970. The most significant social gains for the region occurred in the defense effort

(+18.1 percent) and political participation (+17.4 percent) subindexes. Net gains were achieved on four other subindexes as well. Moderate social losses were found on the women's status (−12.5 percent) and demographic (−4.9 percent) subindexes. The women's status subindex losses, as in North America, reflect the continued absence of constitutional equal protection amendments for women in some European nations. Overall though, the levels of social protection found in Europe continue to be the highest in the world.

In order of achievement, the subregions with the most favorable 1983 ISP averages are Western Europe (average = 188.4), Northern Europe (average = 186.8), Southern Europe (average = 158.6), and Eastern Europe (average = 152.9).

Western Europe

Western Europe is the most socially advanced of Europe's four subregions and, hence, the most socially advanced subregion in the world. ISP scores for the six nations that make up this subregion averaged 188.4 in 1983, an increase of 6.7 percent over 1970 levels. Social gains in Western Europe over the 14-year period were especially high in the political participation (+32.6 percent), economic (+22.9 percent), and defense effort (+17.1 percent) subindexes. Significant improvements also occurred in health (+7.8 percent) and education (+3.2 percent) subindexes. Subregional losses on the geographic (−10.6 percent), women's status (−6.7 percent), and welfare effort (−0.4) subindexes were modest relative to gains in other parts of the ISP.

The West European nations with the largest 14-year advances were Austria (+8.9 percent), France (+8.6 percent), Germany (+8.7 percent), and Switzerland (+8.5 percent). Belgium increased its ISP score by 6.4 percent. The Netherlands remained at about the same already high level of social provision that existed in 1970.

In short, Western Europe remains the world's subregional social leader. Its social accomplishments for more than a century have been impressive, and the subregion continues to provide a standard for other subregions to emulate.

Southern Europe

One of the less developed subregions in Europe, Southern Europe is making steady social progress; indeed, subregional ISP averages now exceed those of Eastern Europe. Between 1970 and 1983 the nations of Southern Europe increased their ISP average scores by 8.5 percent to 158.6. Subindex gains were most substantial in the areas of political participation (+46.4 percent), defense effort (+41.4 percent), health

(+12.6 percent), women's status (+8.3 percent), and education (+8.1 percent). The subregion's continuing economic problems are reflected in a loss of 7.5 percent in the economic subindex. Net changes in other areas of the ISP were not significant.

Portugal (+22.6 percent), Greece (+17.6 percent), and Italy (+14.8 percent) are the most rapidly improving nations of the subregion. Substantial gains were also found for Spain (+8.2 percent). Albania and Yugoslavia experienced net social losses on the ISP, however, amounting to 10.3 percent and 3.0 percent, respectively. The most substantial losses for each of these nations were found in the political participation subindex, a net decline of −120.2 percent for Albania and −72.5 percent for Yugoslavia (Table A.1).

As it is the European subregion with the largest percentage of gains on the ISP, Southern Europe's prospects for further rapid social development appear to be especially favorable.

Eastern Europe

Social development trends in the six nations of Eastern Europe have been largely negative since 1970. Overall, average ISP scores for the subregion dropped by 11.6 percent to a 14-year subregional low of 153.1. The most significant losses for Eastern Europe occurred in the political participation (−83.0 percent), economic (−17.2 percent), demographic (−13.9 percent) and education (−12.5 percent) subindexes. Net losses were recorded on three other ISP subindexes as well.

Social losses ocurred for all six nations of the subregion but were especially acute for Poland (−9.6 percent), Bulgaria (−9.6 percent), and Romania (−8.6 percent).

The current social situation in Eastern Europe is especially worrisome given the high levels of social provision that have characterized the subregion in the past. A combination of high levels of defense spending, political oppression, economic downturns, and increases in fertility are adding significantly to the social problems of the subregion. Clearly, further significant developments in Eastern Europe are not likely to occur until such time as basic human rights and escalating defense spending problems are resolved.

Northern Europe

The six nations of Northern Europe have consistently been the most socially progressive nations in Europe. The subregion is made up of the four Nordic states—Denmark, Finland, Norway, and Sweden—plus the United Kingdom and Ireland.[25] ISP scores for the subregion averaged 186.8 in 1983, an increase of 0.8 percent over the 1970 average score of

185.3. Northern Europe ranks second in overall subregional rankings, a drop of one rank from its 1970 position of first place.

Despite its already high level of social provision, significant new social development gains were realized by the Northern European subregion between 1970 and 1983. The most significant increases are found in the political participation (+29.7 percent), economic (+23.1 percent), defense effort (+13.3 percent), and health (+5.2 percent) subindexes. Gains of this magnitude are especially impressive given the already high level of social development that existed in Northern Europe in 1970. However, the subregion's average score on the women's status subindex dropped by 36.5 percent. The sharp decline on this subindex was due to the absence in some nations of Northern Europe of constitutional protections that accord women the same legal rights as men. Less significant social losses were found on the demographic (−7.0 percent) and education (−6.7 percent) subindexes.

The trends in social development summarized in this chapter confirm the existence of a North–South division between the various regions of the world. In effect, the planet is divided between a relative minority of social "have" nations and a very large majority of social "have not" nations. The gap in social development between the world's geographic regions is profound and, for many nations and regions, the gap is continuing to widen.

The geographic division of the world into comparatively rich and poor nations stems, at least in part, from the geographic location of many of these regions. That is to say, many of the world's developing regions continue to be severely disadvantaged by their relative lack of natural resources, by the frequency of major disasters that regularly occur within their borders, and by the comparatively small percentages of arable land that are available to them for food production. Problems of climate, extreme fluctuations in temperature, irregular rainfall, poor soils, and relative inaccessibility to potable water are all part of the environmental problems confronting developing nations.

But problems of the physical environment alone do not fully explain the poor conditions that exist in many developing nations. Rather, lesser developed regions are also disadvantaged by the comparative youthfulness of their political institutions, including their autonomy as independent nation-states, by the high levels of cultural diversity that characterize many of these regions, by centuries-old minority–majority group tensions, by recurrent problems of political and economic instability, and by ongoing wars and conflicts both within their own borders and with neighboring countries. Poorer regions also possess comparatively little in the way of established social infrastructures that can be called upon to provide for the changing social needs of their rapidly expanding populations.

By comparison, the world's more socially advanced regions have arrived at their level of development through sustained incremental improvements that have taken place over a period of decades, indeed over a period of centuries for the majority of nations and regions. Political stability, steady rates of economic expansion, controlled population growth, well-established social programs, and relative cultural homogeneity have each added to steady social progress within the world's more affluent regions. The history of social experimentation within these regions is also long, and their experiments have resulted in the emergence of comprehensive national and regional comprehensive social safety nets.

Chapter 4 presents more detailed analysis for each of the 124 nations included in this study.

NOTES

1. Sixteen of these nations are either developing ($n = 11$) or least developing countries ($n = 5$); ten are located in Asia.

2. The "worlds of development" concept was formulated by Louis Irving Horowitz in *Three Worlds of Development: The Theory and Practice of International Stratification* (New York: Oxford University Press, 1966). Since the publication of Horowitz's book, however, a "Fourth World" of development has been identified. This world is made up of the "poorest of the poor," nations which, in this and other studies, are referred to as least developing countries (LDCs).

3. United Nations, *The State of the World's Population* (New York, 1987).

4. For discussions of the geographic location of the "Third World" as well as nations of the "South," see J. P. Dickenson et al., *A Geography of the Third World* (New York: Methuen, 1983) and Harry F. Young, *Atlas of U.S. Foreign Relations* (Washington, D.C.: U.S. Department of State, 1983).

5. Independent Commission on International Development Issues, *North South: A Program for Survival* (Cambridge, MA: MIT Press, 1980), pp. 49–50.

6. As cited in the Hunger Project, *Ending Hunger: An Idea Whose Time Has Come* (New York: Praeger, 1985), p. 315.

7. For a discussion of this issue see J. P. Dickenson et al., *A Geography of the Third World*.

8. The profound levels of poverty in Africa have been widely discussed. For one of the most important recent documents on the subject see Lawrence Eagleburger and Donald F. McHenry (co-chairs), *Compact for African Development* (Washington, D.C.: Council on Foreign Relations and the Overseas Development Council, 1985). Also see the Hunger Project, *Ending Hunger*.

9. G. Carter and P. O'Meara, *African Independence: The First Twenty-Five Years* (Indianapolis, IN: University of Indiana Press, 1986).

10. For further discussions see S. Ungar, *Africa* (New York: Simon and Schuster, 1985); H. Bernstein (ed.), *Contradictions of Accumulation in Africa: Studies in Economy and State* (Beverly Hills, CA: Sage, 1985); R. Onwuka and A. Sesay, *The*

Future of Regionalism in Africa (New York: St. Martin's Press, 1985); R. Sandbrook, *Politics of Africa's Economic Stagnation* (Cambridge: Cambridge University Press, 1985).

11. A brief history of the struggles leading to African independence can be found in I. William Zartman, "Africa," in *World Politics: An Introduction*; edited by James N. Rosenau et al. (New York: The Free Press, 1976), pp. 569–94.

12. R. Sandbrook, *Politics of Africa's Economic Stagnation* (Cambridge: Cambridge University Press, 1985); Organization for Economic Cooperation and Development, *Crisis and Recovery in Sub-Saharan Africa* (Paris, 1985).

13. For an overview of the political history of Latin America see Kalman H. Silvert and Morris J. Blachman, "Latin America," in Rosenau, *World Politics*.

14. R. Wesson, *The Latin American Military Institution* (New York: Praeger, 1986); M. Blachman et al., *Confronting Revolution* (New York: Pantheon, 1986).

15. For a discussion of these trends see Charles Humana, *World Human Rights Guide* (New York: Facts on File, 1986).

16. P. Claudon, *World Debt Crisis* (Cambridge, MA: Ballinger, 1985); Brian Kettell and George A. Magnus, *The International Debt Game* (Cambridge, MA: Ballinger, 1986).

17. A. Brimmer and R. Hawkins, *The World Banking System: Outlook in a Context of Crisis* (New York: New York University Press, 1985).

18. A. Varas, *Militarization and the International Arms Race in Latin America* (Boulder, CO: Westview, 1985).

19. See Editors, "Trinidad and Tobago: A *South* Special Report," *South* (September 1985): 231–47.

20. P. Gomes, *Rural Development in the Caribbean: Selected Essays* (New York: St. Martin's Press, 1985).

21. For valuable readings on the nations of the region see I. Norlund et al., *Rice Societies: Asian Problems and Prospects* (New York: Riverdale, 1986); L. Pye and M. Pye, *Asian Power and Politics: The Cultural Dimensions of Authority* (Cambridge, MA: Harvard University Press, 1985); D. Horowitz, *Ethnic Groups in Conflict* (Berkeley, CA: University of California Press, 1985).

22. C. Mackerras and N. Knight, *Marxism in Asia* (New York: St. Martin's Press, 1986); A. L. Dommen, *Laos* (Boulder, CO: Westview, 1985); G. Tanham, *Communist Revolutionary Warfare: The Vietminh in Indochina* (Boulder, CO: Westview, 1985).

23. For histories of social development in Europe see Gaston V. Rimlinger, *Welfare Policy and Industrialization in Europe, America, and Russia* (New York: John Wiley, 1971); Peter Flora and Arnold J. Heidenheimer (eds.), *The Development of Welfare States in Europe and America* (New Brunswick, NJ: Transaction Books, 1981); Alfred Kahn and Sheila Kamerman, *Social Services in International Perspective* (Washington, D.C.: U.S. Department of Health, Education, and Welfare, 1976).

24. Alfred J. Kahn and Sheila Kamerman, *Not For the Poor Alone* (Philadelphia, PA: Temple University Press, 1975); Gerald Handel, *Social Welfare in Western Society* (New York: Random House, 1982).

25. Not to be confused with Northern Ireland, which is currently part of the United Kingdom.

4

NATIONAL SOCIAL PROGRESS

Changes in the capacity of nations to provide for the basic needs of their populations are of considerable interest to specialists in social development research. Indeed, the conceptual and empirical literature that attempts to describe and explain the processes that influence social development worldwide has increased substantially over the past two decades and is now extensive.[1] The interest in better understanding of the international social dynamics that influence social development, however, is more than academic. In the main, social development researchers examine the social progress of nations for at least four reasons: (1) to describe development trends as they are occurring; (2) to learn from the experiences of individual nations; (3) to extract principles concerning the effectiveness of particular national, regional, and international development strategies; and (4) to use the knowledge acquired through research to effect the transfer of social innovations developed in one area of the world to other nations.[2] Hence, the underlying purpose of all social development research is to promote the further social and economic development of nations, both individually and within the context of social development worldwide.

This chapter reports five types of nation-specific social development data. First, social progress index and subindex scores are presented for all 124 countries studied. These scores cover the full 14-year time frame of the investigations. Second, patterns of social development occurring within individual nations are analyzed on the basis of national trend data. In the main, percentage changes in ISP, WISP, and subindex scores are used as the basis for discerning these trends. Third, the chapter identifies those nations that experienced the most significant net social

Table 4.1
Scores and Percentage Change on the Index of Social Progress for Selected Countries ($n = 7$)

COUNTRY	INDEX OF SOCIAL PROGRESS (ISP)	Education	Health	Women	Defense	Economic	Demographic	Geographic	Participation	Cultural	Welfare	WEIGHTED INDEX OF SOCIAL PROGRESS
Albania												
1970	136	16	15	12	11	19	15	13	10	15	10	61
1980	116	16	15	12	5	13	16	14	-2	14	12	54
1983	122	14	17	11	11	14	16	14	-2	14	13	55
% 1970-1980	-14.7	0.6	0.6	0.8	-54.2	-31.3	7.3	8.4	-120.2	-6.1	21.1	-11.5
% 1980-1983	5.2	-12.5	13.3	-8.3	120.0	7.7	0.0	0.0	0.0	0.0	8.3	1.9
% 1970-1983	-10.3	-12.0	14.0	-7.6	0.8	-26.0	7.3	8.4	-120.2	-6.1	31.2	-9.8
Burundi*												
1970	35	1	-10	-2	16	7	2	14	0	5	2	5
1980	41	-1	-5	-4	13	9	4	19	-2	3	5	8
1983	45	-2	-5	-3	13	9	5	19	1	3	6	10
% 1970-1980	17.1	-209.9	50.4	-91.4	-18.3	30.2	109.4	36.6	-212.2	-38.9	161.8	60.0
% 1980-1983	9.8	-100.0	0.0	25.0	0.0	0.0	25.0	0.0	150.0	0.0	20.0	25.0
% 1970-1983	28.6	-319.8	50.4	-43.5	-18.3	30.2	161.8	36.6	100.0	-38.9	214.1	100.0
Chad*												
1970	25	-7	-10	-1	9	5	6	13	11	-7	6	3
1980	7	-8	-9	-4	10	3	6	10	0	-7	8	-4
1983	13	-10	-10	-6	14	8	6	10	0	-7	8	-3
% 1970-1980	-72.0	-12.8	10.8	-267.0	12.2	-38.9	1.5	-22.5	-100.0	-1.3	35.4	-233.3
% 1980-1983	85.7	-25.0	-11.1	-50.0	40.0	166.7	0.0	0.0	0.0	0.0	0.0	-25.0
% 1970-1983	-48.0	-41.0	-0.9	-450.5	57.1	62.9	1.5	-22.5	-100.0	-1.3	35.4	-200.0

Malaysia													
1970	80	10	13	8	11	10	7	8	12	-4	5	36
1980	102	14	16	9	11	13	12	12	13	-3	5	46
1983	102	16	16	8	10	13	12	12	13	-3	5	46
% 1970-1980	27.5	41.3	23.9	13.8	0.8	31.2	73.7	51.7	9.2	26.7	1.8	27.8
% 1980-1983	0.0	14.3	0.0	-11.1	-9.1	0.0	0.0	0.0	0.0	0.0	0.0	0.0
% 1970-1983	27.5	61.5	23.9	1.1	-8.3	31.2	73.7	51.7	9.2	26.7	1.8	27.8
Nicaragua													
1970	81	7	12	10	16	8	3	-8	11	18	4	38
1980	68	9	9	9	9	1	5	-3	9	15	7	33
1983	63	12	9	11	3	-3	4	-3	7	15	7	33
% 1970-1980	-16.0	30.2	-24.4	-9.2	-43.4	-87.4	71.8	62.9	-17.5	-16.2	79.0	-13.2
% 1980-1983	-7.4	33.3	0.0	22.2	-66.7	-400.0	-20.0	0.0	-22.2	0.0	0.0	0.0
% 1970-1983	-22.2	73.7	-24.4	11.0	-81.1	-137.9	37.5	62.9	-35.8	-16.2	79.0	-13.2
South Africa													
1970	120	10	8	21	14	13	8	19	13	-5	19	51
1980	100	7	12	10	13	11	9	12	7	3	16	43
1983	94	5	12	8	12	11	9	12	7	3	16	41
% 1970-1980	-16.7	-29.4	51.7	-52.2	-6.5	-14.8	13.8	-36.5	-45.8	158.9	-15.4	-15.7
% 1980-1983	-6.0	-28.6	0.0	-20.0	-7.7	0.0	0.0	0.0	0.0	0.0	0.0	-4.7
% 1970-1983	-21.7	-49.5	51.7	-61.7	-13.7	-14.8	13.8	-36.5	-45.8	158.9	-15.4	-19.6
United States													
1970	124	21	20	21	-3	23	13	-20	22	13	14	72
1980	147	20	21	20	9	18	16	-12	26	16	13	77
1983	145	19	21	19	8	19	15	-12	25	16	13	76
% 1970-1980	18.5	-4.4	5.5	-4.4	391.3	-21.4	23.9	40.3	18.7	23.9	-6.5	6.9
% 1980-1983	-1.4	-5.0	0.0	-5.0	-11.1	5.6	-6.3	0.0	-3.8	0.0	0.0	-1.3
% 1970-1983	16.9	-9.1	5.5	-9.1	358.9	-17.1	16.2	40.3	14.1	23.9	-6.5	5.6

Notes:

1. Index and subindex scores and percentage changes for all 124 of the nations studied are reported in Table A.1 of Appendix A. Asterisks indicate nations classified by UN as LDCs.

gains and net social losses between 1970 and 1983. Again, percentage changes on the study's 12 indexes are used to identify those nations for which significant shifts are occurring in social development, both improvements and deteriorations. Fourth, the chapter reports a ranking of nations in terms of their overall success in providing for the basic social and material needs of their populations. These rankings reflect not only the degree of success experienced by individual nations relative to the social achievements of other countries, but also their current success in comparison with earlier levels of social performance. In the process of reporting these rankings, the world's comparative "social leaders" (SLs) and "socially least developing countries" (SLDCs) will be identified. And finally, this chapter contains a brief discussion of the prospects for future world social development in relation to the patterns that occurred between 1970 and 1983 and between 1980 and 1983.[3]

NATIONAL TRENDS

Detailed information concerning social development trends for each of the study's 124 nations is reported in Table A.1 of Appendix A. That table summarizes all index and subindex scores for each country as well as the percentage change observed in these scores over the 14-year time frame. Nations are clustered by development groupings and, within groupings, they are listed alphabetically. Readers with a special interest in one or another subset of nations, then, are referred to Table A.1. Table 2.3 contains index and subindex average scores for the four socioeconomic development groupings. Social trend data for each grouping on the basis of net percentage changes in index and subindex scores over time are also reported in Table 2.3.

This section reports on general development trends that are occurring within individual nations. Somewhat more detailed analyses are reported for the social changes occurring in Albania, Burundi, Chad, Malaysia, Nicaragua, South Africa, and the United States. These countries were selected to illustrate development trends for four reasons. First, they represent a broad range of social, economic, and political systems. Second, their change scores reflect "middle range" changes that are typical of the social change patterns observed for their respective development groupings. Third, these nations are divided between those that experienced significant net social gains over the 14-year period (i.e., Burundi, Malaysia, the United States) and those in which significant net social losses were found (i.e., Albania, Chad, Nicaragua, and South Africa). Fourth, the countries were selected because of their broad geographic distribution.

Table 4.2
Frequency Distribution of Countries with Net Changes on the Index of Social Progress in Excess of 10 Percent, by Socioeconomic Development Grouping, 1970–1983 (*n* = 124)

Grouping	Percentage ISP POSITIVE Change		Percentage ISP NEGATIVE Change		! TOTALS	
Developed Market Economy Nations (N=25)	24.0	(6)	4.0	(1)	! 28.0	(7)
Eastern Trading Area (N=8)	-----		50.0	(4)	! 50.0	(4)
Developing Countries (N=67)	34.3	(23)	17.9	(12)	! 52.2	(35)
Least Developing Countries (N=25)	40.0	(10)	36.0	(9)	! 76.0	(19)
All Countries (N=124)	31.5	(39)	21.0	(26)	! 52.4	(65)

Notes: For some countries change scores could be reported for the period 1980–1983. See Table 4.3 for a country-specific listing.

Source: Compiled by the author.

General Patterns

Between 1970 and 1983 scores on the Index of Social Progress changed by more than 10 percent for 65 of the nations studied (52.4 percent). Analysis of the index scores of the remaining 59 nations revealed that either no changes had taken place in comparison with their earlier ISP scores or that the changes that did occur were less than 10 percent. Net index score changes were considered substantively significant if they exceeded 10 percent in either direction.

Data concerning the net social gains and losses of individual nations are reported in Table 4.2. These data indicate that for the majority of nations in which significant ISP changes occurred, the changes tended to be of a positive nature—they reflect net improvements in the ability of many countries to provide for the basic needs of their populations. More specifically, significant social gains were found for 39 countries

(31.5 percent); conversely, significant social deterioration took place in 26 countries (21.0 percent).

Nations for which the most substantial 14-year net social gains and losses were observed are identified in Table 4.3, where they are clustered by development grouping. (Subindex and WISP scores, as well as percentage change for these indexes, are reported for each country in Table A.1.)

ISP Changes in the LDCs

Between 1970 and 1983 significant changes on the ISP occurred for 19 of the 25 LDCs (76.0 percent). The index scores of more than half of these 19 countries ($n = 10$) reflect significant net *improvements* over the 14-year period. Further, the rate at which positive social changes are occurring within some of these countries is impressive indeed.

As reported in Table 4.3, for example, the LDCs with the most substantial social gains are the Central African Republic (+29.4 percent), Tanzania (+29.3 percent), Togo (+28.9 percent), Burundi (+28.6 percent), Burkina-Faso (+28.6 percent), Niger (+20.6 percent), Benin (+16.3 percent), Nepal (+14.3 percent), and Rwanda (+12.9 percent). A net change of 84 percent was found in the ISP scores of Arab Yemen for the four-year period 1980–1983.

Closer analysis of the country-specific subindex data in Table A.1 reveals that the changes observed for these ten LDCs reflect improvements across a broad range of social sectors, but especially in the areas of education (+148.5 percent), women's status (+131.9 percent), political participation (+110.6 percent), and welfare effort (+95.0 percent). Substantial improvements also were found on the economic subindex (+16.1 percent) for these countries; group scores on the health subindex declined, however. This latter finding reflects the generally uneven pattern of social development worldwide.

The net social gains observed on the ISP for Burundi between 1970 and 1983 are typical of those found for other socially improving LDCs.

Burundi

A comparatively small country of approximately 4.7 million people, Burundi achieved its independence from Belgium in 1962; the country's monarchy was overthrown in 1966. Following nearly a decade of bloody civil wars between ethnic minorities, the nation has achieved a degree of stability in recent years under a strong, albeit politically oppressive, central government. Male life expectancy in Burundi averages 45.2 years and literacy is barely at the 25 percent level. Burundi's economy reflects a substantial net trade imbalance; per capita income is approximately

$235, among the world's lowest. The rate of infant mortality in Burundi exceeds 121 per 1,000 live-born infants; the rate of population increase is approximately 2.6 percent, resulting in a net doubling of the population approximately every 27 years.[4]

Burundi's ISP score in 1970 was 35, well below the average of 45 calculated for the LDCs as a group (Table 2.3). The majority of Burundi's subindex scores were also well below those observed for the other LDCs. Burundi's 1970 defense effort, geographic, and cultural diversity subindex scores, however, were more favorable than those found for the LDCs as a group.

Between 1970 and 1983, Burundi's ISP score increased by 29 percent from 35 to 45, a score 5 percent higher than the LDCs 1983 group average of 43. Significant 1970–1983 improvements occurred on six of the ten ISP subindexes: health (+50.0 percent), economic (+30.2 percent), demographic (+161.8 percent), geographic (+36.6 percent), political participation (+100.0 percent), and welfare effort (+214.1 percent). Significant net subindex losses were seen in the areas of education (−319.8 percent), women's status (−43.5 percent), cultural diversity (−38.9 percent), and defense effort (−18.3 percent). Even so, Burundi's subindex gains were considerably greater that its subindex losses, with the result that the country's composite ISP score increased between 1970 and 1983.

Burundi's social progress is, indeed, impressive. Its accomplishments reflect major social investments on the part of the Burundian central government in the nation's social development. Burundi's progress also reflects positive outcomes from the large volume of sustained financial and technical assistance contributed to the nation by international assistance organizations (through a great variety of bi- and multi-lateral development assistance agreements).[5] Indeed, the net improvements that are occurring on some of the ISP subindexes are of such a magnitude that Burundi can be thought of as one of the more rapidly progressing of the LDCs. It is clearly a nation that is "on the move," and one can only hope that these positive trends will be sustained for Burundi into the future.

Though the level at which social gains are taking place in some LDCs is impressive, one must remember that the overall social standing of even the most successful LDCs, including Burundi, remains very low compared with ISP levels in other groupings, even in comparison to levels in the DCs. The 1983 ISP average for the group of ten LDCs in which positive changes have been reported, for example, is only 50.3. This score is well above that of the LDCs in general (1983 average = 43), but significantly below the 1983 average of 91 for the DCs.

Tables 4.2 and 4.3 show that significant net social losses occurred in nine (36 percent) of the LDCs. For the most part, these losses reflect

Table 4.3
Nations with Percentage Change in Excess of 10 Percent on the Index of Social Progress, 1970–1983

	Percentage ISP POSITIVE Change	Percentage ISP POSITIVE Change	Percentage ISP NEGATIVE Change
DEVELOPED MARKET ECONOMY NATIONS			
Israel	32.1		
Portugal	22.6		
Greece	17.6		
United States	16.9		
Italy	14.8		
Japan	12.3		
South Africa			-21.7
EASTERN TRADING AREA			
Soviet Union			-28.4
Albania			-10.3
Bulgaria			-9.6
Poland			-9.6
DEVELOPING COUNTRIES			
Indonesia	288.5		
Nigeria	278.9		
Jordan	131.7		
Vietnam	104.9		
Mozambique‡	54.5		
Egypt, UAR		27.1	
Singapore		20.0	
Thailand		19.6	
Morocco		19.2	
Dominican Republic		17.9	
Angola‡			-133.3
Mauritania			-39.7
Liberia			-29.4
Zambia			-29.2
Senegal			-28.9

Libya	48.9	Lebanon	16.2	Saudi Arabia#	-22.6
Iran	38.5	Ecuador	13.0	Nicaragua	-22.2
India	33.3	Venezuela	12.0	Iraq	-21.0
Syria	32.9	Colombia	11.9	Ghana	-15.8
Zaire	32.6	Korea, Dem. (N)#	11.4	El Salvador	-15.7
Congo, PR#	27.8	Trinidad-Tobago	9.8	Kampuchea	-14.6
Malaysia	27.5			Chile	-10.4

LEAST DEVELOPING COUNTRIES

Yemen, Arab*#	84.6	Ethiopia*	-91.4
Cen. African Rep.*	29.4	Somalia*	-52.5
Tanzania*	29.3	Guinea*	-50.0
Togo*	28.9	Sierra Leone*	-49.4
Burundi*	28.6	Chad*	-48.0
Burkina-Faso*	28.6	Mali*	-26.7
Niger*	20.6	Lao PDR*#	-22.6
Benin*	16.3	Malawi*	-19.0
Nepal*	14.3	Bangladesh*#	-14.3
Rwanda*	12.9		

Notes:
1. Asterisks (*) indicate officially designated Least Developing Countries (LDCs).
2. The number mark (#) indicates that the percentage change reported is for 1980-1983 only.

95

social deteriorations sustained over the full 14-year period of the study. The most substantial net social losses occurred in Ethiopia (-91.4 percent), Somalia (-52.5 percent), Guinea (-50.0 percent), Sierra Leone (-49.4 percent), Chad (-48.0 percent), Mali (-26.7 percent), Laos (-22.6 percent), Malawi (-19.0 percent), and Bangladesh (-14.3 percent). The average 1983 ISP score for these nine countries is 24.4, an average that is considerably lower than that of the LDCs as a group.

Significant losses within this group of LDCs occurred on nine of the ISP subindexes. The most dramatic losses, however, occurred on five subindexes: women's status (-235.1 percent), health (-165.9 percent), education (-126.7 percent), political participation (-116.3 percent), and demography (-47.1 percent). Even the relatively impressive gains achieved by this subgroup on the welfare effort ($+35.2$ percent) subindex were not sufficient to offset the staggering losses found in so many other social sectors in these countries. The pattern of social losses that took place in Chad are typical of those found for all nine LDCs for which major social declines were found.

Chad

Located in central North Africa, Chad has a population of approximately 5.1 million, 40.7 percent of whom are under the age of 15. A land-locked country with comparatively few natural resources, Chad's chief products are cotton and uranium. The country's 1976 per capita income was $73, one of the world's lowest. Infant mortality in Chad is among the highest in the world, at 146 per 1,000 live births. Further, Chad's population is increasing at the rate of 2.1 percent (a projected doubling in size every 33 years). Average male life expectancy is very low, at 41.5 years. About 15 percent of the population is literate.

The country is under oppressive military domination. Since 1965 the violence between the Moslem Arabic northerners and the Christian black southerners has taken at least 21,000 lives.[6] Chad is also one of the sub-Saharan nations that has been the most seriously affected by the African famines of the late 1970s and early 1980s; ten of thousands of persons are known to have perished as a result of these related disasters.

Chad's ISP score in 1970 was 25; by 1983 it had plummeted to 13— among the worst in the world. Unrelenting civil wars, political oppression, rapid population growth, and tragic natural disasters combined between 1970 and 1983 to weaken the country's already fragile economic and social systems. Indeed, significant 14-year declines occurred on six of the ISP subindexes for Chad: women's status (-450.5 percent), political participation (-100.0 percent), education (-41.0 percent), geographic (-22.5 percent), cultural diversity (-1.3 percent), and health (-0.9 percent). Net gains on the defense effort ($+57.1$ percent), economic (+62.0 percent), and welfare effort (+35.4 percent) subindexes were not sufficient to offset the substantial losses in other areas of the index.

While not the poorest nation on earth, Chad nonetheless remains one of the most tragic, given the high levels of human deprivation that exist in the country. In light of current trends, Chad's prospects for a significantly improved future seem pessimistic indeed.

Already listed among the "poorest of the poor" countries in both 1970 and 1980, these nine LDCs have slipped even further into unimaginable levels of poverty and human deprivation. Even worse, the rate of social decline within these countries is accelerating. For the majority of LDCs experiencing significant net social losses, given the enormity of the social, political, and economic calamities that are confronting them, it may well be the case that they will be unable to recapture earlier levels of social development, let alone surpass those levels by the year 2000.

Eastern Trading Area Nations

Unfortunately, the data reported in Tables 4.2 and 4.3 show that the only significant changes occurring among the group of eight ETA nations reflect net social losses. In fact, significant losses were found for four of the ETA nations: the Soviet Union (−28.4 percent), Albania (−10.3 percent), Bulgaria (−9.6 percent), and Poland (−9.6 percent). Net social losses for the ETAs occurred on seven of the ISP subindexes; the most significant losses, however, are found on the political participation (−94.1 percent), defense effort (−51.0 percent), and economic (−26.8 percent) subindexes. Less dramatic, but also significant, were ETA losses on the education (−12.1 percent), women's status (−9.0 percent), and cultural diversity (−12.9 percent) subindexes. As with the LDCs, gains achieved by these ETA nations on the welfare effort (+10.8 percent) and health (+6.5 percent) subindexes were not sufficient to offset the net impact of the substantial losses found on the other subindexes. The pattern of social losses observed for Albania between 1970 and 1983 is typical of current development trends in the ETAs.

Albania

One of the world's smaller nations, with a 1983 population just under 3 million persons, Albania has consistently been one of the economically lesser developed ETA nations. The country is highly homogeneous culturally, however, and in comparison with the LDCs, Albania has had a stable political history since Communist partisans assumed control of the country in 1944.

Per capita income in Albania is approximately $830. The country's infant mortality rate is 86.8 per 1,000 live-born; population doubling time is approximately 34.7 years, with an annual population growth rate of 2.0 percent and average male life expectancy exceeding 69 years. Approximately 75 percent of the population is literate. In 1983 Albania allocated about 13 percent of its GNP to defense spending.

Social development in Albania, even when compared with that of other ETA nations, has been slow. The country achieved an ISP score of 136 in 1970 compared with an ETA group average of 158, with the most favorable ratings found on the welfare effort, education, demographic, health, and geographic subindexes. Between 1970 and 1983, however, Albania's ISP scores dropped by 10.3 percent, with the most significant declines occurring on the political participation (−120.2 percent), economic (−26.0 percent), and education (−12.0 percent) subindexes. As with other nations, net increases on the welfare effort (+31.2 percent) and health (+14.0 percent) subindexes were not sufficient to halt the serious erosion in Albania's post–1970 ISP scores.

The major factors contributing to Albania's current social difficulties are related to high levels of political oppression and increasing levels of central government allocations for military spending. Considered together these factors are depriving Albania of the economic and social resources that are needed to promote its development in other sectors. Recent drops in economic and technical assistance from both the Soviet Union and China have also added to the net social losses already being experienced by the country.

What is reasonably clear from these data is that sharp increases in military spending are adding enormously to the broad range of social declines occurring in the ETAs. These increases have been especially steep in the Soviet Union, whose scores on the defense effort subindex declined by 204.7 percent between 1970 and 1983. Military spending at current levels is beginning to be reflected in seriously worsening social conditions within all ETA nations. Without significant decreases in current military spending patterns, combined with appreciably more open political environments, it is unlikely that significant gains will be achieved by the ETA nations as a group, at least as measured by the social indicators that make up the ISP.

Developed Market Economy Nations

Significant social improvements occurred in six DMEs: Israel (+32.1 percent), Portugal (+22.6 percent), Greece (+17.6 percent), the United States (+16.9 percent), Italy (+14.8 percent), and Japan (+12.3 percent). As noted in the previous section of this chapter, South Africa is the only DME nation for which significant net social declines were found between 1970 and 1983 (−21.7 percent).

Within the group of six forward–moving DMEs improvements occurred on seven of the ISP subindexes. The most significant improvements were found on four subindexes, however: defense effort (+ 168.8
percent), political participation (+ 465.3 percent), women's status (+ 40.9
percent), and education (+ 21.8 percent). Lesser degrees of improvement
took place on the health (+ 6.7 percent) and welfare effort (+ 12.4 percent) subindexes. The substantial improvement in the defense effort
subindex for both Portugal and the United States is especially noteworthy (a net increase of + 580.6 percent and + 358.9 percent for Portugal
and the United States, respectively). Currently, social trends in the
United States are typical of those occurring in the other DMEs for which
net social gains were found.

United States

Having celebrated its 200th anniversary as an independent nation in
1976, the United States is among the world's largest nations, with a 1983
population exceeding 230 million. The country's current rate of natural
population increase is 0.6 percent, resulting in a population doubling
time of approximately 115 years. Though predominately a white society
(85.7 percent), the United States is racially and ethnically mixed; this
pattern of cultural diversity contributes significantly to racial tensions
within the country.[7]

The world's most economically advanced nation, per capita income
in the United States exceeds $12,000. Nevertheless, the rate of infant
mortality in the United States, at 11.5 per 1,000 live-born, is the sev-
enteenth highest worldwide, a rate that is substantially higher than that
of most other DMEs and even higher than that of some DCs (e.g.,
Taiwan, Hong Kong, Singapore). Approximately 99 percent of the adult
population is literate. Geographically extensive, the United States experiences one-third of all the world's major natural disasters. Compared
with the DCs and the LDCs, however, the U.S. death rate from natural
disasters is low.

The ISP score for the United States in 1970 was 124, well below the
DME group average of 163. In 1980 ISP levels rose to 147 but declined
slightly in 1983 to 145, a level that continues to be considerably lower
than the 1983 DME average of 172. This discrepancy in ISP levels between
the United States and other DMEs—especially given the enormity of the
nation's economic wealth—is due, to a large degree, to inconsistent
commitments on the part of the country to social investments. This lack
of commitment to sustained social expenditures at the national level is
especially visible in the human services. The United States, for example,
continues to be the only DME nation without either a national health
service or a universal form of national health insurance for its citizens.

It is also a nation whose social safety net is so full of holes that more than 14 percent of the population are officially classified as poor.[8]

An amalgam of human service programs, federally subsidized, but financed, sponsored, and administered by states and private entities, add significantly to the inefficiencies of the network of human service systems that exist in the United States.[9] Continuing high levels of national spending for defense, combined with centuries-old deprivation of the country's racial minorities, also contribute to the lower social rating of the United States relative to other DME nations.

Nonetheless, significant social improvements occurred for the United States between 1970 and 1983. The most significant changes occurred on the defense effort (+358.9 percent), geographic (+40.3 percent), cultural diversity (+23.9 percent), and political participation (+14.1 percent) subindexes. Problems of inflation and slowed economic growth are reflected in net losses amounting to 17.1 percent on the economic subindex. Smaller amounts of losses were also found on the education (−9.1 percent), women's status (−9.1 percent), and the welfare effort (−6.5 percent) subindexes.

In comparison with the highly advanced social status of the majority of DME nations, the United States must be regarded as something of a social anomaly. Its comparatively less favorable social ratings stem from the long-standing pattern of social inequality that exists between the country's minority and majority populations. For example, rates of infant mortality, unemployment, accidental death, illiteracy, poverty, and criminal offenses average from two to four times higher for the black minority than for the white majority population.[10] The current rate of black infant mortality, for example, is a 19.6 per 1,000 live-born compared with a rate of 10.1 deaths for white infants. In fact, on many of the ISP indicators, the social well-being of racial minorities in the United States more closely resembles patterns found in the higher-income DCs than those that exist in DME nations. Consequently, the United States should be regarded as a social laggard relative to other more socially advanced DME nations.

South Africa

South Africa was the only DME nation for which significant net social losses occurred between 1970 and 1983. In fact, these losses were found on seven of South Africa's ISP subindexes: women's status (−61.7 percent), education (−49.5 percent), political participation (−45.8 percent), geographic (−36.5 percent), welfare effort (−15.4 percent), economic (−14.8 percent), and defense effort (−13.7 percent). A great many of these subindex losses reflect the inclusion of only recently available social indicator data for the country's majority black population. Even so, the highly negative trends reflected in these subindex scores provide insights into the dimensions of the human costs that are associated with South Africa's system of racial apartheid. Net social gains on the cultural diversity (+158.9 percent), health (+51.7 percent), and demographic (+13.8 percent) subindexes were insufficient to offset the steep losses found in the majority of the country's social sectors.

South Africa's social and political history, especially in relation to its anti-human policy of racial apartheid, is already well known and does not need to be restated here.[11] Analysis of the negative social development trends occurring in South Africa reveals two fundamental patterns that are most responsible for the country's continuing and rapid social decline: (1) the extraordinary social, economic, and political disparities that exist between white South Africans and South Africans "of color," both those who are black and those of mixed racial origin; and (2) the increasing levels of militarism and other forms of political oppression that are being used by the white minority government to suppress black liberation movements. Changes on all of the ISP subindexes (Table A.1) indicate that levels of social provision in South Africa are falling at a precipitous rate, for both its black majority and white minority populations. Given current trends, it is highly improbable that South Africa will again move forward until the desperate circumstances under which the majority of South Africans live are dramatically improved.

Developing Countries

Twenty-three DCs (34.3 percent of total) experienced significant social gains between 1970 and 1983; 12 DCs experienced net social deteriorations (17.9 percent) over earlier levels of social progress, however. Table 4.3 identifies the 35 DCs for which significant social gains and losses were found. Included among the DCs with the largest net increases over the 14-year period are Indonesia, which experienced the highest of gains of any nation (+288.5 percent), Nigeria (+278.9 percent), Jordan (+131.7 percent), Vietnam (+104.9 percent), Libya (+48.9 percent), Iran (+38.5 percent), India (+33.3 percent), Syria (+32.9 percent), and 15 others. Social gains in these nations occurred across a broad spectrum of the ISP indicators, including those found on the demographic (+20.0 percent), welfare effort (+15.0 percent), women's status (+13.3 percent), and geographic (+11.3 percent) subindexes. Gains were also realized on the education (+10.0 percent), economic (+5.0 percent), and political participation (+2.2 percent) subindexes. Social trends observed for Malaysia are typical of those found in other forward-moving DCs.

Malaysia

Malaysia is a culturally diverse nation populated by some 15.5 million Malays (50 percent), Chinese (36 percent), and Indians (10 percent). With an annual rate of natural increase of 2.2 percent, the population doubling time for Malaysia is 31.5 years. The per capita income level for Malaysia in 1984 was $1,980. Life expectancy averages 64 years; the rate of infant mortality is 31.8 per 1,000 live-born. Malaysia was created in 1963 from several neighboring territories but was reorganized in 1965 following Singapore's successful campaign for independence from the Federation.

Development trends in Malaysia have improved steadily since 1970. The nation's ISP scores, for example, increased from 80 in 1970 to 102 in 1980 and 1983, a net gain of 27.5 percent during the 14-year period. The most significant improvements for the country have occurred on the demographic (+73.7 percent), education (+61.5 percent), economic (+31.2 percent), cultural diversity (+26.7 percent), and health (+23.9 percent) subindexes. Scores on the political participation subindex also rose by 9.2 percent over the period. In general, the only negative trends for Malaysia have been in the area of defense spending; net losses in this area have been moderate and are reflected in a 8.3 percent subindex decline.

Malaysia is a nation rich in natural resources and has been the center of considerable foreign investment in industrial development for more than a decade.[12] The country's current strategy of multicultural social and economic development, in combination with a highly stable and participatory political environment, is succeeding in advancing development objectives.

In comparison with Malaysia, the DCs with the most significant 14-year social losses are Mauritania (−39.7 percent), Liberia (−29.4 percent), Zambia (−29.2 percent), Senegal (−28.9 percent), Nicaragua (−22.2 percent), Iraq (−21.0 percent), Ghana (−15.8 percent), El Salvador (−15.7 percent), Kampuchea (−14.6 percent), and Chile (−10.4 percent). Angola and Saudi Arabia experienced four-year ISP losses, averaging −133.3 percent and −22.6 percent, respectively. Social development trends in Nicaragua are typical of those occurring in other DCs for which 1970–1983 net social losses were observed.

Nicaragua

The population of Nicaragua numbers fewer than 3 million. About half (55.3 percent) live in the nation's urban areas. Like Malaysia, the country is ethnically diverse: Mestizo (69 percent), Caucasian (17 percent), black (9 percent), and Indian (5 percent). The country is religiously homogeneous, however, with a predominately Roman Catholic population. Per capita income averaged $804 in 1980. Infant mortality is 37.0 per 1,000 live-born, and approximately 87 percent of the population is literate. Male life expectancy averages 56 years; Nicaragua's population is projected to double in size every 20.4 years (3.4 percent).

Nicaragua became an independent republic in 1838. Since independence, however, the country has been the locus of considerable regional political turmoil. Following a period of intense civil conflicts, the Marxist-oriented Sandinista government assumed military control in 1979; political dissension within the country and military conflicts with Nicaragua and neighboring nations are continuing.

Nicaragua's ISP scores have fallen steadily since 1970, from 81 in 1970 to 68 in 1980 and, most recently, to 63 in 1983—a net 14-year decline of 22.2 percent. The most substantial losses occurred on the economic (−137.9 percent), defense effort (−81.1 percent), and political participation (−35.8 percent) subindexes. Substantial losses are also reported for the health (−24.4 percent) and cultural diversity (−16.2 percent) subindexes. However, significant gains occurred on the welfare effort (+79.0 percent), education (+73.7 percent), geographic (+62.9 percent), and demographic (+37.5 percent) subindexes. Women's status subindex scores also increased by 11.0 percent. Despite impressive gains on these last five subindexes, the overall pattern of social development in Nicaragua is on the decline.

The most fundamental problem that is inhibiting Nicaragua's further development is the state of military conflict that continues to exist within Nicaragua and between Nicaragua and its neighbors. These conflicts consume an inordinate amount of the nation's available economic and human resources, including much of the estimated $114,000,000 in direct aid given to Nicaragua by OECD and OPEC nations in 1984.[13] Clearly, future development of the country's social infrastructure will depend on Nicaragua's ability to achieve peace with its neighbors and political stability within its borders.

WORLD RANKINGS

Using scores obtained on the Index of Social Progress, individual countries were *ranked* in terms of their overall level of social provision for each of the study's three comparison years. The use of rankings, in addition to index and subindex scores, adds to the analysis in two ways. First, they make it easier to compare the impact of the various social gains and losses that take place within individual nations with those of other countries. In this way, social rankings, in combination with ISP and WISP scores, can be used to identify those nations that can be classified as world "social leaders" and those that are "socially least developing nations" (SLDCs). This is possible by placing all nations on a single "adequacy of social provision" continuum that reflects the social position of each nation relative to all other countries at particular moments in time. Thus, this type of analysis results in an international ranking of nations in terms of their level of comparative social development. Second, rankings also make it possible to compare the current social situation of a nation against its own historical performance. By this I mean that a particular country's unique pattern of net social gains and losses can be assessed in terms of its own historically changing capacity to provide for the basic social and material needs of its population.

National rankings are reported in two tables. First, Table 4.4 contains an alphabetical listing of national rankings on both the ISP and the WISP for all three time periods. Nations are ranked in order of relative social standing from 1 (most favorable) to 124 (least favorable). An exception to the general ranking scale occurs for 1970 rankings inasmuch as only 107 nations could be included in the study for this time period; consequently, the overall social rankings reported for 1970 range from 1 (most favorable) to 107 (least favorable). Table 4.5 reports the national ranks in numerical order; however, these rankings are for 1983 only. The reader is also referred to Table A.2, which contains 1983 national rankings on each of the ISP subindexes for all 124 nations.

A variety of findings emerge from an analysis of the comparative social ranks of nations. The international social ranking of the United States, for example, improved from 37th position in 1970 to 28th place in 1980 and, then, to 27th place in 1983, a net increase of ten ranks over the study's 14-year time period. The 1980–1983 advance in rank for the United States occurred despite a slight drop in the country's ISP score during the period. Similarly, the comparative social rankings of Malaysia, India, Syria, and 26 other nations reflect advances in their social standing worldwide, for example, for Malaysia an increase from 61st place in 1970, to 56th place in 1980, to 55th place in 1983.

The nations for which the most impressive 14-year rank shifts were found include Indonesia (+ 49 ranks to 56th position), Jordan (+ 37 ranks to 59th position), Nigeria (+ 28 ranks to 79th position), Vietnam (+ 27 ranks to 70th position), and Portugal (+ 14 ranks to 19th position). Substantial 1970–1983 social rank improvements were also found for Iran, Lebanon, the Dominican Republic, Syria, Italy, Japan, Greece, and others. In all, 30 of 107 nations (28 percent)[14] increased their international social standing by more than three ranks between 1970 and 1983. Within each of these countries rank changes reflect substantial increases in the capacity of nations to provide a more adequate level of social provision for their populations. The social accomplishments of these nations have been steady and, in the main, are continuing.

Table 4.4

Alphabetical Listing of Countries by Scores on the Index of Social Progress (ISP83) and the Weighted Index of Social Progress (WISP) by Year ($n = 124$)

ISP70	ISP80	ISP83	RANK ISP70	RANK ISP80	RANK ISP83	COUNTRY	WISP70	WISP80	WISP83	RANK WISP70	RANK WISP80	RANK WISP83
NA	24	26	NA	118	120	Afghanistan*	NA	4	3	NA	121	121
136	116	122	30	49	48	Albania	61	54	55	32	48	45
85	86	88	56	66	66	Algeria	36	36	36	61	74	73
NA	15	-5	NA	122	124	Angola	NA	5	0	NA	119	122
136	128	132	28	41	36	Argentina	61	60	62	33	35	34
172	176	173	14	15	16	Australia	80	82	81	13	14	15
179	197	195	8	4	4	Austria	83	90	90	8	5	4
NA	49	42	NA	105	109	Bangladesh*	NA	18	16	NA	101	105
173	190	184	12	8	10	Belgium	81	89	85	11	8	9
43	52	50	90	101	97	Benin*	14	17	16	92	105	103
81	91	82	60	63	73	Bolivia	35	37	34	63	67	79
123	131	128	38	36	42	Brazil	56	57	56	35	41	44
166	151	150	17	27	25	Bulgaria	77	72	71	18	23	24
35	46	45	100	107	106	Burkina-Faso* (UV)	3	11	11	107	111	111
78	66	72	63	84	78	Burma	36	27	29	59	84	82
35	41	45	102	111	105	Burundi*	5	8	10	104	117	113
60	59	57	80	91	91	Cameroon	23	22	21	82	92	95
157	166	168	22	18	18	Canada	76	78	80	19	18	17
34	40	44	103	112	108	Cen African Rep*	10	12	14	99	109	107
25	7	13	106	123	122	Chad*	3	-4	-3	106	123	123
135	112	121	31	53	49	Chile	62	54	58	30	49	42
NA	69	74	NA	79	77	China	NA	36	37	NA	73	71
118	131	132	42	37	39	Colombia	50	57	59	44	40	40
NA	54	69	NA	96	84	Congo, PR	NA	22	30	NA	91	81
137	155	142	27	25	28	Costa Rica	60	69	63	34	28	30
139	122	126	25	46	44	Cuba	67	59	61	26	37	35
165	154	152	18	26	23	Czechoslovakia	79	72	71	16	24	25
196	208	207	1	1	1	Denmark	91	92	92	2	3	3
112	129	132	47	40	37	Dominican Republic	47	53	55	51	52	48
108	121	122	49	47	47	Ecuador	49	53	54	47	51	49
70	81	89	70	68	65	Egypt, UAR	35	37	39	62	68	66
115	109	97	45	54	57	El Salvador	48	43	38	50	58	68
35	-8	3	101	124	123	Ethiopia*	4	-10	-6	105	124	124
167	178	175	16	13	14	Finland	80	81	80	14	15	16
175	193	190	11	6	6	France	81	90	88	10	7	6
NA	161	156	NA	21	22	Germany, Dem (E)	NA	75	73	NA	21	23
183	201	199	7	3	3	Germany, FDR (W)	85	94	93	6	1	2
57	56	46	82	94	104	Ghana	22	18	14	83	99	106
136	164	160	29	20	21	Greece	64	76	75	29	20	20
64	67	59	76	82	89	Guatemala	30	30	27	68	80	85

105

Table 4.4 (cont.)

ISP70	ISP80	ISP83	RANK ISP70	RANK ISP80	RANK ISP83	COUNTRY	WISP70	WISP80	WISP83	RANK WISP70	RANK WISP80	RANK WISP83
42	22	21	94	119	121	Guinea*	14	5	4	94	118	120
72	68	67	68	80	85	Haiti*	28	25	24	72	89	90
88	80	92	55	69	63	Honduras	40	35	41	56	75	63
NA	129	132	NA	39	38	Hong Kong	NA	59	60	NA	38	37
173	165	162	13	19	20	Hungary	79	75	74	15	22	21
54	70	72	83	78	80	India	19	27	28	86	85	84
26	95	101	105	60	56	Indonesia	9	42	45	101	60	59
65	76	90	75	72	64	Iran	32	38	43	67	66	60
62	61	49	78	90	99	Iraq	32	35	37	66	76	70
184	187	185	6	10	8	Ireland	84	85	85	7	11	11
84	104	111	57	55	53	Israel	55	63	62	37	32	31
176	203	202	10	2	2	Italy	81	93	93	12	2	1
68	65	63	72	85	87	Ivory Coast	24	24	23	79	90	91
129	141	137	34	30	31	Jamaica	55	62	60	38	34	36
155	178	174	23	12	15	Japan	73	86	85	22	10	10
41	62	95	96	89	59	Jordan	29	39	47	70	65	56
48	41	41	87	110	112	Kampuchea	23	12	11	81	108	112
68	63	65	73	86	86	Kenya	27	26	26	74	86	87
NA	70	78	NA	77	75	Korea, Dem (N)	NA	40	41	NA	63	65
103	117	112	51	48	52	Korea, Rep (S)	49	55	53	49	46	51
NA	53	41	NA	97	110	Lao PDR*	NA	20	12	NA	96	109
117	137	136	44	31	33	Lebanon	53	64	64	41	30	29
NA	95	88	NA	62	67	Lesotho*	NA	36	35	NA	71	76
63	53	48	74	98	102	Liberia	24	20	17	78	97	98
47	90	70	88	64	83	Libya	21	40	35	84	62	77
81	76	83	58	73	72	Madagascar	30	31	34	69	79	78
42	28	34	93	116	116	Malawi*	11	4	6	98	120	119
80	102	102	61	56	55	Malaysia	36	46	46	60	57	57
45	35	33	89	115	118	Mali*	13	8	7	95	115	117
63	21	38	77	121	115	Mauritania	23	10	14	80	113	108
NA	133	136	NA	35	32	Mauritius	NA	56	58	NA	45	43
119	116	114	41	50	51	Mexico	50	51	51	46	54	54
NA	71	75	NA	75	76	Mongolia	NA	37	38	NA	70	69
73	88	87	67	65	69	Morocco	29	36	38	71	72	75
NA	22	34	NA	120	117	Mozambique	NA	2	9	NA	122	115
49	57	56	85	93	92	Nepal*	13	17	16	96	104	104
185	188	184	4	9	9	Netherlands	87	87	85	4	9	8
176	176	176	9	16	13	New Zealand	82	81	82	9	16	14
81	68	63	59	81	88	Nicaragua	38	33	33	57	78	80
34	39	41	104	113	111	Niger*	6	8	10	103	116	114
19	72	72	107	74	79	Nigeria	6	26	25	102	87	88
184	192	186	5	7	7	Norway	89	90	86	3	6	7
53	50	50	84	104	98	Pakistan	20	18	17	85	103	100
125	125	129	36	43	40	Panama	56	56	58	36	43	41

Table 4.4 (cont.)

ISP70	ISP80	ISP83	RANK ISP70	RANK ISP80	RANK ISP83	COUNTRY	WISP70	WISP80	WISP83	RANK WISP70	RANK WISP80	RANK WISP83
NA	71	71	NA	76	81	Papua New Guinea	NA	29	29	NA	83	83
113	123	123	46	44	45	Paraguay	49	54	54	48	50	50
79	77	82	62	71	74	Peru	38	37	39	58	69	67
97	93	92	54	61	62	Philippines	42	41	41	55	61	62
167	157	151	15	23	24	Poland	78	71	68	17	25	26
133	158	163	33	22	19	Portugal	62	70	73	31	26	22
162	155	148	20	24	26	Romania	74	70	67	21	27	27
62	62	70	79	87	82	Rwanda*	17	18	22	89	102	93
NA	62	48	NA	88	101	Saudi Arabia	NA	29	26	NA	82	86
76	57	54	66	92	93	Senegal	27	18	18	75	98	97
77	45	39	65	108	113	Sierra Leone*	25	12	8	77	110	116
105	127	126	50	42	43	Singapore	50	60	59	45	36	39
59	36	28	81	114	119	Somalia*	19	10	6	87	112	118
120	100	94	40	58	60	South Africa	51	43	41	43	59	64
158	176	171	21	17	17	Spain	72	78	76	24	17	18
118	129	128	43	38	41	Sri Lanka	51	55	55	42	47	47
48	53	52	86	99	95	Sudan*	18	18	17	88	100	101
195	194	192	2	5	5	Sweden	95	91	90	1	4	5
164	180	178	19	11	11	Switzerland	75	83	82	20	13	13
70	81	93	71	67	61	Syrian Arab Rep	32	40	43	64	64	61
NA	96	87	NA	59	68	Taiwan	NA	58	55	NA	39	46
41	52	53	95	100	94	Tanzania*	12	20	21	97	95	96
102	123	122	53	45	46	Thailand	45	52	52	52	53	52
38	44	49	98	109	100	Togo*	9	15	17	100	106	102
122	134	134	39	34	34	Trinidad/Tobago	54	57	59	40	42	38
108	114	117	48	51	50	Tunisia	44	48	49	53	56	55
102	114	105	52	52	54	Turkey	44	49	46	54	55	58
134	101	96	32	57	58	USSR	67	56	52	25	44	53
43	49	44	92	106	107	Uganda*	14	14	12	93	107	110
186	177	177	3	14	12	United Kingdom	87	84	83	5	12	12
124	147	145	37	28	27	United States	72	77	76	23	19	19
147	135	142	24	33	29	Uruguay	66	63	66	27	31	28
125	142	140	35	29	30	Venezuela	55	63	62	39	33	33
41	79	84	97	70	70	Vietnam	28	33	36	73	77	74
NA	26	48	NA	117	103	Yemen Arab Rep* (N)	NA	10	21	NA	114	94
37	52	39	99	102	114	Yemen,* PDR (S)	17	22	17	90	93	99
138	137	134	26	32	35	Yugoslavia	65	64	62	28	29	32
43	55	57	91	95	90	Zaire	15	21	22	91	94	92
72	51	51	69	103	96	Zambia	27	25	24	76	88	89
78	67	84	64	83	71	Zimbabwe	32	29	37	65	81	72

Note: See Appendix B for a discussion of the methodology and factor analytical techniques that were used to derive the system of statistical weights for all three sets of WISP scores.

Source: Compiled by the author.

Table 4.5
1983 Country Rankings on the Unweighted Index of Social Progress (ISP83)

ISP83 RANK	ISP83 SCORE	COUNTRY		ISP83 RANK	ISP83 SCORE	COUNTRY		ISP83 RANK	ISP83 SCORE	COUNTRY
1	207	Denmark		46	122	Thailand		91	57	Cameroon
2	202	Italy		47	122	Ecuador		92	56	Nepal‡
3	199	Germany, FDR (W)		48	122	Albania		93	54	Senegal
4	195	Austria		49	121	Chile		94	53	Tanzania‡
5	192	Sweden		50	117	Tunisia		95	52	Sudan‡
6	190	France						96	51	Zambia
7	186	Norway		51	114	Mexico		97	50	Benin‡
8	185	Ireland		52	112	Korea, Rep (S)		98	50	Pakistan
9	184	Netherlands		53	111	Israel		99	49	Iraq
10	184	Belgium		54	105	Turkey		100	49	Togo‡
				55	102	Malaysia				
11	178	Switzerland		56	101	Indonesia		101	48	Saudi Arabia
12	177	United Kingdom		57	97	El Salvador		102	48	Liberia
13	176	New Zealand		58	96	USSR		103	48	Yemen Arab Rep‡ (N)
14	175	Finland		59	95	Jordan		104	46	Ghana
15	174	Japan		60	94	South Africa		105	45	Burundi‡
16	173	Australia						106	45	Burkina-Faso‡ (UV)
17	171	Spain		61	93	Syrian Arab Rep		107	44	Uganda‡
18	168	Canada		62	92	Philippines		108	44	Cen African Rep‡
19	163	Portugal		63	92	Honduras		109	42	Bangladesh‡
20	162	Hungary		64	90	Iran		110	41	Lao PDR‡
				65	89	Egypt, UAR				
21	160	Greece		66	88	Algeria		111	41	Niger‡
22	156	Germany, Dem (E)		67	88	Lesotho‡		112	41	Kampuchea
23	152	Czechoslovakia		68	87	Taiwan		113	39	Sierra Leone‡
24	151	Poland		69	87	Morocco		114	39	Yemen,‡ PDR (S)

108

21	160	Greece	65	89	Egypt, UAR	111	41	Niger*
22	156	Germany, Dem (E)	66	88	Algeria	112	41	Kampuchea
23	152	Czechoslovakia	67	88	Lesotho*	113	39	Sierra Leone*
24	151	Poland	68	87	Taiwan	114	39	Yemen,* PDR (S)
25	150	Bulgaria	69	87	Morocco	115	38	Mauritania*
26	148	Romania	70	84	Vietnam	116	34	Malawi*
27	145	United States	71	84	Zimbabwe	117	34	Mozambique
28	142	Costa Rica	72	83	Madagascar	118	33	Mali*
29	142	Uruguay	73	82	Bolivia	119	28	Somalia*
30	140	Venezuela	74	82	Peru	120	26	Afghanistan
31	137	Jamaica	75	78	Korea, Dem (N)	121	21	Guinea*
32	136	Mauritius	76	75	Mongolia	122	13	Chad*
33	136	Lebanon	77	74	China	123	3	Ethiopia*
34	134	Trinidad/Tobago	78	72	Burma	124	-5	Angola
35	134	Yugoslavia	79	72	Nigeria			
36	132	Argentina	80	72	India			
37	132	Dominican Republic	81	71	Papua New Guinea			
38	132	Hong Kong	82	70	Rwanda*			
39	132	Colombia	83	70	Libya			
40	129	Panama	84	69	Congo, PR			
41	128	Sri Lanka	85	67	Haiti*			
42	128	Brazil	86	65	Kenya			
43	126	Singapore	87	63	Ivory Coast			
44	126	Cuba	88	63	Nicaragua			
45	123	Paraguay	89	59	Guatemala			
			90	57	Zaire			

NOTES:

Asterisks (*) indicate countries officially classified as "Least Developing Countries" (LDC).

But improvements in overall social position did not occur for all nations; in fact, net social rank losses in excess of three or more positions occurred for 60 (56 percent) of the 107 nations for which 1970 and 1983 comparisons could be made. The ranks of ten nations remained identical for both time periods.

As reported in Table 4.4, the most substantial losses were found for Sierra Leone (−48 ranks to 113th position), Mauritania (−38 ranks to 115th position), Somalia (−38 ranks to 119th position), Nicaragua (−29 ranks to 88th position), Mali (−29 ranks to 118th position), among others. Further, lower social rankings were assigned to 19 of the 20 LDCs in 1983 than in 1970. The LDCs with the most significant social rank losses were Sierra Leone, Mauritania, Somalia, Mali, Guinea (−27 ranks to 121th position), Malawi (−23 ranks to 116th place), and Ethiopia (−22 ranks to 123rd place). Social rank losses were also substantial for Haiti, Chad, Uganda, PDR Yemen, the Sudan, Niger, Benin, Nepal, Burkina-Faso (previously Upper Volta), the Central African Republic, Rwanda, and Burundi. The only LDC to improve was Tanzania, which was able to raise its rank by one position from 95th place in 1970 to 94th place in 1983.

WORLD SOCIAL LEADERS AND FOLLOWERS

Of the 124 nations studied, which countries have been the most successful in providing for the basic social and material needs of their populations? Which have been the least successful? To what extent does the membership of these groupings of world social leaders and, by comparison, the world's SLDCs remain stable? What are the factors that best predict the likelihood of a nation, or set of nations, moving into either a social leadership or socially least developing position?

Beginning answers to these questions are contained in the data reported in Table 4.6, which summarizes ISP scores and social rank data for the world's ten social leaders and eight SLDCs.

Social Leaders

Viewed from an international comparative perspective, the world's 1983 social leaders are, from 1 to 10, Denmark, Italy, Germany, Austria, Sweden, France, Norway, Ireland, the Netherlands, and Belgium. Eight of these nations were on the list of social leaders in 1970 (France and Belgium were not) and all ten appear on the list for both 1980 and 1983. Note, however, that the rankings of individual nations tend to fluctuate somewhat over time; for example, Italy ranked tenth place in 1970 but second place in both 1980 and 1983. Conversely, the social rankings for

Table 4.6
Index of Social Progress Scores and Ranks for World Social Leaders and
Socially Least Developing Nations, 1970–1983 ($n = 124$)

Country	ISP 1970	Rank 1970	Country	ISP 1980	Rank 1980	Country	ISP 1983	Rank 1983
WORLD SOCIAL LEADERS								
Denmark	196	1	Denmark	208	1	Denmark	207	1
Sweden	195	2	Italy	203	2	Italy	202	2
United Kingdom	186	3	Germany	201	3	Germany	199	3
Netherlands	185	4	Austria	197	4	Austria	195	4
Norway	184	5	Sweden	194	5	Sweden	192	5
Ireland	184	6	France	193	6	France	190	6
Germany	183	7	Norway	192	7	Norway	186	7
Austria	179	8	Belgium	190	8	Ireland	185	8
New Zealand	176	9	Netherlands	188	9	Netherlands	184	9
Italy	176	10	Ireland	187	10	Belgium	184	10
LEAST SOCIALLY DEVELOPING COUNTRIES								
Nigeria*	19	107	Ethiopia*	-8	124	Angola	-5	124
Chad*	25	106	Chad*	7	123	Ethiopia*	3	123
Indonesia	26	105	Angola	15	122	Chad*	13	122
Niger*	34	104	Mauritania	21	121	Guinea*	21	121
C. African Rep.	34	103	Mozambique	22	120	Afghanistan*	26	120
Burundi*	35	102	Guinea*	22	119	Somalia*	28	119
Ethiopia*	35	101	Afghanistan*	24	118	Mali*	33	118
Burkina-Faso*	35	100	Yemen, Arab*	52	117	Mozambique	34	117
AVERAGE SCORE ALL COUNTRIES	100			100			100	

* Countries officially classified as LDCs by the United Nations.

Source: Compiled by the author.

Ireland reflect a more variable pattern: sixth position in 1970, tenth place
in 1980, and eighth place in 1983.

What do the social leaders have in common? First, they are all DME
nations. Second, they are all physically located in Europe.[15] More particularly, five of the ten nations are geographically situated in Northern
Europe (Denmark, Germany, Sweden, Norway, and Ireland), four are

located in Western Europe (Austria, France, Netherlands, and Belgium), and one, Italy, is Southern European.[16] Indeed, it is not until New Zealand surfaces on the list, in 13th place (Table 4.5), that a non-European country appears at or near the top of the list of world social leaders. The dominant social philosophy, social policies,[17] and even the bulk of New Zealand's population (85 percent),[18] however, are essentially European in origin.

In effect, the countries identified as the world's social leaders share a rather rich, dynamic, and unique history of European social innovation that began more than a century ago.[19] These social experiments have resulted in the emergence of societies which, to a very great extent, are succeeding in providing a more secure social safety net for the majority of their citizens, albeit not without predictable financial and related political problems from time to time.[20]

A third factor that the world's social leaders share is that they are comparatively small demographically. The 1983 population size of the top ten nations, for example, averaged only 22.6 million persons. In fact, six of the social leaders have populations that are either at or below 10 million: Denmark (5 million), Austria (8 million), Sweden (8 million), Norway (4 million), Ireland (4 million), and Belgium (10 million). The relatively small size of the populations of these countries compares favorably with that of both the remaining 15 DME nations (average = 41.4 million) and the group average for the DCs (average = 47.0 million).

For the most socially progressive nations, then, size contributes to their ability to develop social infrastructures that respond effectively to the changing social needs of their populations. The depth of commitment of these nations to social progress is documented in their average 1983 welfare effort subindex score of 26.9, the highest such score identified for any subgroup of nations. This score compares favorably with that achieved by the remaining group of 15 DME nations (average = 18.8), and the group of eight ETA nations (average = 22.1). Given all of the other dynamics that inform welfare development, certainly population size, at least for this subset of nations, has been a significant factor for enhancing further social development in the social leaders.

A fourth factor that the social leaders share is their comparatively high level of cultural homogeneity. By this I mean that the majority of the country's inhabitants of the social leaders share more or less the same language and religious traditions, and the same or similar racial and ethnic group origins (Table 2.3). The average 1983 cultural diversity subindex score for this group of ten nations, for example, was 17.5, again a subgroup score that is considerably higher than that found for either the remaining group of 15 DME nations (average = 13.4), the ETAs (average = 12.1), the DCs (average = 9.9), or the LDCs (average = 4.9).

Socially Least Developing Countries

The world's ten socially least developing nations (SLDCs) are Angola (rank = 124), Ethiopia (rank = 123), Chad (rank = 122), Guinea (rank = 121), Afghanistan (rank = 120), Somalia (rank = 119), Mali (rank = 118), Mozambique (rank = 117), Malawi (rank = 116), and Mauritania (rank = 115). Also near the bottom of the list are PDR Yemen (rank = 114), Sierra Leone (rank = 113), Kampuchea (rank = 112), and Niger (rank = 111).

With the exception of Afghanistan, SLDCs are located in Africa. Indeed, 16 of the bottom 20 nations are African nations; the remaining four are Asian (Table 4.5). Further, six of the SLDCs have been officially designated by the United Nations as LDCs. The data presented here would suggest that the United Nations should also designate Angola, Afghanistan, Mozambique, and Mauritania as LDCs, thereby making it possible for these nations to receive international development assistance on a priority basis.

As a group, the world's SLDCs also are small, with an average 1983 population size of 11.1 million. This is a demographic characteristic that the SLDCs share with the world's socially leading nations, but the SLDCs have not been able to exploit their comparatively small size to realize significant social gains. The reasons for this are complex but stem principally from seven factors: their relative youthfulness as nations, the relative scarcity of natural resources within these countries, the fragile nature of their economies, their high levels of cultural diversity, burgeoning rates of population growth, the absence of an established history of national social infrastructures, and the high level of militarism, including political oppression, that characterizes nearly all of these countries.

Especially important to an understanding of the relative underdevelopment of the SLDCs is the fact that most have been politically autonomous nations for less than 30 years. Indeed, only until the early and middle 1960s, the majority of SLDCs were political dependencies of European colonial powers. Further, for the majority of SLDCs independence was achieved only through devastating civil and regional wars; these decades-long conflicts consumed many of the scarce economic and human resources that were needed by these nations to advance social development.

The emergence of the SLDCs as autonomous nation-states was possible only through an amalgamation of peoples and geographic territories that the majority of the inhabitants of many of these nations, even today, find disquieting (e.g., Angola, Chad, Ethiopia).[21] The great mix of languages, religions, and ethnic diversity that characterizes the SLDCs is reflected in their average 1983 cultural diversity subindex score of 4.2, an average well below that of the LDCs as a group (average = 4.9), and one that is considerably lower than that of the world's social leaders (average = 17.5). In response to their considerable cultural diversity, many SLDCs continue to conduct the official business of government in three or more languages, one of which typically is the mother tongue of the former colonial power. In Angola, for example, fewer than 38 percent of the population share the same mother tongue.[22]

Formal welfare programs and services are at their poorest in the SLDCs. These nations achieved an average welfare effort subindex score of only 4.1. Similarly, subgroup subindex scores in the areas of health (−4.6), education (−2.4), women's status (−2.1), economic status (4.9), demographic trends (2.4), and political participation (−1.0) are all well below those averages reported for the LDCs as a group. Subgroup scores on the defense effort subindex (average = 8.2) were also less favorable than that of the group average for the LDCs of 12.0.

In summary, the world's SLDCs tend to be comparatively youthful and culturally diverse nations that lack the basic social, economic, and welfare infrastructures that exist in more socially advanced nations. The majority of these SLDCs are also at war internally and, in some cases, with other nations in the region. SLDC expenditures for military and defense purposes, as a result, often tend to exceed central government social expenditures; for example, in Mali 1983 central government expenditures for health care amounted to 2.5 percent while expenditures for the military exceeded 7.9 of all expenditures.[23]

The analysis of nation-specific trends in social development reveals a variety of patterns concerning worldwide social gains and losses. The great majority of nations are moving forward in their ability and willingness to provide a more secure social net for the bulk of their population. The social gains realized by many of these nations have been impressive, and they are continuing to accumulate at a more or less steady pace.

For a substantial minority of nations, however, net social losses occurred between 1970 and 1983. The diminished capacity of many of these nations to sustain already inadequate levels of social provision is very worrisome indeed. The current world social situation is especially desperate in those already deeply impoverished LDCs and some lower-income DCs. The absence of significant social progress within these countries, let alone the continuing downward spiral that has been observed in this study, means that yet another generation of inhabitants of "fourth world" nations is doomed to unimaginable levels of human suffering and deprivation.

The next chapter will discuss several of the most critical social dilemmas that will influence social development worldwide through the year 2000.

NOTES

1. For a beginning listing of the major studies in this body of research see Richard J. Estes, "Toward a Quality-of-Life Index: Empirical Approaches to Assessing Human Welfare Internationally," in *The Third World: States of Mind and Being*, edited by James Norwine and Alfonso Gonzalez (London: George Allen & Unwin, 1987).

2. For examples of research on the transfer of social technologies between countries see Harvey W. Wallender, *Technology Transfer and Management in the Developing Countries: Company Cases and Policy Analyses in Brazil, Kenya, Korea, Peru, and Tanzania* (Cambridge, MA: Ballinger, 1979); Wilberne H. Persaud, "Technology Transfer: Conceptual and Development Issues," *Social and Economic Studies* 3(1981): 1–17; Jacques Perrin, "The Production of Know-How and Obstacles to Its Transfer," *Prospects* 14(1984):479–85.

3. Seventeen nations were added to the analysis for the first time in 1980 (Table 1.2); hence, 1970 ISP scores were not available for them. Changes in ISP levels for these countries, then, are reported only for the four-year period 1980–1983.

4. Population doubling time is computed by dividing 69.31 by the annual population growth rate; thus, the time required to double the 1983 population of the LDCs is 26.6 years—that is, 69.31/2.6 percent = 26.65 years (see Ehrlich and Ehrlich 1972 for a fuller discussion of the origins of this formula).

5. A minimum of $140,000,000 was contributed to Burundi by OECD and OPEC nations during 1984. These dollars amounted to 15.0 percent of Burundi's total GNP, or $30.7 for each of Burundi's 4.6 million population in 1984. World Bank, *World Development Report, 1986* (Washington, D.C., 1986), Table 21, p. 220.

6. Don Podesta, "Ethnic Conflicts: Toll Mounts," *Washington Post*, May 26, 1987, pp. A1, A17.

7. As examples see P. Burstein, *Discrimination, Jobs, and Politics: The Struggle for Equal Employment* (Chicago, IL: University of Chicago Press, 1985); A. Morris, *The Origins of the Civil Rights Movement: Black Communities Organizing* (New York: The Free Press, 1986).

8. United States Bureau of the Census, *Current Population Reports*, series P–60, 145 (Washington, D.C.: Government Publications Office, 1983).

9. Michael Katz, *In the Shadow of the Poorhouse: A Social History of Welfare in America* (New York: Harper & Row, 1986); Richard Cloward and Frances Fox Piven, *Regulating the Poor: The Functions of Public Welfare* (New York: Pantheon, 1971).

10. Evidence in support of this conclusion is plentiful. As examples, see Margaret M. Heckler, *Report of the Secretary's Task Force on Black and Minority Health*, Vol. 1 (Washington, D.C.: Department of Health and Human Services, 1985); Melvin Rudov and Nancy Santangelo, *Health Status of Minorities and Low Income Groups* (Washington, D.C.: Department of Health, Education, and Welfare, 1979); United States Department of Commerce, *Statistical Abstracts of the United States, 1987* (Washington, D.C.: U.S. Government Printing Office, 1987).

11. For example see Leonard Thompson, *The Political Mythology of Apartheid*

(New Haven, CT: Yale University Press, 1986); C. Mayson, *A Certain Sound: The Struggle for Liberation in Southern Africa* (New York: Orbis Books, 1985); H. Giliomee and L. Schlemmer, *Up Against the Fences: Poverty, Passes, & Privilege in South Africa* (New York: St. Martin's 1985).

12. For a special report on economic developments in Malaysia see "Malaysia: Moving Into the Big League," *South* (September 1985): 215–28.

13. World Bank, *World Development Report*, p. 220.

14. Reflects net rank changes among only the 107 nations for which both 1970 and 1983 ISP data are available.

15. A fuller discussion of this finding can be found in Richard J. Estes, "Trends in European Social Development," *Europe* (November 1986).

16. See Table 1.2 for a complete listing of countries by geographic subregion.

17. P. R. Kaim-Caudle, *Comparative Social Policy and Social Security: A Ten Country Study* (Port Washington, NY: Kennikat Press, 1973); John Dixon, *Social Security Traditions and Their Global Applications* (Canberra, Australia: International Fellowship for Social and Economic Development, 1986).

18. Hana Umlauf Lane (ed.), *The World Almanac and Book of Facts, 1986* (New York: Newspaper Enterprise Association, 1985), p. 587.

19. For interesting histories of these developments see: Peter Flora and Arnold J. Heidenheimer (eds.), *The Development of Welfare States in Europe and America* (New Brunswick, NJ: Transaction Books, 1981); Gaston V. Rimlinger, *Welfare Policy and Industrialization in Europe, America, and Russia* (New York: Wiley, 1971); Robert Erikson et al., *The Scandinavian Model: Welfare States and Welfare Research* (Armonk, NY: M. E. Sharpe, 1987).

20. Organization for Economic Cooperation and Development, *The Welfare State in Crisis: An Account of the Conference on Social Policies in the 1980s* (Paris, 1981); *Social Expenditures, 1960–1990: Problems of Growth and Control* (Paris, 1985).

21. Don Podesta, "Ethnic Conflicts: Toll Mounts," *Washington Post*, May 26, 1987, pp. A1, A17.

22. Lane et al., *The World Almanac and Book of Facts, 1986*, p. 536.

23. United Nations Children's Fund, *The State of the World's Children, 1987* (London: Oxford University Press, for UNICEF, 1987), Table 6, pp. 138–39.

5

SINCE 1984

During the closing months of 1987 the following headlines appeared in the world press:

- Population increases to 5 billion; world population expected to exceed 6 billion by the year 2000 and 10 billion by the middle of the next century; 90 percent of world population increases will occur in the poorest nations.
- Famine again in Africa; millions more predicted to die from a new wave of starvation; Western nations move slowly to provide critically needed pre-emergency food and other assistance.
- Massacre in Mozambique leaves 386 dead; toll from continuing civil war exceeds 100,000 dead and 1.5 million refugees. African civil wars threaten the continent's stability.
- Corazon Aquino survives sixth coup attempt to oust her from Philippine presidency; political turmoil returns to the nation with thousands imprisoned and hundreds dead in the streets.
- Tens of thousands of black South African miners strike; the country's economy is thrown into yet more chaos as possible end to apartheid nears; neighboring Southern African nations fear retaliation for their support of striking workers and opposition military forces.
- The United States Navy bombs two Iranian oil rigs in retaliation for Iran's attack on a Kuwaiti oil vessel sailing under protection of an American flag; Iran threatens massive retaliation against the United States and other NATO members assisting in protecting international shipping lanes in the Persian Gulf.
- Major financial markets collapse in New York, Tokyo, Hong Kong, and London; rising interest rates, economic protectionism, and widening imbalances in trade thought to be responsible; new global economic recession feared.

- Oscar Arias Sanchez, president of Costa Rica, awarded Nobel Peace Prize for efforts to achieve peace among the five Central American nations of Honduras, Guatemala, Nicaragua, El Salvador, and Costa Rica.
- Soviets face a reassessment of their political goals and the economic costs of occupying Afghanistan; Gorbachev said to "want out" of political quagmire.
- Radioactive fallout from Chernobyl nuclear accident represents continuing threat to Northern and Western Europe; environmental consequences for rest of world still unknown.
- World Health Organization declares AIDS (Acquired Immune Deficiency Syndrome) to be the single greatest threat to world development; by the year 2000 more lives are expected to be lost to the disease than from the century's two world wars.

Since 1970 considerable progress has been achieved throughout the world in improving the conditions under which people live. Social progress has been most apparent among the world's already economically advanced nations, but substantial changes have already occurred and are continuing to take place in many of the planet's developing and least developing nations. Certainly a greater proportion of the people living today are having their basic social and material needs satisfied than was the case 50, 40, 30, 20, or even 10 years ago. While taking place unevenly throughout the world, social progress will, nonetheless, continue to occur worldwide. Governments, international development organizations, private citizens, and others who have contributed to past successes in the social sectors should feel justifiably satisfied with what their labor has accomplished. But more work needs to be done. Much of this work is of critical importance; indeed should the urgent social problems facing the world today go unresolved it is highly probable that the accomplishments of earlier decades will be substantially eroded.

In this chapter I will discuss what I consider to be the most pressing social problems confronting humanity as the present century draws to a close. I will attempt to identify the various forces that sustain these problems and, where possible, I will suggest some alternative approaches to their resolution. More particularly, in this chapter the reader's attention will be directed to the following worldwide social dilemmas: militarism, war, and the spread of nuclear weapons; population growth; world hunger, malnutrition, and famine; the international debt crisis and developing nations; women and development; the crisis in welfare; AIDS and development.

MILITARISM, WAR, AND THE SPREAD OF NUCLEAR WEAPONS

Is the world of 1987 a safer one than that which existed in 1970, or 1980, or even 1983? Are the number of wars, civil and regional, being fought around the world on the decline? Is there evidence for believing that further expansions in nuclear weapons are beginning to come under control? Are fewer people dying from the economic consequences of a more militant world than was the case in earlier years?

In a word, the answer to each of these questions is, no! Indeed, the profound development problems reported throughout this volume are being exacerbated through increases in each of the categories listed above. Consider the following facts for example:

1. Today wars are being waged in or between at least 40 countries. The most devastating conflicts, as in 1980, continue to be fought by developing nations including Iran, Iraq, Angola, Ethiopia, Mozambique, El Salvador, Nicaragua, Costa Rica, Guatemala, Lebanon, Afghanistan, Chad, Kampuchea, and so on. The death toll from these wars is staggering, as is the cost of financing them, in terms of funds that otherwise could have been spent on the peaceful development of these nations.

2. In March 1983 President Reagan announced the start of a new Strategic Defense Initiative (SDI). The SDI would result in the construction in space of a series of "doomsday" devices so lethal that neither superpower would dare to initiate a first-strike nuclear attack. Nicknamed "Star Wars" because of its fantastic proportions, the proposal has been condemned repeatedly as "unworkable," "overly simplistic," "too expensive," "doomed to failure from the outset," and so on. Nonetheless, the President and Congress authorized several billion dollars to begin research and development work on the project. The political repercussions of the decision to initiate development of SDI resulted in an immediate worldwide destabilization of relations between the two superpowers.

   a. Regarded as blatantly offensive in nature, the decision to pursue development of SDI was directly responsible for the failure of the hastily called Reykjavik summit between President Reagan and General Secretary Mikhail Gorbachev.

   b. Not persuaded by critics of the SDI, Reagan pledged to commit whatever funds are necessary to establish the system. According to Ruth L. Sivard, "the Pentagon put the five-year research cost at about $30 billion. Recent overall cost estimates by independent authorities range from $500 to $1,000 billion, with former Secretaries of Defense, representing both major political parties, agreeing on the top range."[1]

      The figure of $1,000 billion for the SDI exceeds the total combined social spending of virtually every nation on earth. Were such funds committed to promoting social development in the Third World, poverty, malnutrition, homelessness, and the other major social catastrophes confronting these countries could be eliminated overnight. Many of the national and regional problems contributing to international political instability could also be eliminated through a redirection of the funds already allocated to SDI's development.

   c. Thousands of defense specialists worldwide agreed that, even if a system approximating the SDI could be developed, the system would not be 100 percent leakproof. Should only as few as 1 percent of targeted weapons get through the system—a conservative estimate of the leakage—a minimum of 100 U.S. cities could be destroyed and as many as 35 million to 56 million people would be killed immediately.

To suggest that the SDI is pure folly is an understatement at best.

3. In 1986 the world experienced its most serious nuclear disaster to date, at the Chernobyl nuclear power plant in the Soviet Union. The impact of the disaster was far-reaching and its total consequences, in terms of the ill health of people exposed to its radiation, may not be known for decades.

Chernobyl had made eminently clear that there is no safety in nuclear energy, as there is none to be found in nuclear weapons. As the number of nuclear power plants increases around the world, inevitably there will be more nuclear accidents. The problems of the safe disposal of nuclear waste is another matter entirely but nuclear waste, too, poses a serious and lingering threat to humanity's safety that will last at least hundreds, probably thousands of years.

Since the accident many nations have called a halt to the construction of new plants; pressures exist in many countries to close down existing plants and, in others, a higher level of oversight on the operation of nuclear power plants has been imposed.

But the extraordinary danger of nuclear power plants, even just one, is only beginning to sink into people's consciousness. A return to the use of alternative non-nuclear forms of energy, including significantly reducing current consumption levels, remains an urgent global priority.

4. In 1986 the number of political refugees worldwide, as in 1980, continued to exceed more than 10 million. Nearly all of these persons are without homes either because of either civil wars being fought in their nations or because of regional wars with neighboring states. The majority of refugees continue to be from the world's most impoverished nations:[2]

Afghanistan	3.66 million
Palestine	2.01 million
Mozambique	1.50 million
Ethiopia	1.21 million
Uganda	.31 million
Angola	.30 million
El Salvador	.24 million

The desperate situation of the world's refugees continues unabated. The vast majority of refugees are women, dependent children, and aged men. Deprived of permanent homelands, these stateless people live under conditions of squalor in the resettlement camps of receiving nations while awaiting permanent homes in yet other countries. For the majority of these persons invitations to resettle elsewhere will never come.

5. The social budgets of the majority of even affluent nations are collapsing under pressures to increase defense spending. The situation is most acute in the DCs and LDCs of Africa and the DCs of Latin America. But defense spending is virtually bankrupting the Soviet Union as well, a country in which lines of people have again begun to form in order to purchase daily essentials that are in short supply (e.g., meat, bread, shoes, petroleum, and so on).[3]

In the United States accelerated defense spending has been achieved at the expense of domestic social programs; as a result, the number of impoverished Americans increased from 12.1 million in 1981 to about 15.0 million in 1986.[4] The country also has large numbers of hungry people, homeless persons, as well as people unable to receive basic medical and psychiatric services because of sharp cuts in government support for these programs.

In Europe sharp cuts are occurring in domestic social spending in order to accommodate NATO pressures for European nations to share a larger percentage of the financial costs involved in their defense—minimally estimated to be about $200 billion annually.[5] Japan is in the process of rearming. Israel, South Korea, and Singapore are already spending 27.8, 29.7 and 20.1 percent, respectively, of their central government budgets on defense.[6] The military budgets of both the United States and the Soviet Union, in the absence of agreements on disarmament, are escalating. The social and economic costs accruing to all of these nations as a result of fewer resources available for social development are enormous.

6. Nuclear weapons, nuclear stations, and the number of nuclear warheads are proliferating throughout the world.[7] The most rapid increases are occurring in the Third World, where in exchange for cash, preferential trade status, or limited conventional military protection, developing nations are leasing bases to First and Second World nuclear nations.[8] As of 1986 "the U.S. stocked nuclear weapons in two Third World countries—South Korea and Turkey. But 65 nations housed support installations: 40 for the U.S., 11 for the Soviet Union, 12 for the U.K., and nine for France."[9] In effect, these nations have targeted themselves as the "nuclear battlefields" of the future.

All in all, the state of peace in the world of 1987 is much more precarious than it was in 1980. Clearly, major new breakthroughs are needed if a higher level of security is to come into being. At a minimum the following actions are needed:

1. A complete moratorium needs to be enacted on the building of any new or expanded nuclear weapons systems.

2. Serious discussions concerning disarmament must be initiated as quickly as possible.

3. The use of the Third World for nuclear storage sites and as nuclear bases needs to be brought to an end.

4. Further work on the Strategic Defensive Initiative needs to be halted and the funds allocated to this project used to promote social development in the United States and in other nations.

5. The size of conventional armies and navies must be sharply reduced.

6. An extraordinarily attractive "incentive system" must be developed that will encourage the leaders of developing nations to devote more of their resources to development than to war.

7. The use of nuclear energy as a primary energy source in many nations should be abandoned at the earliest possible date.

If these minimal steps are not implemented, it is likely that an increasing number of wars, civil disruptions, and regional conflicts will emerge in the decade just ahead. Certainly without progress in any of these areas the world of the future will be more dangerous than that which exists today.

POPULATION GROWTH

Second only to the threat of nuclear war, uncontrolled population growth continues to be the most serious obstacle to further development worldwide. The nature of the threat is threefold:

1. Rapid growth in population size places increasing demands on the always scarce resources of developing nations, which already find it difficult to provide for the needs of their existing populations.
2. Population growth contributes to and exacerbates the high level of political instability that characterizes the majority of developing nations.
3. Rapid increases in population size erode—and in many cases negate entirely—the modest gains that some poorer countries have been able to achieve during previous decades of development.

Conversely, reductions in fertility make it possible for developing nations:

1. to commit a higher share of national resources to meeting the basic needs of children;
2. to increase the range of educational and career opportunities for women;
3. to enlarge the pool of total resources that can be used to develop improved social infrastructures, especially in the areas of health care, education, transportation, communications, and agricultural development; and
4. to reduce considerably the level of intra-national conflict that results from competition between groups for resources in short supply.

Unfortunately, however, rather than a prospect of fertility reductions, the prognosis nationwide is for even sharper increases in the global population. The rate of increase is expected to be greater in the early part of the next century, given the exponential population growth projected for the planet by the end of the century. The global population reached 5 billion people sometime during 1986, for example, and is expected to exceed 6 billion by the end of the century. The most conservative estimates project a global population size exceeding 10 billion by the middle to end of the next century. In the future, as now, more than 90 percent of all net population increases will take place within developing nations. Even more rapid increases are expected to occur in the "poorest of the poor" nations of Africa and Asia.[10]

On the positive side, population growth in China, the world's most populous nation, is beginning to come under control, although not without periodic setbacks and considerable international controversy concerning the involuntary nature of some of China's fertility control methods. During the 15-year period 1965 to 1980, for example, the average rate of natural population increase for China was 2.2 percent, resulting in a projected population doubling time (PDT)[11] for the period of 31 years. For the period 1980–1985 the rate of population increase declined to 1.2 percent; between 1985 and the year 2000 the rate is expected to stabilize at about 1.3 percent with a projected population doubling time of more than 53 years—a favorable PDT increase of some 70 percent in just six years. China's population is expected to level off at about 1,683 million by the year 2000, by which time a net reproduction rate equal to 1 percent is expected to be achieved.

China's success in this remarkable turnaround in population growth is to be commended. This success, however, has been achieved only as a result of a nationally organized program of locally monitored fertility control. The Chinese efforts in this area have no parallel in other nations of the world, but other nations do not anticipate the same drastic consequences as China, should it fail to stabilize population growth among its nearly 1.2 billion people—more than 20 percent of the world's total population. The reason for China's substantial commitment to fertility control is obvious—China recognizes that it cannot move forward as a nation without halting the extraordinary rates of population increase that have hampered past development efforts. Data reported in the preceding two chapters of this volume confirm that China is now beginning to reap substantial benefits from its successes in population control. Indeed, China is among the list of "most rapidly developing" Asian DCs and the momentum of that development is increasing appreciably each year.

The current population situation in India, the second most populous nation, is quite different from that found in China. Like China, India has been able to slow the rate of natural increase of its now 810 million people. Between 1965 and 1980, for example, the rate of population increase in India averaged 2.3 percent, with a PDT of 30 years. For the period 1980–1985 the rate of natural increase dropped slightly to 2.2 percent and is expected to continue to decline gradually until the year 2000, when an average of 1.8 percent is expected to be achieved. A population growth rate of 1.8 percent will lengthen India's PDT from 30 years to somewhat more than 39 years.

The progress is impressive. But still, India has a very long road to travel if it is to succeed in achieving a level of population stability that will make possible dramatic moves forward in its overall levels of social and economic development. A nation that is already less affluent than

China with a 1985 per capita income level of $270 per annum versus $310 for China, the economic situation in India is expected to steadily worsen as its population continues to increase to more than 1,678 million by the year 2010. India's population at that time is expected to equal, and probably exceed, that of China's. In direct response to increases in population size coupled with reduced rates of economic expansion, future levels of social and economic prosperity in India are expected to drop considerably below those of today; further, they are expected to fall substantially below those projected for China in 2010, given China's current economic trends. These countervailing trends will result in a considerably more advanced China while India, given its special set of circumstances, steadily loses ground nationally and internationally.

Today India is at a critical juncture in deciding what it must do to halt further increases in its population and thereby retain the possibility of a better life for its citizens over the foreseeable future. As the world's largest democratic nation, India cannot implement the same spectrum of authoritarian fertility control methods that have yielded positive results in China. And yet voluntary methods of contraception and sterilization are not achieving the results that India seeks. The challenges to India, given both its current level of living and dominant political traditions, are enormous. The solutions to the problem of achieving stability in population growth, given the high level of social instability that presently exists in the country, are not in sight but must be found if India is to keep from sliding, a birth at a time, into becoming a least developing country. The prognosis of a substantially more impoverished India by the year 2010 is one that neither Indian leaders nor the leaders of other democratic societies can accept without first exercising every conceivable option.

Other developing nations with high rates of population growth include (the first figure is the yearly percentage increase; the figure in parentheses is the PDT): Ivory Coast, 5.0 (14 years); Kenya, 3.9 (18 years); Oman, 3.6 (19 years); Venezuela, 3.5 (20 years); Iraq, 3.4 (20 years); Iran, 3.2 (22 years); Rwanda, 3.3 (21 years); Somalia, 3.3 (21 years); and Tanzania, 3.3 (21 years). The global disparities that result from extraordinary population trends such as these, especially given the low levels of socioeconomic development that exist in the majority of developing nations, was noted by futurist Lester R. Brown, President of Worldwatch Institute. Writes Brown, "[T]he projected growth for North America, all of Europe, and the Soviet Union is less that the additions expected in either Bangladesh or Nigeria."[12]

To halt the present trend of a substantially more populous world by the year 2000—especially given the global unwillingness to meet even the basic needs of the current 5 billion inhabitants—existing efforts at fertility control must continue and new ones need to be implemented.

A significantly strengthened program of international fertility control directed at developing countries should contain at least all of the following elements:

1. Public education and increased awareness concerning safe and reliable methods of fertility control must be the centerpiece of any effective program. Such a strategy must also include education on the need for fertility control from both a national and global perspective. The need for such programs is all the more apparent when one recognizes that, ultimately, lasting choices about family size rest with individual couples and not with the state. Such choices can only be made in an environment that encourages people to reduce their family size so that they, as well as others in the society, can benefit from the improved living conditions that can be expected to result from population stability.

2. A great variety of incentives must be developed that will encourage couples to either remain childless or, at a maximum, to limit the number of their children to two, that is, the net population replacement rate (NRR). Incentives for reduced fertility may take many forms, including financial rewards, preferential access to scarce goods and services (e.g., housing, education, employment, etc.), public recognition, higher social status, etc.

3. Governmental ensured systems of social welfare and income security must be developed, or expanded, that will provide for the long-term care of childless couples who become physically or economically dependent, as well as the needs of those who choose to limit the size of their families to the NRR. Without such public assurances, it is improbable that many couples will be persuaded to remain childless in situations where no one will be able to provide for them in their old age or during periods of solitary survivorship, or should they become ill or incapacitated. In virtually every nation of the world dramatic declines in population have occurred in tandem with the establishment of social programs and services that provide a reasonably secure social safety net for persons who are unable to provide for themselves directly.

4. At a minimum, safe and effective forms of contraception must be made available on an affordable or free basis everywhere. Voluntary abortions, sterilization, and other dramatic forms of population limitation that present a broader range of fertility control for couples need to be expanded.

5. Research on new, more effective, less costly, and more convenient forms of male and female contraception must be undertaken. Current fertility control methods are still rather primitive given the "high tech" nature of most societies. The total resources currently spent on research in this area are pitifully small.

6. Finally, government leaders and citizens alike must be helped to recognize that reductions in fertility contribute significantly over both the long and short terms to improvements in living standards and national economic development.

The need for new initiatives in defusing the global population bomb is self-evident. Certainly, no blueprint for improving the social conditions of people can ignore this important dimension of national development.

WORLD HUNGER, MALNUTRITION, AND FAMINE

In September 1987 the Marxist government of Ethiopia announced officially that famine was once again an imminent reality for the world's poorest nation. Drought had returned to the countryside, fields of grain were wilting, and hundreds were already dead. More than 5 million persons were believed to be at imminent risk of starvation from yet another famine, the fourth to strike the country since the ousting of Emperor Haile Selassie I by a military coup in 1974.[13] An urgent plea was made by the Ethiopian government for Western nations to come forward with large donations of foodstuffs, emergency medical supplies, and other assistance to prevent a recurrence of the human devastation that swept the country during the famine of 1984–1985. At least 1 million Ethiopians perished during that famine, with countless more left chronically disabled and homeless. The belief among world food relief organizations was that the Ethiopian government's requests substantially underestimated the seriousness of the nation's new food crisis.

By the end of 1987 the return of widespread famine to other areas of Africa also appears imminent. Only the great Soviet famines of 1918–1922 and 1932–1934, in which an estimated 5 to 10 million persons died from starvation, compares in magnitude to the suffering already experienced by the nations of the Sahel and sub-Sarahan regions during the decade.[14] All reports indicate that the current droughts may prove to be even more intractable than earlier ones; ultimately, more Africans are expected to die from famines that will occur during the last 20 years of the century than died from hunger during the preceding 80 years.[15]

As devastating as the current famines in Africa have been, the incidence of hunger and malnutrition is greater in the poorest nations of Asia than in Africa. In *The State of the World's Children, 1987*, for example, UNICEF Executive Director James Grant notes that "in the last two years more children died [from hunger-related causes] in India and Pakistan than in all the 46 nations of Africa together. In 1986, more children died in Bangladesh than in Ethiopia, more in Mexico than in Sudan, more in Indonesia than in all eight drought-stricken countries of the Sahel."[16] During the June 1987 ministerial meeting of the United Nations' World Food Council, held in Beijing, the Food and Agricultural Organization (FAO) revised its estimates of the number of hungry people in the world upward to more than 475 million; a World Bank study reported at the same meeting placed the number closer to 720 million. Both organizations agreed that children were among the most severely affected and that, each day, more than 40,000 children die of hunger-related causes.

The extent of world hunger is staggering. The authors of *Ending World Hunger* estimate that, as of 1985:

- more than 1 billion people worldwide are chronically hungry;
- every year 13 to 18 million people die as a result of hunger and starvation; and
- every 24 hours, 35,000 human beings die as a result of hunger and starvation— 24 every minute, 18 of whom are children under five years of age.

By comparison:

- more people died from hunger between 1983 and 1985 than were killed in World War I and World War II combined;
- the number of people who die every few days of hunger and starvation is equivalent to the number who were killed instantly by the Hiroshima bomb; and
- the worst earthquake in modern history, in China in 1976, killed 242,000 people. Hunger kills that many people every seven days.

Slowed economic growth in industrial nations, political instability in the famine-affected nations, and failed efforts at social development are all believed to be major factors responsible for the recent escalations in the numbers of hungry people worldwide.[17] Even in the richest nation on earth, the United States, the number of hungry people is estimated to exceed 20,000,000 persons, about 9 percent of the total population. A Harvard University Physicians' Task Force on Hunger in America found that the majority of the hungry in America (15,000,000) were people living below the poverty line without food stamp or other forms of nutritional assistance.[18] In the United States, as in many developing nations, the problems underlying hunger have less to do with food scarcity than with the price and accessibility to food that is available.[19] Overdependence on the exportation of cash crops to other nations in exchange for hard currencies has added considerably to the food shortage problems of some developing nations, including Ethiopia, India, and China. In many food-"deficit" nations, foodgrains and other agricultural products are produced in sufficient quantities but are not available for local consumption.[20]

The Hunger Project, as well as other international organizations concerned with world hunger, predict that the number of hunger-related deaths will continue to rise until the end of the century.[21] Each group has advocated its own program of emergency and long-term assistance to food-deficit nations. All agree, however, that only a combination of carefully implemented approaches *over the long term* can succeed in significantly reducing the causes of malnutrition worldwide.[22] In addressing the problem of world hunger prior to the recent African famines, the Brandt Commission on International Development Issues concluded:

Mankind has never before had such ample technical and financial resources for coping with hunger and poverty. The immense task can be tackled once the necessary collective will is mobilized. What is necessary can be done, and must be done.

Within the United States, the 1980 Presidential Commission on World Hunger arrived at the same conclusion: "If decisions and actions well within the capability of nations and people working together were implemented, it would be possible to eliminate the worst aspects of hunger and malnutrition by the year 2000."[23]

In December 1986 the Council on Foreign Relations and the Overseas Development Council issued a joint *Compact for African Development* in which they encouraged a highly activist posture on the part of the United States in contributing to the resolution of the world hunger situation:

America has an opportunity to use publicly supported bilateral and multilateral programs, together with its universities, foundations, corporations, and private voluntary organizations, to help Africa in a coherent, lasting way. We urge private groups to marshal their own resources and to advocate a greater public response. We urge Congress and the Executive Branch to act with foresight to express our country's long-term interests in an Africa that can both survive short-term crises and assume its place as a full participant in the world economy.[24]

Similar sentiments have been echoed for their governments by scholars and political leaders the world over.[25]

The following recommendations are offered as a beginning approach to reducing hunger throughout the world:

1. Social reform in the context of international social development must begin with recognition that the most fundamental problems confronting humanity, including the dual problems of poverty and hunger, are political, social, and moral in nature. They are not exclusively problems of resource supply or resource scarcity although, indeed, real and serious limitations in available resources do exist. The vast bulk of the evidence confirms that the planet already possesses the material and technological resources that are needed to permanently rid the world of hunger.

2. Global reforms in dealing with problems of world hunger will require acceptance of our shared responsibility for one another's welfare. The world simply has become too interdependent for any of us to turn our back on the needs of our neighbors living in other areas of the world. To do so bankrupts

us morally; ultimately, the tragic deprivations experienced by others can be expected to spread to our homes as well.

3. Global food reforms will require a speedier and more complete implementation of the economic reforms contained in the various approaches that seek to establish a "New International Economic Order."[26] At a minimum, the initiatives that are adopted must emphasize:

   a. global cooperation rather than competition;

   b. global sharing rather than squandering;

   c. more generous and better sustained international subsidies and programs of international development assistance to the world's food-deficit nations.

   Ideally, implementation of these strategies will be carried out on a multilateral basis. They should also be formulated on an expanded system of internationally financed agricultural loans, grants, and technical assistance.

4. Global food reforms will require as well a significant shift from nationalistic attitudes to those that place increased emphasis on regionalism and internationalism.

5. Necessarily, existing international food and agricultural institutions will need to be strengthened, and new ones that focus on the underlying causes of hunger will need to be developed. Within the next decade, for example, more effective global institutions will be needed to:

   a. promote global peace and cooperation, especially so that a global plan for food security can be developed and implemented;

   b. promote, monitor, and control the use of nuclear energy for peaceful purposes, including food production;

   c. oversee international efforts at arms control and reduction so that a greater share of the world's resources can be committed to the survival of the human race rather than its destruction;

   d. promote and protect internationally guaranteed human rights of individual citizens against oppressive governments;

   e. manage the global economy, especially in relation to the flow of development and other resources between the world's rich and poor nations;

   f. promote access on the part of all nations to the food and other resources that exist in the earth's seas and oceans and, in time, in space;

   g. implement a coherent international food policy for feeding all of the world's hungry;

   h. halt the high rates of population growth in food-deficit nations; and

   i. manage problems related to the preservation and conservation of the world's physical environment, especially those elements that are essential to a stable food supply.

6. To be effective, a global food strategy must respect national sovereignty, and must promote the three objectives on which concerned people everywhere agree: war prevention, economic security, and social justice.

7. A new and more dramatic approach to closing the ever widening gap in development between the world's richest and poorest nations must be embarked upon. To be successful, such an approach must emphasize

a. people working for and on behalf of themselves and for one another within the context of their own history, traditions, and national objectives;

b. nations, especially food-deficit countries, must decide for themselves what their needs are and how the satisfaction of those needs should best be pursued;

c. the international community must perceive its role to be that of a "partner" in development, not as that of a decision-maker or planner acting for or on behalf of what they perceive to be in the best interests of food-deficit nations;

d. an invigorated strategy leading to international food reforms must emphasize the accomplishment of a broad range of varied, but interrelated, social and economic objectives. The simple reality is that, over the decade, many developing nations have slipped more deeply into poverty as a result of their efforts to emulate patterns of development found in economically advanced nations;

e. regionalism among developing nations should be strongly encouraged as a basis for developing programs of mutual aid, self-help, and cooperation.

8. To be effective on a global level, national agricultural and dietary reforms must take place within the context of a larger, more fully integrated, plan of world social development. To achieve its objectives, this global social development strategy must

a. encompass development planning for all nations, not just those of the South;

b. differentiate between the specialized development needs and objectives of individual nations and groups of agriculturally similar nations;

c. specify specific objectives that can be completed within designated time intervals;

d. include a mechanism for ongoing review and revision of planning efforts once implemented;

e. include a mechanism for continuous reporting to the world community concerning progress in achieving world food security objectives;

f. contain the mechanisms necessary to generate the financial and human resources needed to finance development worldwide.

9. The new strategy for global food reform must

a. foster maximum self-reliance within each nation for planning and implementing its own program of national development;

b. foster mutual participation and cooperation among all the world's nations in a co-equal partnership focused on improving the adequacy of social provision for people everywhere;

c. advance creative and flexible solutions to matters of subnational, national, regional, and global social development;

d. emphasize working for the benefit of all of humanity, while advocating and advancing the right of each nation to develop its own approach to social development that does not do harm to others.

To eliminate the current food crisis, serious consideration must be given to the implementation of each of the following actions:

Immediate Actions

1. The flow of international food, financial, technical assistance, and other es-

sential supplies to food-deficit nations must continue; so, too, must the flow of medical assistance, help with the resettlement of famine refugees, and help with other difficult physical, social, and economic problems experienced by persons facing imminent starvation.

2. Methods for increasing food production in food deficit nations must be found. Consideration should be given to such methods as
   a. the cultivation of new lands;
   b. the use of less costly organic fertilizers;
   c. increasing the supply of water for agricultural use;
   d. improved food and water collection, distribution, and storage facilities.

Actions for the Near Term (3–7 Years)

1. Food-deficit nations need help in developing agricultural reforms that provide economic supports to small farmers and to women farmers, groups that have been all but ignored in earlier development plans.

2. An increased emphasis must be placed on
   a. vegetarianism, for North and South nations alike, rather than the consumption of meat (production of each pound of beef requires 20 pounds of grain);
   b. a return to breast-feeding for infants rather than the use of expensive and widely misused commercially packaged formulae.

3. Critical attention must be given to the development of effective water management policies and infrastructures within food-deficit nations that depend either exclusively or primarily on rainfall for crop irrigation. At a minimum such policies must include
   a. the establishment of underground water storage facilities and irrigation networks; and
   b. the creation of cross-national irrigation systems that make possible the transfer of critically needed water from water-surplus nations to water-deficit nations.

4. Emphasis must also be placed on the conservation of food that is already being produced in food-deficit countries. Currently, between 20 and 40 percent of the total food production of developing nations is lost to pests, blight, and other forms of shrinkage because of inadequate food storage, transportation, and distribution systems.

5. The steady migration of rural workers into the cities must be either reversed or substantially slowed down so that the numbers of food-dependent persons living in cities will be reduced and those available to engage in food production will be increased.

Actions for the Long Term

1. Multinational planning for ensuring global food supplies over the long term must begin. Past efforts in these areas have faltered over political or economic issues, but the global stakes are such that the planning process must begin once again.

2. An international grain reserve designed to minimize the effects of local crop failures must be established. With it, the volume of per capita daily global food reserves must be increased.

3. Economically advanced nations need to cooperate with food-deficit nations in establishing Agricultural Research Institutes within the borders of LDC nations. The research agenda of these institutions, among other topics, should focus on:

   a. the development of new varieties of grains and other foods that are resistant to drought, infestations, rodents, molds, and other environmental stresses;

   b. the development of highly nutritious foodstuffs other than grains and starches that can be grown quickly within the limited growing seasons available to the arid nations of the Sahel and sub-Saharan Africa;

   c. improved methods of cultivation, harvesting, storage, and food transportation;

   d. the development of more technologically appropriate farming equipment, implements, and irrigation methods.

The research agenda of these institutes should also devote a major share of their attention to studies of the transferability potential of the agricultural methods that succeeded in helping 41 developing nations become food self-sufficient since 1960.[27] Through the use of agricultural extension workers, these institutes should also serve as centers of technical assistance to local farmers.

Nothing less than a major international commitment to eliminating world hunger will prove effective in solving this most tragic of human problems. Fortunately, the tools and resources needed to eliminate hunger are already available to us; all that is required is for the nations of the world to join together in pursuit of the goal. And only then can the World Food Conference's Declaration on the Eradication of Hunger and Malnutrition, a document to which the majority of nations have already committed themselves, be implemented:

Every man, woman and child has the inalienable right to be free from hunger and malnutrition in order to develop fully and maintain their physical and mental faculties. . . . Accordingly, the eradication of hunger is a common objective of all the countries of the international community, especially of the developed countries and others in a position to help.

THE INTERNATIONAL DEBT CRISIS AND DEVELOPING NATIONS

The global economy of the second half of the 1980s has been characterized by considerable instability, even by a certain degree of chaos. Double-digit inflation, once thought to be under control, has again surfaced; unemployment is on the increase nearly everywhere; trade protectionism, with its deeply divisive political consequences, is being widely practiced; interest rates are rising; and significant imbalances in trade between otherwise friendly nations have produced overt animosity and threats of economic reprisal.[28] Affluent nations have become more dependent on international loans to finance their current expenses; the deepening national debts of these countries have added considerably to internal political tensions and, early in the decade, have resulted in the election of more financially conservative governments. In Western nations, as elsewhere, pressures exist for increased nationalism, for greater economic protectionism,[29] and for withdrawal from all but essential international activities. Some countries are denying continuation visas and work permits to foreign workers living within their borders; in some cases visas have been withdrawn from persons on whose relatively cheap labor many Western nations, especially in Europe, have depended for decades. Some nations have sealed their borders to foreign workers entirely; other countries currently are attempting to locate and expel workers who entered their borders illegally in search of work.

In the last several years the United States, the world's largest economy, has become a major "debtor nation." In 1985, for example, imports to the United States exceeded exports by $148.5 billion, or by 70 percent of exports ($213.1 billion in exports versus $361.6 billion in imports). The country's gross international reserves, as measured in months of import coverage, fell to 3.1 months in 1985 from 4.0 months of coverage in 1983.[30] Both inflation and unemployment are increasing in the United States, as are interest rates. Economic growth for the period 1980–1985 averaged only 2.5 percent, higher than that of many other DME nations but well below what is needed to promote economic recovery. A recent survey of investment in the United States found that foreign individuals and companies owned the equivalent of all the wealth of the country's top 100 corporations. As with other nations experiencing high levels of external indebtedness, slow rates of economic growth, and increasing trade imbalances, rapidly increasing pressures exist in the United States for greater protectionism in the international marketplace.

Continuing economic problems in the United States have contributed to a sharp decline around the world in the value of the dollar. Some of this decline was deliberate on the part of the U.S. Treasury Department, but much of it was not. Used for decades as the primary medium for settling international accounts, the dollar lost in excess of 30 percent of its international purchasing value between 1981 and 1986. Increasingly, many nations have turned away from the dollar to conduct international business and, instead, are using a "basket" of more financially stable European and Japanese currencies.[31] Some economists and political leaders have even advocated at least a partial return to the use of gold and other precious metals in international exchanges. Lack of confidence in the U.S. economy, including the dollar, was fueled by the mid-October

1987 crash of the New York Stock Market. The most precipitous decline since "the Great Crash" of 1929, the paper value of stocks listed on the New York exchange plummeted by more than 500 points in a single day, resulting in a loss of more than 25 percent of the market's total value. Panic was felt around the world. Within hours, equally dramatic losses were reported by exchanges in London, Tokyo, Hong Kong, Sydney, and elsewhere. Most observers regarded the crash (one popular weekly magazine referred to it as the "meltdown of 1987") as the start of an expected new worldwide recession.[32] The stock markets were regarded as merely reflecting the underlying instabilities that characterized the majority of Western economies. Despite the partial recovery of pre-crash prices that occurred in the days that followed the catastrophe, the financial crisis of "Black Monday" made clear the need for a new approach to international finance, at least among the world's economically advanced nations. As of this writing, neither the essential elements nor the direction of that new course has been chartered.

As problematic as global economic trends have been for the economies of advanced nations, the impact of these trends on the fragile economies of developing countries has been nothing short of devastating. As a group, the DCs and the LDCs have fallen steadily into deeper debt, much of which has resulted from development loans and related financial obligations to Western nations.[33] Trade imbalances stemming from a combination of declines in exports and increases in imports have added substantially to their economic problems. Shortfalls in productivity, sharp drops in the value of oil exports, inflation, rising interest rates, an overdependence on food imports, and significant reductions in levels of financial assistance from richer countries[34] have also compounded the economic problems of developing nations. So, too, have recurrent natural disasters, the persistence of now decades-long civil and regional wars, continuing internal political unrest and, currently, the rapid spread of AIDS and other highly contagious diseases with their extraordinary financial and human costs.

Table 5.1 identifies those nations with 1985 external debt levels that exceed $10 billion; all but five of the 22 countries listed are developing nations. In fact, the ten countries with the highest debt levels are all developing nations; four are located in Latin America (Brazil, Mexico, Argentina, Venezuela) and five are in Asia (South Korea, Indonesia, India, Philippines, and Turkey). The country with the tenth largest level of external indebtedness, Egypt, is located in North Africa. Israel, Yugoslavia, Greece, and Portugal were the four DME nations with external debts exceeding $10 billion; among the eight ETA nations included in this study, only Hungary had an external debt level exceeding $10 billion.

All 25 of the LDCs included in this study are deeply in debt. As reported in Table 5.2, the combined external public and private debt of

Table 5.1
Countries with External Debt Exceeding $10 Billion, 1985

Country	Debt (in billions of U.S.$)
Brazil	$106.7
Mexico	$ 94.4
Argentina	$ 48.4
Korea, Republic	$ 48.0
Indonesia	$ 35.8
India	$ 35.5
Venezuela	$ 32.1
Philippines	$ 26.2
Turkey	$ 26.1
Egypt	$ 24.3
Israel	$ 23.9
Chile	$ 20.2
Yugoslavia	$ 19.4
Greece	$ 18.6
Nigeria	$ 18.3
Thailand	$ 17.5
Algeria	$ 15.5
Portugal	$ 14.6
Colombia	$ 14.0
Peru	$ 13.7
Hungary	$ 13.0
Pakistan	$ 12.7

Source: World Bank (1987b), Table 16, pp. 232–33.

these countries exceeds $23.3 billion, with an average long-term national indebtedness in excess of $1.2 billion. LDC 1985 debt levels averaged 55.4 percent of total GNP. The aggregated interest paid by the LDCs to service this debt was $340 million, an amount greater than the national budgets of some of these countries. On average, LDC long-term debt consumes the equivalent of 20 percent of LDC exports.

The LDC nations with the highest debt levels are Bangladesh ($6.0 billion), Tanzania ($3.0 billion), Arab Yemen ($1.9 billion), Ethiopia ($1.7 billion), PDR Yemen ($1.4 billion), and Mali ($1.3 billion). The LDC nations with the highest debt/GNP ratios are PDR Yemen (135 percent), Mali (127 percent), and Togo (121 percent). Arab Yemen (56 percent), Somalia (45 percent), and PDR Yemen (42 percent) have the highest equivalent share of their earnings from exports obligated to servicing long-term debt obligations.

Given the desperate socioeconomic circumstances under which all

Table 5.2
Total External Public and Private Debt and Debt Service of Least Developing Countries, 1985 (n = 25)

Country	Millions of Dollars ($)	As Percentage of GNP	Total Interest Paid (Mil $)	Long-Term Debt as % of:	
				GNP	Exports
Afghanistan*	. . .	. . .	. . .	. . .	
Bangladesh*	$5,968	37.2	$89	1.3	16.7
Benin*	$677	66.9	$9	2.2	. . .
Burkina-Faso*	$496	46.4	$10	2.5	. . .
Burundi*	$415	39.7	$9	2.0	16.6
Central African Rep*	$296	44.9	$7	2.0	11.8
Chad*	$150	9.9	$2	. . .	. . .
Ethiopia*	$1,742	37.1	$35	2.2	10.9
Guinea*	. . .	. . .	. . .	. . .	
Haiti*	. . .	. . .	. . .	. . .	
Laos PDR*	. . .	. . .	. . .	. . .	
Lesotho*	$172	30.1	$4	3.2	6.2
Malawi*	$775	75.7	$28	7.4	
Mali*	$1,327	122.1	$13	3.5	16.6
Nepal*	$527	22.5	$6	0.5	4.0
Niger*	$990	64.4	. . .	. . .	. . .
Rwanda*	$324	19.1	$4	0.9	4.3
Sierra Leone*	$390	32.6	$3	0.8	5.7
Somalia*	$1,309	53.5	$17	2.3	44.8
Sudan*	. . .	. . .	. . .	. . .	. . .
Tanzania*	$2,988	48.6	. . .	. . .	. . .
Togo*	$787	121.0	$39	13.7	27.5
Uganda*	$726	. . .	$27	. . .	. . .
Yemen, Arab Rep (N)	$1,868	45.6	$19	3.1	55.8
Yemen, PDR (S)	$1,446	134.7	$19	10.6	42.3
TOTAL	$23,373.0		$340.0		
AVERAGE	$1,168.7	55.4	$18.9	3.6	20.2

Source: World Bank (1987b, Table 18, pp. 236-37).
Note: Asterisks indicate LDCs; blanks indicate missing data.

LDC nations exist, it seems folly indeed to expect that these countries can meet their long-term obligations to foreign creditors and, at the same time, increase the level of national prosperity. The majority of countries are food-deficit nations, most have staggering rates of population growth, and their rates of early death and infant mortality are the highest in the world, resulting from inferior living conditions. This study and others confirm the reality that many LDCs are in a weaker economic position today than they were 10, 15, or even 20 years ago.[35] The LDC debt situation, compared to that of the rest of the world, is made all the more ridiculous when one recognizes that many of these starving and near-starving nations are exporting foodgrains as cash crops to generate the foreign exchange required to service their foreign debts. The situation is further compounded by an overall decline in the relative levels of international development assistance flows to the LDCs from OECD and OPEC nations between 1980 and 1985. Recent efforts at reducing the need for foreign borrowing by concentrating on accelerated South–South trade[36] and bartering[37] between developing countries appear to have been unsuccessful.

The sad reality is that the majority of the LDCs now find themselves in the position of having to choose between paying interest on their long-term debts or dealing with starvation (or building schools for their children, or purchasing fertilizers needed for food production, or manufacturing medicines that are desperately needed to treat their sick, or constructing roads that will facilitate economic development, etc.). International lending institutions have offered comparatively few options to the LDCs in dealing with their debt crisis, with the exception of extending repayments over a longer period of time. The exercise of these options, however, will leave the LDCs even more impoverished over the long term as their level of past and future indebtedness continues to mount. Ad hoc solutions to the crisis will not help the problems of LDC debt.

The following suggestions are offered to help the poorest developing countries begin to unravel their international debt problems. They do not reflect a set of recommendations for all debtor nations. Nor are they offered as panaceas that will solve all of the complex financing problems confronting the LDCs.

1. Current debts owed by the LDCs to the World Bank, the International Monetary Fund, and other international development-oriented financial institutions should be forgiven entirely. Instead, receipts from the monies owed by the LDCs to these institutions should be placed in a special account within the LDC country and administered jointly by the loan-granting institution and the LDC for the following broad purposes:

    a. To finance the development of new economic infrastructures at a higher level than possible while debt repayments were being made (e.g., for new or expanded loan and loan-related programs to local farmers and small business persons; for the establishment or expansion of credit unions, cooperatives, small businesses, and other self-help-oriented economic enterprises; and to finance the development of other local, regional, and national activities that contribute directly to national economic development).

b. To provide financial incentives for the development of new product lines, food-stuffs, equipment, processes, and methods of production that are more appropriate to the farming, industrial development, and service development needs of the LDCs. The notion is to encourage LDCs to develop innovative methods and approaches to economic development that best reflect their own needs, rather than those of the more economically advanced nations.

c. As possible and appropriate, to finance the turning over of state-run enterprises and monopolies to the private sector.

d. To attract foreign investment and enterprise to establish business and other joint ventures within the LDC. These funds should only be used to help subsidize investments however in which the LDC itself has either a co-equal or controlling interest in the joint venture. The funds should also be used to subsidize the development of those businesses from which the bulk of profits realized from the joint venture will remain in the LDC, ideally for reinvestment in other similarly successful initiatives.

e. To provide assistance to local farmers, manufacturers, and others during periods when temporary price fluctuations threaten the viability of their operations.

2. The LDCs need generous infusions of new capital into their economies. These infusions should take two forms:

a. Some of this new capital should be provided as direct "no strings" grant-in-aid from donor nations.

b. The bulk of assistance should continue to be tied to the achievement of specific economic goals and objectives. While possible, incentives for additional amounts of goal-oriented funding should be included in this type of assistance so as to both ensure the likelihood of project success and reward nations for their achievements.

c. Donor nations need to make commitments to development in the LDCs for longer than the usual 3- to 5-year time span of most projects.

3. The economically advanced nations of the world—both DMEs and the ETAs—need to grant the poorest LDCs preferential status as trading partners. Such status should include

a. free or substantially subsidized LDC access to the technology of the North;

b. opportunities for joint ventures and partnerships in the exploration and exploitation of the seas, space, and other untapped areas where needed resources are believed to be plentiful;

c. stable and more realistic currency exchange rates that better reflect the human effort expended by LDCs to produce their goods and services;

d. significantly increased opportunities for large numbers of persons from LDC nations to study in and learn from the North;

e. significantly reduced or eliminated trade tariffs on LDC-produced goods and services;

f. assistance to LDCs in promoting and finding new and expanding markets for their products;

g. expansion, as possible and appropriate, of "debt-equity swaps"[38] and similar schemes that permit LDCs to settle their financial obligations in local rather than foreign currencies.

4. Inasmuch as 80 percent of the populations of the LDCs live in rural areas, financial assistance to the LDCs should encourage investment in rural rather than urban development. Necessarily, an emphasis on rural projects should include improved agricultural methods; improved seed strains; more effective transport, irrigation, communication, and related infrastructures; and adequate food processing, storage, and distribution systems.

5. Increased South–South economic cooperation must be encouraged and nurtured. As formulated by Zhang Peiji and Cheng Yugui at the 1983 Beijing South–South Conference, South–South economic cooperation must occur within the context of the following principles:

   a. Equality and mutual benefit must be the fundamental guidelines on which South–South cooperation occurs, especially in respect for national sovereignty and non-interference in the affairs of other nations of the South.

   b. Stress must be placed on practical results, especially in the areas of technological innovation, research, and finding of solutions to the most pressing social and economic problems confronting the nations of the South.

   c. Diversity in form, especially in response to the differing socioeconomic conditions that exist among the nations of the South.

   d. Attainment of common development must be the ultimate goal of South–South cooperation.[39]

While not a complete list of all the options that are available to assist LDCs with their staggering debt problems, the implementation of these recommendations by the international development assistance community would represent a solid first step toward finding more permanent solutions.

WOMEN AND DEVELOPMENT

A popular Chinese expression says that "Women hold up one-half of the sky"—meaning, of course, that women are as important as men in all aspects of life. And yet in China, as elsewhere in the world, the status of women continues to be substantially inferior to that of men.[40] Worldwide, for example, women continue to have the highest rates of illiteracy, to earn significantly less money than men even when performing the same work, and to have fewer legal protections available to them for help in resolving disputes. In many parts of the world women continue to be unable to own property in their own names, cannot travel without the written approval of a male head of household, and may not divorce of their own volition. In situations where divorces are approved, a substantial number of women worldwide may not even have access to their children, let alone retain parental rights. The small number of women worldwide who occupy important positions of political or policymaking power is already well established.

Further, even the crude women's status subindex used in this investigation makes clear that during the past 15 years the social gains achieved by women worldwide have tended to be modest. Certainly, the majority of women in developing countries have not realized the minimal economic objectives, legal protections, and political aspirations that were sought as part of the International Decade of Women. The reasons for lack of more substantial social progress for women over the past two decades are many but center on the facts that: (1) development efforts, in the main, continue to be directed at improving the social and economic conditions of men in developing countries; (2) the role of women as co-partners, let alone as leaders, in development has been grossly underestimated by the international development community; and (3) the assistance strategies of the majority of international development organizations, intentionally or not, have functioned to perpetuate social and economic inequalities which, for centuries, have retarded the social progress of women.

Irene Tinker, in a *CARE Brief* prepared in cooperation with the Overseas Development Council,[41] identifies six myths commonly held by development planners that work to the disadvantage of social progress for women.

MYTHS	FACTS
Women are dependent on men.	Women—as well as men and children—work to contribute to the survival of poor rural and urban families in the Third World. Far from being dependent, it is estimated that women are the heads of one out of every three families worldwide.
Women do not work.	Generally, rural women in the Third World work between 10 and 12 hours a day, collecting water and fuel as well as growing, processing, and marketing food. Urban women most often work in small businesses and services.
Women are not farmers.	In many countries, women produce most of the food for family consumption. Women provide nearly half of all agricultural labor in the world.

Animal work is a man's domain.	Wherever animals such as cows, sheep, and goats are raised for consumption, women rather than men are likely to be responsible for their care.
A woman's income is incidental.	In many countries, a woman's income is critical to the survival of the family. Typically, the poorer the family, the greater the proportion of its income is provided by women.
Women do not understand business.	In Southwest Asia, West Africa, and Central America, women have traditionally dominated local markets. In many countries women have moved into large-scale production and trade—especially in textiles and clothing—as well as into small industry.

The reason that myths such as these persist despite readily available evidence to the contrary is simply that they serve the purposes of myth-holders, that is, males and other females who benefit from the subjugation of comparatively powerless women. Certainly economic considerations are at the core of the problem. A recent study of the attitudes of Asian electronic firm managers who favored the hiring of women over men found, for example, that these managers believed that

• Women are more industrious, obedient, and able to do delicate work because they are more deft and patient, and their fingers are smaller.

• They are less likely to organize into trade unions.

• They are easier to recruit because other types of employment are virtually nonexistent.

• They are flexible in their work hours and available for day and night shifts.

The authors of the study concluded that the preference for female workers is no doubt largely a function of the relatively low cost of their labor."[42]

And so it is for women in all sectors of social, economic, and political life in virtually all areas of the world, including many women residing in the highly advanced industrial nations of both the East and the West. The perpetuation of gender-based myths works to the detriment of women everywhere; they also impose an undue and unnecessary burden on men while keeping both genders in social and economic relationships which, over the long term, work to the benefit of neither (e.g., earlier death and higher rates of illness among stress-prone men).

The gap in social progress between men and women worldwide continues to be enormous, and closing it in the foreseeable future seems doubtful. Among the objectives that should continue to be pursued through to the end of the current century include the following:

1. Every effort must continue to be made to help women achieve legal guarantees, rights, protections, and entitlements equal to those accorded to men. Today, some 40 nations, including seven otherwise socially advanced European countries, continue to make unavailable to women the same constitutional protections that are available to their male citizens.[43] In some developing countries, male children enjoy a higher standard of legal protection than do either their mothers or sisters.

2. Women need to be able to share ownership of the land that they work and to reap the economic profits that result from their labor.

3. Women need increased access to basic and higher education, to skills training, to basic health care (including prenatal and maternity care), and to safe and reliable methods of contraception.

4. Women in developing countries, like men, also require assistance in establishing and operating their own businesses, and need access to viable channels for influencing the political decisions and social policies that affect their well-being and that of their children.

5. Women must be integrated fully into all levels of development planning and implementation.[44] Development plans that fail to take into account the critical contribution of women to national and international social development will not succeed in achieving the social transformations that they seek.

6. In all respects, women must be viewed as co-equal with men in considering alternative courses of action, in participating in the decisions that directly affect their welfare, and in taking the actions that are necessary to improve their standard of living. Nothing short of equality between the genders will make possible the improvements that are urgently needed in the social standing of women throughout the world.

The relative neglect of women in development over the past three decades serves neither the interests of development planners nor those of men in general over the long term. Certainly, nations are poorer that fail to recognize the myriad and dynamic contributions that women can and do make to the development process. Nations are poorer still if their political leaders insist on perpetuating gender stereotypes that disadvantage the social progress of their own mothers, sisters, lovers, wives, and daughters.

THE CRISIS IN WELFARE

For more than a decade international concern has been expressed about the ability of national governments to continue to meet the escalating personal service needs of their populations (e.g., for food, housing, health care, basic education, and so on).[45] Much of the focus of this concern has centered on the public provision of welfare services that persons living in industrialized nations currently take more or less for granted (e.g., pensions for the aged, services to the disabled, income support for the poor, etc.).[46] Critics of these programs suggest that they are overly expensive, inefficient and, more fundamentally, represent an unnecessary drain on national economic resources that are needed for "other" activities (usually defense). Even the socially progressive "welfare states" of Northern Europe and Scandinavia have come under attack as operating social programs that promote public dependency among persons for whom greater self-sufficiency is possible.[47] By implication, governments have more pressing challenges with which to concern themselves than providing assurances that the basic social needs of their citizens will be met.

In response to recurrent economic problems many governments have substantially reduced the level of their financial commitments to human service programs. Recent data from the World Bank, for example, confirm that reductions in central government expenditures for human service activities have been occurring steadily since 1972.

Government cutbacks in the human services have been most dramatic in health and education; however, severe reductions have also occurred in housing, social security, and formal welfare as well. As summarized in Table 5.3, between 1972 and 1985 public expenditures for education and health declined by an average of 23.6 and 21.0 percent, respectively. Cutbacks in government funding in these sectors were especially high among those nations for which increases in health and education services, not reductions, are the most urgently needed, that is, the low- and middle-income DCs and LDCs. But central government reductions for education were also substantial among the affluent industrial market nations of the West (− 29.6 percent) and the high-income oil-exporting countries of the Middle East (− 27.0 percent). In the case of the latter group of nations, expenditures for defense rose by an unparalleled 162.2 percent, at the same time that the governments of these nations chose to reduce their commitments to education.

Government expenditures for housing, social security, and general welfare services also declined during the period, but by a smaller percentage (− 2.5 percent) than in either health services or education; cutbacks were most significant among lower-, middle- (− 29.9 percent) and upper-middle-income nations (− 17.4 percent). During the same time

Table 5.3
Central Government Expenditures in Selected Sectors, 1972 and 1985 ($n = 119$)

Economy Level	Percentage of Total Expenditures											Total Expenditures as Percentage of GNP		
	Defense			Education			Health			Housing, Social Security and Welfare					
	1972	1985	% CHANGE	1972	1985	% CHANGE	1972	1985	% CHANGE	1972	1985	% CHANGE	1972	1985	% CHANGE
Low Income (N=37)	17.2	18.6	8.1	13.2	7.6	-42.4	4.9	3.7	-24.5	5.4	7.2	33.3	18.0	20.3	12.8
Lower Middle Income (N=36)	15.7	14.2	-9.6	16.4	13.8	-15.9	5.2	3.8	-26.9	12.7	8.9	-29.9	19.4	24.8	27.8
Upper Middle Income (N=23)	14.4	9.7	-32.6	12.3	10.6	-13.8	7.9	4.6	-41.8	23.0	19.0	-17.4	19.7	22.7	15.2
High-Income Oil Exporters (N=4)	9.0	23.6	162.2	15.2	11.1	-27.0	5.5	6.4	16.4	14.1	14.1	0.0	21.1	29.1	37.9
Industrial Market (N=19)	20.9	16.8	-19.6	5.4	3.8	-29.6	10.0	11.4	14.0	36.6	35.5	-3.0	22.9	29.1	27.1
All Countries (N=119)	16.5	15.4	-4.3	12.8	9.6	-26.3	6.4	5.2	-21.0	16.3	14.7	-2.5	19.6	23.8	20.9

Source: World Bank (1987b, Table 23, pp. 246-47).

period, however, low-income nations succeeded by increasing investments in welfare spending by 33.3 percent, all the more impressive given
the more negative trends in this sector occurring in all other areas of
the world.

Overall, the sharpest reductions in public expenditures for human
service programs occurred during the early and mid–1980s. During the
same time period steep reductions also occurred in public spending in
non-welfare sectors. No longer do governments feel compelled to accept
complete responsibility for the provision of such diverse services as
ensuring adequate public transportation systems, subsidized housing,
libraries and related community educational and cultural services, the
development and maintenance of national communication networks,
opportunities for higher education, programs of life-long learning, scientific research and development, and so on. The price tag associated
with the financing of these public goods simply has become too expensive for many governments to afford, or at least to the same extent that
they were able to prior to 1980. Problems of rising unemployment,
mounting inflationary pressures, and balance of trade deficits, as well
as shrinking export opportunities have forced governments to search
for non-government approaches to financing many of these services.
Raising individual and corporate taxes to support an ever increasing
range of more expensive services is no longer perceived to be a viable
solution.

In discussing the crisis in welfare it is important to recognize that the
crisis has little to do with whether welfare programs and services should
or should not continue to exist. Nor is the crisis related to whether these
services should be provided by governments or by private entities, or
by some combination of the two. Even in the United States—a welfare
"laggard" in comparison with virtually all other modern states—surveys
repeatedly find that Americans want their central government to provide
more human services, not less.[48] Rather, the problem is squarely one of
governments being able to offer an expanded system of services while
remaining fiscally solvent.

One solution to the problem of financing public services is that em-
bodied in the current privatization movement. This involves the shift of
fiscal responsibility for the provision of public goods and services from
governments to the private sector. Under a variety of schemes, governments may continue to carry ultimate responsibility for ensuring that
public needs are met (e.g., for the arrest, conviction, and incarceration
of adjudicated criminals), but the approaches taken to meet these needs
can include a combination of private, semi-private, quasi-private, and
voluntary arrangements (e.g., the creation of for-profit prisons built and
managed by private corporations). The notion is one of a shared partnership between the private and public sectors in delivering goods and

services that governments are no longer able to provide directly, or alone. The public/private partnership is expected to result in a new "welfare mix" that will both improve the administration of these services while also substantially reducing their costs (e.g., through lower overhead expenses, fewer numbers of salaried workers, more competitive financing methods, more efficient use of privately raised resources, etc.).[49]

Privatization is being pursued vigorously by the majority of Western nations.[50] Even the centrally planned nations of Eastern Europe[51] and Asia[52] are searching for ways to transfer some of their public services to private entities. Privatization is also perceived to be a viable approach for accelerating the development of critically needed social infrastructures in the Third World.[53]

Whatever results from the current initiative for the privatization of some public services, it is clear that governments are being forced to find new solutions to recurrent social problems. The following recommendations are offered as guidelines in choosing between various alternative models of service financing and delivery that are expected to emerge during this period of experimentation.

1. Despite the financial pressures confronting them, governments *cannot* transfer their responsibilities for meeting basic human needs, including basic social welfare services, from the public to the private sector. Responsibility for the satisfaction of basic needs is part of the social contract that exists between governments and their citizens; governments should not be permitted to reassign their responsibilities in these areas to non-public organizations or entities.

2. Together with the private sector, governments need to experiment with alternative methods, including privatization, for achieving a new mix of welfare financing. At a minimum these approaches should include

   a. maximum use of general tax revenues to underwrite the basic costs of operating a more efficient system of services;

   b. financial contributions from individuals, employers, and others for whom participation in the support of basic public services is appropriate;

   c. the establishment of more fiscally secure private and public insurance trusts, provident funds, and other long-term welfare financing methods that can be used to provide economic "safety nets" that will assist persons during predictable periods of financial hardship (e.g., illness, injury, disability, joblessness, early death, retirement, and solitary survivorship, etc.);

   d. the establishment of private and public "catastrophic" social funds that will provide assistance to individuals during unanticipated periods of financial hardship (e.g., resulting from natural and human-made disasters, crimes of violence, incarceration, acts of terrorism, riots, etc.).

3. Trade unions, professional associations, and other organizations of workers need to play a more prominent role in the design, financing, and implementation of social welfare programs and services.

4. Professionally administered voluntary organizations that already exist in great numbers in many countries need to be greatly expanded and more securely financed (e.g., Red Cross, credit unions, service coordination and planning councils, national personal service organizations, etc.). A combination of public and private resources should be used to achieve this objective.

5. Informal systems of care need to be significantly expanded and strengthened virtually everywhere in the world. The most critical components of informal welfare services include the following:

   a. families, especially those providing high levels of basic care for dependent family members (e.g., dependent children, disabled persons, the sick, the aged, etc.);

   b. neighbors, especially those who provide basic human services to dependent persons without family or whose families are unable or unwilling to provide for them;

   c. volunteers, including persons who provide face-to-face services without expectation of remuneration;

   d. self-help and mutual aid groups, especially those that provide high-quality alternative services to persons or groups of persons who share a similar or related social problem or need;

   e. other citizens interested in working toward the improvement of welfare in their communities, including those who contribute to service planning, policy setting, organization, fundraising, and oversight at the community level.

   The majority of people working in the informal care sector do not require financial remuneration for their services. However, governments, in partnership with private entities, need to develop adequate supportive structures and networks that facilitate the activities of informal caregivers. Supportive services for unpaid caregivers should include respite care services, paid assistants when needed, opportunities for scheduled vacations, public recognition, and a functioning psychoemotional support network to which caregivers can turn during periods of great emotional stress, physical exhaustion, or economic hardship.

6. Working together, the new private/public partnership should seek to achieve a dramatically restructured system of human services. At a minimum, a more fully integrated system of human services would be characterized by

   a. One "front door" to the service system. This door should be open wide, and should be accessible to all persons who can make legitimate demands of the system.

   b. On entering the system, all consumers should be exposed to the same high-quality approach to care, to a system that offers the best possible range of effective services to all people regardless of their age, gender, race, social status, or their capacity to pay for these services.

   c. The reorganized system must also possess greater capacity for better assessing, planning for, and responding to the most critical needs of persons using the system. To accomplish this objective, service providers must upgrade their diagnostic skills, implement a more goal-oriented approach to service delivery, and adopt even more rigorous approaches to peer review and quality assurance.

   d. Further, service providers must develop better and more effective approaches to case monitoring and follow-up, especially for consumers whose conditions require post-discharge supervision.

e. Necessarily, the establishment of a more comprehensive system of human services will require a full integration of social, medical, and mental health services—a goal that has eluded most countries since the formal division of these services into separate administrative and fiscal divisions since World War II.

In moving toward the next century it is critical that governments and their citizens be mindful that welfare programs and services are not luxury items in national budgets. Nor are welfare services palliatives that can be used to appease a disgruntled citizenry. They are also not programs of social control that are intended to keep an aberrant population in check. To the contrary, welfare services are essential to the functioning of societies everywhere. In a real sense, welfare programs and services embody the collective ideals and values that join people together in a social contract with one another. As such, welfare services contribute substantially to the social development of nations and provide the mechanism through which social justice for all can be achieved. Governments would be foolish indeed to either divest themselves of such a powerful tool for promoting social development, or to transfer its responsibilities to entities that exist outside public influence and control.

AIDS AND DEVELOPMENT

AIDS (Acquired Immune Deficiency Syndrome) has become the new scourge of humanity. It has also emerged during the second half of the 1980s as the most potentially devastating health threat to worldwide development, especially among the poorest nations of Africa. The World Health Organization (WHO) estimates that approximately 10 million people worldwide were infected with the deadly virus as of February 1987 and that by 1991, without an effective vaccine, the number of infected persons could exceed as many as 100 million, or 2 percent of the world's population. Without an effective treatment or cure for the disease, the WHO expects that at least 30 to 50 percent of those with the infection will develop an active form of the disease within five years and ultimately will die. The prognosis for infected persons who do not develop the active stage of the disease within five years is unknown; it is anticipated that the majority of these persons will fall victim to AIDS and die within 10 years of contracting the infection.

So virulent is AIDS that it has been compared to the Black Death of the Middle Ages which, according to biophysicist John Platt, "swept through Europe along the trade routes from Italy to Sweden in 1347–1350, killing some 30 million people out of a population of 75 million in four years." Writing in *The Futurist* about the impact of AIDS on countries, Platt states that "by the end of this century, AIDS could have the impact of a world war, producing recession and a stay-at-home society at the same time that it transforms world health and demographics."[54] It is almost certainly the case that the AIDS epidemic already has resulted in more serious global social dislocations than those caused by other epidemics including yellow fever, malaria, tuberculosis, bubonic plague, and others.

Historically, AIDS appears to have originated as a mutant virus somewhere in equatorial Africa during the second half of the 1970s.[55] Spread primarily through the exchange of body fluids, in Africa AIDS spread quickly among the heterosexual populations of Burundi, the Central African Republic, the Congo, Kenya, Rwanda, Tanzania, Uganda, Zaire, and Zambia—the so-called AIDS belt of Africa.[56] By the early 1980s the infection had spread to North America, the Caribbean, Latin America, and Europe. AIDS infections in these regions were transmitted primarily through homosexual contacts, the use of contaminated needles by drug users, infected blood supplies, and from infected mothers to their newborn infants. As of this writing a more limited number of AIDS cases has been reported for Asia, but the incidence of AIDS in Asia is also known to be increasing rapidly.

By July 1987 some 53,000 active cases of AIDS had been reported officially to the World Health Organization.[57] This number is estimated to reflect only a small portion of the total number of active AIDS cases worldwide, especially given the reluctance of many nations to report the true extent of the problem within their borders. Whatever the actual number of active AIDS cases, the prevalence of clinically dormant AIDS-infected people is estimated to be 30 to 50 times the number of diagnosed cases.

In Africa, epidemiologists estimate that approximately 25 percent of the populations of Central and East Africa already have been infected with the disease. The incidence is particularly high among urban dwellers, soldiers and sailors, pregnant women, and persons who frequently travel across national borders. Further, the number of fatal AIDS cases is doubling every 4 to 6 months in Africa, which is about twice as fast as the rate of infection in the United States. By the end of the century a majority of Africans are expected to have been exposed to the virus. And the estimates keep increasing.

Though there is no reason for believing that infected Africans are more sexually promiscuous than sexually active Europeans or North Americans, it is the case that the populations of Africa are younger, more sexually active, and are still predominantly in their child-bearing years. Africans also marry at an earlier age and produce more offspring than do Westerners. Rather than sexual promiscuity explaining the high rates of AIDS infection in Africa, the rapid spread of the disease would appear to better accounted for by the presence of the mutant virus on the continent for a longer period of time and the entrenched nature of the disease there prior to discovery of the HIV virus. Longer exposure to the virus, combined with generally poor or incomplete knowledge concerning the disease, would leave the spread of the disease virtually unchecked. The absence of minimally protective sexual practices, cultural biases against condom use, and widespread misunderstanding concerning how the disease is spread from one community to the next have also added to the problem. Severe reductions in government expenditures for health and education services in many of the affected countries has also compounded the problem and added to the rapid spread of the disease across the continent.

Among the industrialized nations of the West, the United States has the highest incidence of AIDS infection. The Center for Disease Control in Atlanta, Georgia, reported that of the 38,000 Americans known to have contracted AIDS by July 1987, over 22,000 had already died. The National Academy of Sciences conservatively estimates that the number of active AIDS infections will increase to approximately 270,000 cases by 1991, with the actual number of infected persons increasing to more than 1 million.[58] In Europe, as of March 1987, approximately 5,000 active AIDS cases were officially identified; the number of active cases is expected to increase steadily to 300,000 by 1991, with an additional 10 million asympomatic carriers of the disease.[59] As in Africa, the economic costs of the AIDS infection to these nations, let alone its human toll, are incalculable.

One certain thing about the AIDS epidemic is that it is with us, and a cure is not. Indeed no cure and, for the moment, no vaccine to protect currently uninfected persons from infection have been found. Those already infected are almost certainly doomed to a wasting death from what Africans call "the slimming sickness." Virologists and other specialists working on the problem have indicated that no cure or vaccine will be available before the 1990s, by which time the worldwide epidemic is expected to engulf as many as 100 million people.

AIDS can be expected to produce profound social, economic, and political dislocations worldwide. It sems reasonable to expect, for example, that more lives will be lost to the AIDS epidemic than to all of the century's wars and famines. The major portion of the health budgets of many developing nations, and a substantial share of the health resources of economically advanced nations as well, can be expected to be redirected to provide public health education and clinical care for people afflicted with the disease. The economic costs associated with the treatment of AIDS will be exceedingly high and, in the end, the vast majority of infected persons will die. It is also probable that many governments will be forced to redirect resources committed to other sectors of national development to AIDS-related activities; the immediate consequence of these reallocation decisions will be that the implementation of existing plans of national development will need to be postponed, including those leading to the establishment of basic health infrastructures. Further, given the disproportionate concentration of AIDS infections among the urban elites of many developing countries, substantial numbers of the most educated persons in developing nations will perish from the disease. The deaths of so many educated professionals in developing nations can be expected to have a profound impact on the development capacity of these countries for decades.[60]

Prospects for a more optimistic outcome for the AIDS epidemic internationally appear to be dim indeed. Working with governments, health authorities, private citizens, and others, development specialists need to consider a variety of approaches that can be used to help minimize the most negative social consequences of the disease. In the absence of a cure or effective vaccine, such strategies must center on containment of the disease, on methods and approaches that governments and individual citizens can take to reduce the risk of infection in as yet non-exposed populations. Necessarily, however, these action steps are only suggestive; more effective actions can be recommended as knowledge about the disease and its transmission becomes available.

1. Hysteria and panic associated with the rapid spread of the disease should be kept to a minimum. It is important for people, and their governments, to recognize that they can take positive actions that are likely to prevent them from coming in contact with the virus.

2. The most powerful tool currently available in the fight against the AIDS epidemic is mass education. Ignorance, irrationality, and denial or panic will do nothing to prevent the spread of AIDS to persons who are unfamiliar with the life-threatening nature of the disease. Every conceivable forum for mass education must be used to provide people with accurate knowledge concerning all aspects of the disease and how exposure to the AIDS virus can be minimized.

3. Young people must be encouraged to abstain from initiating sexual activity for the longest time possible.

4. An inexpensive test for AIDS must be found for use in the Third World.

5. Sexually active persons must be instructed in the nature of "safe sex" practices and be encouraged to use them.

6. Fresh syringes and practical information concerning effective and easily available methods for sterilizing needles must be made available to intravenous drug users.

7. Communal supplies of blood and blood products must be carefully monitored and controlled so that the risk of AIDS infection to persons requiring emergency blood transfusions will be reduced to the lowest levels possible.

8. Severe actions must be taken against infected persons who knowingly expose

others to the disease without their knowledge. In the most serious situations criminal prosecution and confinement may be required.

9. National and international efforts at combating AIDS, to the fullest extent possible, must be coordinated and their resources pooled so as to produce the greatest results in the shortest possible period of time.

The only lasting solution to the AIDS epidemic is a cure for the disease; at a minimum, an effective vaccine is needed that will protect persons exposed to the virus from contracting the disease. The search for an AIDS cure should be an urgent priority on the agendas of all nations. Working in cooperation with national and international health organizations, research institutes, and independent scholars, governments need to do all that they can to ensure that research for a cure for the disease will go forward.

PROSPECTS FOR THE FUTURE

In this chapter I have discussed what I consider to be the most important social problems confronting specialists working in international development. The problems identified are many, and they are complex. They are also persistent and will not readily yield to short-term or piecemeal solutions. Rather, sustained social investments over a long period of time will be needed to bring about their resolution.

Necessarily, effective strategies for global social reform will require close cooperation between governments, individual citizens, and other aggregates of people working together toward the same objectives. No one set of persons or institutions can be expected to accomplish the task alone. The social problems that we now face are not so far out of control that they will not respond to thoughtful and carefully planned interventions. To achieve the goal of creating a more just world, each of us, acting alone and with others, must commit ourselves to the task. The time to act is now; the course is a just one; and the means for the accomplishment of our goals are within our reach.

NOTES

1. Ruth Sivard, *World Military and Social Expenditures, 1985* (Washington, D.C.: World Priorities, 1985), p. 18.

2. Hana Umlauf Lane (ed.), *The World Almanac and Book of Facts, 1986* (New York: Newspaper Enterprise Association, 1986), p. 629.

3. Charles Wolfe, Jr., "The Costs of the Soviet Empire," *Science*, November 29, 1987, pp. 997–1002.

4. U.S. Bureau of the Census, *Current Population Reports*, series P–60 (Washington, D.C.: U.S. Government Printing Office, 1987).

5. "Other Items on the Agenda: Western Europe Needs to Rearm," *The Economist* (1987).

6. World Bank, *World Development Report, 1987* (Washington, D.C.: 1987), Table 23, pp. 246–47.

7. Altaf Gauhar, "The Nuclear Race: Who Wants the Bomb?" *South* (September 1985): 14–18; Sivard, *World Military and Social Expenditures.*

8. William M. Arkin and Richard M. Fieldhouse, *Nuclear Battlefields: Global Links in the Arms Race* (Boston, MA: Ballinger, 1986).

9. "Plugging Into the Nuclear Frontline," *South* (March 1986):89.

10. All population data cited here, including projections, were abstracted from World Bank, *World Development Report, 1987* (Washington, D.C.: World Bank, 1987), Table 27, pp. 254–55.

11. Population doubling time (PDT) is computed by dividing 69.31 by the annual population growth rate (Ehrlich and Ehrlich, 1972).

12. Lester R. Brown, *State of the World, 1985* (New York: W. W. Norton and Company, 1985), p. 204.

13. Blaine Harden, "Ethiopia Faces Famine Again, Requests Massive Food Relief," *Washington Post*, September 14, 1987, pp. A1, A26.

14. Paul Ehrlich et al., *Ecoscience: Population, Resources, and Environment* (San Francisco, CA: W. H. Freeman and Company, 1971), p. 187.

15. Hunger Project, *Ending Hunger: An Idea Whose Time Has Come* (New York: Praeger, 1985).

16. James P. Grant, *The State of the World's Children, 1987* (New York: Oxford University Press, for the United Nations Children's Fund, UNICEF, 1987).

17. Paul Lewis, "World Hunger Found Still Growing," *New York Times*, June 28, 1987.

18. Hunger Project, "Taking Care of Our Own," *A Shift in the Wind*, September 1987, p. 4.

19. Jonathan Power, "Food Plenty, Yet Hunger is Rising," *Baltimore Sun*, June 22, 1987; Glenn Frankel, "Zimbabwe's Farms Prosper, Yet Many Young Go Hungry," *Washington Post*, July 14, 1986, pp. A1, A16.

20. Nigel Twose, *Cultivating Hunger* (Oxford: OXFAM, 1984); John Tanner, "Cash Crops and Empty Plates," *South* (April 1986): 99.

21. For a discussion of alternatives to this scenario see Medard Gabel, *Ho-Ping: Food for Everyone* (New York: Doubleday, 1979); Lester R. Brown, *Building a Sustainable Society* (New York: W. W. Norton & Company, for the Worldwatch Institute, 1981).

22. As examples see Independent Commission on International Development Issues, *North–South: A Program for Survival* (Cambridge, MA: MIT Press, 1980), p. 16; Alan Berg, *Malnutrition—What Can be Done?* (Washington, D.C.: World Bank, 1987); J. Price Gittinger et al., *Food Policy* (Washington, D.C.: World Bank, 1987); Hunger Project, *Ending Hunger.*

23. U.S. Presidential Commission on World Hunger, *Overcoming World Hunger: The Challenge Ahead* (Washington, D.C.: U.S. Government Printing Office, 1980), p. x.

24. Lawrence Eagleburger and Donald F. McHenry (co-chairs), *Compact for African Development* (Washington, D.C.: Council on Foreign Relations and the Overseas Development Council, 1985), p. 22.

25. See Asbjorn Eide et al., *Food as a Human Right* (Tokyo: United Nations University, 1984); United Nations, Food and Agriculture Organization, *Agriculture: Toward 2000* (New York, 1979), report no. C 79/24.

26. See Sauvant and Hasenflug, *The New International Economic Order* (Boulder, CO: Westview, 1977); Wassily Leontief, *The Future of the World Economy: A United Nations' Study* (New York: Oxford University Press, 1977); Jyoti S. Singh, *A New International Economic Order: Toward a Fair Distribution of the World's Resources* (New York: Praeger, 1977).

27. As reported in the Hunger Project, *The Ending Hunger Briefing Workbook* (San Francisco, CA: The Hunger Project, 1984), p. 30.

28. For a fuller discussion of these trends see Peter Dicken, *Global Shift: Industrial Change in a Turbulent World* (London: Harper & Row, 1986); Peter Jay and Michael Stewart, *Apocalypse 2000* (London: Sidgwick and Jackson, 1987).

29. Max Corden, *The Revival of Protectionism*, Occasional Paper 14 (New York: Group of Thirty, 1984); David Greenaway, *Trade Policy and the New Protectionism* (New York: St. Martin's Press, 1983); Susan Strange, "Protectionism and World Politics," *International Organization* 39, no. 2 (1985).

30. World Bank, *World Development Report, 1987*, Table 15, pp. 230–31; World Bank, *World Development Report, 1985*, Table 14, pp. 200–201.

31. For a fuller discussion of the issues involved in these trends see "Everybody's Business: International Monetary Reform—A Survey," *Economist*, October 5, 1985, pp. 5–32, 41–68.

32. Jay and Stewart, *Apocalypse 2000*.

33. World Bank, *World Debt Tables, 1986–1987* (Washington, D.C., 1987); Gordon W. Smith and John T. Cuddington, *International Debt and the Developing Countries* (Washington, D.C.: World Bank, 1987).

34. Although the actual dollar volume in development assistance increased between 1980 and 1985, the purchasing power of these additional dollars has not kept pace with inflation. Consequently, the amount of net assistance flowing to the LDCs actually declined. Assistance losses were most significant from the group of OPEC nations, from 1.79 percent of OPEC GNP in 1980 to 1.06 percent of GNP in 1985.

35. World Bank, "Short-Term Outlook for the Developing Countries and the International Economy." Staff Paper (Washington, D.C., 1987).

36. Oli Havrylyshyn (ed.), *Exports of Developing Countries: A World Bank Symposium* (Washington, D.C., 1987); Refrik Erzan et al., *On the Potential for Expanding South–South Trade Through the Extension of Mutual Preferences Among Developing Countries*, Discussion Paper 16 (Geneva: United Nations Conference on Trade and Development, 1986).

37. "Revamping the Glass Bead Business," *South* (March 1985):55–57; Miriam Ryan and Melvyn Westlake, "Boomtimes for the Swapshop," *South* (March 1985):60.

38. John Yemma, "Dealing in Discounts: Debt Equity Swaps," *Development International* 1, no. 4 (1987):12–13.

39. Zhang Peiji and Cheng Yugui, "On the Promotion of South–South Cooperation and Its Measures," in *The Rich and the Poor*, edited by Altaf Gauhar (London: Third World Foundation for Social and Economic Studies, 1983), p. 139–58.

40. For detailed data concerning these patterns see Ellen M. Charlton, *Women in Third World Development* (Boulder, CO: Westview Press, 1984); Joni Seager and Ann Olson, *Women in the World: An International Atlas* (New York: Simon and Schuster, 1986); and Richard Anker and Catherine Hein, *Sex Inequalities in Urban Employment in the Third World* (Geneva: International Labour Organization, 1986).

41. As cited in *World Development Forum*, September 15, 1987 (Washington, D.C.: The Hunger Project), p. 3.

42. As cited in *World Development Forum*, November 30, 1985 (Washington, D.C.: The Hunger Project), p. 2.

43. Rebecca Cook et al., *Women: Progress Toward Equality*, wallchart (London: International Planned Parenthood Federation, 1985).

44. A more detailed action agenda of strategies for empowering women can be found in "Women and International Economic Relations," *INSTRAW News* 2, nos. 1, 2 (June 1985):21–31.

45. Organization for Economic Cooperation and Development (OECD), *Social Expenditures, 1960–1990: Problems of Growth and Control* (Paris, 1985).

46. For a careful review of the issues that surround this debate see Helga Nowotny and H. Wintersberger, *Can There Be a New Welfare State? Ideology and Practice in a Situation of Change and Uncertainty* (Vienna: European Centre for Social Welfare Training and Research, 1984); Neil Gilbert, "The Welfare State Adrift," *Social Work* 31, no. 4 (1986):251–56; H. Glennester (ed.), *The Future of the Welfare State* (London: William Heinemann, 1983).

47. Paul Samuelson, "The Failure of the 'Swedish Miracle'—Toting Up the Victories—and Problems," *New York Times*, August 30, 1987; Bent Thorndahl, "Denmark Cuts Back: Agonizing Reappraisals in Tivoli's Shadow," *World Press Review*, January 1986, pp. 32–34; Richard Reeves, "The Welfare State Has a Price Tag," *Philadelphia Inquirer*, January 16, 1987.

48. As an example see "New Spending Priorities," *Newsweek*, September 21, 1987, p. 7.

49. George Yarrow, "Privatization in Theory and Practice," *Economic Policy* (April 1986):323–77.

50. See Dirk Jarre, (ed.) *New Social Initiatives in European Countries* (Vienna: European Centre for Social Welfare Training and Research, 1984); Adalbert Evers, "Intermediate Bodies: Their Role in Coproducing Social Services," *Working Paper* (Vienna: European Centre for Social Welfare Training and Research, 1987); Alan Walker, "The Future of the British Welfare State: Privatisation or Socialisation?" in *The Changing Face of Welfare*, edited by Adalbert Evers et al. (London: Gower & Company, 1987).

51. As an example of these trends in Eastern European nations see Anna Gondos, Gabor Hegyesi, and Maria Herzog, "Integration of Formal and Informal Contribution to Social Services: Professionals and Clients as Coproducers" (Vienna: European Centre for Social Welfare Training and Research, 1987). The paper was originally presented at the Helsinki Seminar on "The Position and Participation of Clients as a Key Question in Advancing Social Policy," August 29–September 3, 1987.

52. Richard J. Estes, *China: The Rusting of the Iron Rice Bowl* (in preparation).

53. As examples see Gabriel Roth, *The Private Provision of Public Services in Developing Countries* (Washington, D.C.: World Bank, 1987); Theodore H. Moran

et al., *Investing in Development: New Roles for Private Capital* (New Brunswick, NJ: Transaction Books, 1986); Peter Robbs, "Privatization in Africa: Neither Pox nor Panacea," *Development International* 1, no. 2 (1987):27–30.

54. John Platt, "The Future of AIDS," *The Futurist* 21, no. 6 (1987):10–17.

55. For an overview of the history, clinical manifestations, epidemiology, and citations of recent international research on the AIDS epidemic see Population Information Program, "AIDS—A Public Health Crisis," *Population Reports*, series L, no. 6 (July–August 1986).

56. Blaine Harden, "AIDS Seen as Threat to Africa's Future," *Washington Post*, May 31, 1987, pp. A1, A18.

57. Renee Sabatier, "The Global Costs of AIDS," *The Futurist*, (November–December 1987):19–21.

58. Platt, "The Future of AIDS," p. 11.

59. Jean-Claude Cherman, "What We Know About AIDS," *Forum* (of the Council of Europe), May 1987, pp. 10–11.

60. Harden, "AIDS Seen as Threat to Africa's Future."

6

EPILOGUE

In the final days of completing work on this book two extraordinary events occurred in the world: U.S. President Ronald Reagan and Soviet General Secretary Mikhail Gorbachev announced agreement on a new initiative that would eliminate all intermediate-range nuclear missiles in Europe; and the State Council of the People's Republic of China announced that the Chinese Communist Party would be officially separated from the day-to-day operations of the government. The U.S.–Soviet accord on intermediate nuclear missiles marks the first step taken by these countries in nearly 40 years that would result in a substantial reduction in the threat of global nuclear war. The political actions taken by the Chinese People's Political Consultative Conference—the most far-reaching since the 1976 death of Mao Zedong—will make possible fuller implementation of the social and economic reforms that are needed to transform China into a major modern state. The separation of the Chinese Communist Party from the government of China can be expected potentially to transform the country into the most influential political and economic power in Asia.

U.S.–SOVIET ACCORD ON INTERMEDIATE NUCLEAR MISSILES

For more than three decades Soviet-American efforts at nuclear disarmament have been fraught with difficulties. Profound ideological differences, political skepticism, mutual distrust, pressures for increased military support from allied nations, substantial capital investments, and other internal and external pressures combined to accelerate confrontations between the two nations. Bilateral efforts at disarmament, given the larger political context, were not perceived to be realistic. Instead, for more than 30 years the two nations have engaged in more or less steady military conflicts with one another, all of them of an indirect nature, and all fought ostensibly on behalf of achieving "liberation" for the inhabitants of Third World countries (i.e., Korea, Cuba, Vietnam, Afghanistan, Nicaragua). The majority of these wars ended in military stalemates, although political victories were claimed by both sides.

The reality has been that neither nation has been able to achieve the level of political trust required to promote more peaceful programs of mutual cooperation. Instead, a series of uneasy "detentes" ensued after each conflict, that is, agreements that placed limits on the pace at which armaments could be increased but which, in themselves, did little to bring about a reduction in the destructive power of either nation that already existed. Though much welcomed, especially in lieu of open and direct military confrontations between these countries, various approaches to detente have done little to increase the sense of security that people around the world experience; indeed, the world has become militarily less secure with the passing of each decade.

Further, the financial, technical, and human costs associated with maintaining the fragile "balance of power" reflected in detente agreements have had the effect of draining the superpowers of the resources needed to promote their own development. Today, both the Soviet Union and the United States are experiencing severe domestic economic problems, nearly all of which have their origin in the extraordinary national expenditures being made to maintain their superpower status. Indeed, the combined military budgets of the United States and the Soviet Union are larger than the combined budgets of nearly all of the world's developing nations. Soviet and U.S. government expenditures for military purposes also exceed their expenditures in the areas of health, education, housing, and the social services. Worse still, the arms race has instilled a sense of hopelessness among young people, a majority of whom in both countries have come to believe that a global nuclear holocaust is inevitable in their lifetime. The social and economic costs to the Third World of the superpowers' race for military supremacy—as measured in regional instabilities, their own escalating military budgets, internal political oppression, and jockeying for "favored nation" status with one or another of the superpowers—also has been nothing short of devastating.

Today reasons exist for feeling more optimistic about the possibilities for a considerably different, more peaceful world. An end to the decades-old cold war may be in sight; mutually destructive confrontations between the Soviet Union and the United States may also be halted; the number and size of superpower military installations around the world may be reduced; and, as a precondition for receiving superpower assistance, developing nations may no longer be asked to choose between East and West, or between capitalism and communism. It is equally conceivable that the financial savings realized by the superpowers from reduced military budgets will enable them to rebuild their failing economies, to provide for the basic needs of their growing numbers of poor people, and to settle the major share of their staggering international debts. It is also hoped that a large share of savings resulting from a substantially less nuclear world will be used to help the poorer nations achieve an accelerated rate of social development. Certainly, substantial reductions in—and eventually the elimination of—nuclear weapons throughout the world will make the planet a safer place in which both people and nations can develop.

The October 1987 understandings reached by U.S. Secretary of State George Shultz and Soviet Foreign Minister Eduard Shevardnadze are expected to be only the first of several steps toward "normalization" of political relations between the two countries. Negotiations concerning reductions in the number of long-range nuclear missiles have already begun; discussions are also beginning on the formulation of a phased timetable leading to an elimination of all chemical and biological weapons.

In December 1987 the General Secretary traveled to Washington to meet with the U.S. president. The meeting resulted in the signing on December 10 of the official Soviet-American agreement on the dismantling of all intermediate nuclear weapons. The meeting also resulted in the establishment of a working framework within which future negotiations will take place that may lead to the eventual elimination of other classes of nuclear weapons.

The chief threat to the current disarmament treaty is that, in the end, the two superpowers will not feel sufficient trust in one another to implement fully what they have agreed to on paper. They may also doubt the political motives of one another, and may even believe that further reductions in the nuclear arsenal will represent too great a destabilization of the nuclear balance that has taken decades to achieve. They may also succumb to pressures from powerful internal political forces that are less committed to the pursuit of a non-nuclear world, even one in which the prospects for a nuclear holocaust are substantially reduced. Alternatively, Reagan and Gorbachev may yield to political pressures from their military allies, especially in Europe, who feel more vulnerable with the raising of the nuclear curtain that has protected them since the end of World War II. European nations can be expected to lobby hard for superpower assurances of more conventional military protection in the event of outside aggression. It is also probable that, over the short term, European nations will increase the size of their own conventional military forces; in doing so, they will be forced to allocate a substantially larger share of their national budgets to military purposes. The worst-case scenario is that one or more non-allied, but nuclear-capable, nations will increase their own production of nuclear weapons and, thereby, re-create the nuclear nightmare that the United States and the Soviet Union are seeking to end.

Whatever the final outcome of these extraordinarily important agreements between the United States and the Soviet Union, certainly, a major positive step forward has been taken to reorder world military priorities. Should these fragile disarmament initiatives succeed, the potential benefits to people everywhere are substantial; their failure will not simply mean a return to pre-disarmament tensions, but to a considerably more destabilized military situation worldwide.

CHINA'S NEW POLITICAL REFORMS

Political developments occurring in China are of a vastly different nature from those taking place between the Soviet Union and the United States. The world's most populous nation, China, is also among the poorest. Poverty in China has been compounded by centuries-long subjugation of the country's population by oppressive dynastic forces, by wars with neighboring states, by internal unrest, and by China's colonial occupation at the beginning of the century. Early death, famines, disease, wars, and civil conflicts each reaped devastating havoc on China.

Following the 1949 War of Liberation, life in China changed dramatically. Under the leadership of Mao Zedong, the Chinese Communist Party implemented sweeping reforms in agriculture, mass education, health care, industrial development, and finance. Major political changes were instituted as well, changes that ultimately were to influence every aspect of life in China. The intention underlying all of these reforms was to create a broadly woven social safety net that would respond effectively to the needs of all of China's population, but especially to those of China's rural peasants which then, as now, comprised 80 percent of the country's population. Only China's ten years of political chaos—the Great Proletarian Cultural Revolution of 1965 through 1975—thwarted its rapid development toward becoming one of the great economic powers of Asia, indeed of the world.

The Cultural Revolution notwithstanding, for 30 years China has succeeded in meeting the basic needs of a larger proportion of its steadily increasing population. China's social safety net—euphemistically referred to as an "iron rice bowl"—has succeeded in eliminating hunger, malnutrition, and famine for the vast majority of the population. Basic health and education services are more or less readily available and accessible throughout all areas of the countryside, and most infectious diseases are under control. Both infant and maternal mortality rates have plummeted; overall life expectancy has increased steadily and now averages 69 years, one of the highest in Asia. Once a food-deficit nation, China no longer faces the threat of starvation from famines.

As a result of recent developments China has also emerged as a major military power; it maintains a large standing army, is an independent nuclear power, and is one of the major exporters of armaments to other Third World nations. Like the Soviet Union and Western nations, China has also made major commitments to the development of aerospace technology and to space exploration. It is fully capable of launching its own satellites, a service that other nations eagerly purchase from China to launch their own telecommunications stations into space. China is rapidly developing into becoming one of the most important new centers of high-tech research and development in Asia, a region that already controls much of current R&D in the computer-related technological fields.

Since 1980 China has also been developing into a major world economic power. Its 1985 GNP exceeded $265.5 billion, an economy substantially larger in size than that of any other developing nation. China's exports to the rest of the world are also substantial; in 1985 foreign sales amounted to approximately $23.7 billion. The amount of China's exports alone exceeds the total GNP of the majority of low- and middle-income nations. China's 1985 gross international financial reserves exceeded 16.9 billion, the largest of any developing nation and among the largest anywhere in the world.[1]

The success of China's far-reaching economic reforms has been achieved through a complex strategy built on strong central planning and control, with actual implementation taking place through a vast network of local committees, communes, production units, civil affairs bureaus, and other collectives of workers. The Chinese Communist Party and local cadres of party members have overseen virtually every aspect of the country's development. China's strong centrist model of ideologically inspired development has obviously served its needs well, especially given the extraordinary levels of poverty and deprivation that existed in the country when Mao Zedong and his followers assumed control of the country.

In recent years, though, China's communist ideology and the country's need for modern approaches to economic reform have not always meshed as comfortably as they did during the decades immediately following liberation. In search of new solutions to China's massive economic difficulties the country reopened its doors to the outside world; in doing so, both China and other nations have been transformed by the extraordinary social and economic events taking place within the country. China and other nations of the world have benefited substantially from developments occurring within the country.

But China's "open door" policy—especially its "flirtations" with various elements of capitalism—have not been without internal political problems. Political dissension within the country has been highly visible among the heterogeneous factions that make up its 46 million-member Communist Party. From time to time these conflicts have threatened to disrupt modernization efforts, and in the process return China to an earlier and more simple, if less affluent, stage of development. These conflicts have been particularly evident in the recent reappearance of political purges, public executions, imprisonment, censorship, restricted travel, public criticisms, and especially in official efforts to "de-Westernize" particular cultural influences that entered China through the open door.

Much of the current political tension in China arises from the widely held belief among influential segments of the Communist Party that the country is moving too quickly toward Western forms of development. Many Party members fear the loss of traditional Chinese values and, even more acutely, fear the loss of control by the Party over the direction of China's development. Many Party members also express deep concern about the absence of a consistent ideological framework that integrates current economic reforms within the context of China's unique approaches to communism and socialism. These concerns are felt deeply in China and in recent years have proven to be significant obstacles in promoting the country's more rapid development. Other factions of the Party, however, believe that China's current development, as rapid as it is, is still too slow and needs to be accelerated, especially given its size and relative underdevelopment compared with other nations. These groups, made up mostly of younger workers, urbanites, and intellectuals are pushing for additional reforms, and want them implemented quickly.

In the middle of all these contradictory political factions is China's massive army of bureaucrats. Most of these people arrived at their positions of authority through membership in the Communist Party, and most have exercised their substantial political power in controlling both the pace and nature of China's development. Over the past five years, though, major disagreements have become apparent between the country's leaders, selected Party officials, and the bureaucrats that are charged by the Party with overseeing that the conduct of China's affairs is consistent with the Party's teachings and the long-term development of China into a fully socialist state. Finding disagreement with many of the current economic reforms some bureaucrats have covertly thwarted development initiatives, while others have pleaded their cases of "ideological inconsistency" at various Party meetings and congresses. Still others lack the education and training that is required to administer a more technologically complex China and have blocked the promotions of more competent younger people. In all situations the effect of China's sluggish bureaucracy has been the same, to retard the pace at which China develops into a modern state comparable in all respects to other world powers.

The events of October and November 1987 promise to change all of that, however; the decisions made during these two months will result in enormous implications for other nations of the world. At the 13th Congress of the Chinese Community Party, the Party gave its official approval to the country's recent economic reforms—including those that clearly reflect a "capitalist" orientation and values—and accepted the recommendation of Prime Minister Zhao Ziyang (heir apparent to Deng Xiaoping) that the Party separate itself entirely from the day-do-day operations of government, industry, and public life.[2] The Party's acceptance of Zhao Ziyang's recommendation should be regarded as nothing short of revolutionary. In effect, the Party has voluntarily removed itself from the role of censor of government actions, and no longer will exercise ideological authority over every aspect of the nation's development.

As part of the Congress Deng Xiaping, in an unprecedented move, announced his own retirement as Chief of the Party and forced the retirement of virtually every other senior leader of the Party as well. Instantly, political leadership of the country was shifted from the revolutionary "old guard" that had marched with Mao Zedong during the campaigns of 1949 to a group of comparatively younger men (and a few women) that had not been directly a part of the country's liberation. The move was an extraordinary one, and its impact on China's short- and long-term future development will be no less extraordinary. In effect, the reigns of official authority in China have now been vested in a better educated group of technically competent political leaders who are less tied to the older, more pure, social, political, and economic ideologies that inspired the country's transformation from a feudal to the beginnings of a modern state. Though the influence of the "old guard" will continue to remain substantial over the next several years the shift in leadership is a significant one.[3]

In effect, the political reforms of October and November 1987 will result in a substantial quickening in the pace of China's economic and political reforms. Further, the Party approved the creation of a new civil service system, which will select government workers on the basis of competitive examinations and technical competence rather than Party affiliation. For the first time in China's modern history, the country will have the opportunity to place in positions of administrative power younger, better qualified workers who can lead the country's development into the next century. Given China's already substantial development gains of the past ten years, its further rapid development into one of the most politically and economically influential nations of Asia seems assured.

My own view is that current political events in China will have a profound impact on its relations with other Asian nations and, indeed, with the rest of the world. With China's most serious political impediments to progress now out of the way, one can reasonably expect that by the beginning of the next century China will have developed into the region's most influential nation. Its importance as East Asia's major economic power can be expected to exceed that currently enjoyed by Japan and the region's four so-called economic "tigers," Hong Kong (which will be reabsorbed into China in 1997), Taiwan (which is in the process of normalizing its relationships with the mainland), Singapore (77 percent of whose population is ethnic Chinese), and South Korea. China, in my judgment, can also be expected to emerge as the region's preeminent military and political power. In all respects, China's development into Asia's superpower will significantly alter the balance of global military and political power. All that remains for China to accomplish is for Zhao Ziyang and his colleagues to put China's economic house in order, a challenge that would humble the leaders of even the world's most economically advanced nations.

NOTES

1. World Bank, *World Development Report, 1987* (Washington, D.C., 1987), Table 15, p. 230.

2. Edward A. Gargan, "More Change Due in China's Economy," *New York Times*, October 26, 1987, pp. A1, A11.

3. Fay Willey and Dorinda Elliot, "China's Changing Guard: The Long March Ends," *Newsweek*, November 16, 1987, p. 78.

APPENDIX A:

SELECTED TABLES OF NATIONAL RANKINGS ON THE INDEXES OF SOCIAL PROGRESS

Table A.1
Scores and Percentage Change on the Indexes of Social Progress (ISP83, WISP83) by Subindex, Development Grouping, Country, and Year ($n = 124$)

COUNTRY	INDEX OF SOCIAL PROGRESS (ISP)	Educa-tion	Health	Women	Defense	Economic	Demo-graphic	Geo-graphic	Partici-pation	Cultural	Welfare	WEIGHTED INDEX OF SOCIAL PROGRESS
DEVELOPED MARKET ECONOMIES (N=24)												
Australia												
1970	172	17	19	26	10	17	17	15	15	13	23	80
1980	176	19	19	15	15	18	18	7	26	18	21	82
1983	173	19	19	14	14	17	19	7	25	18	21	81
% 1970-1980	2.3	12.4	0.5	-42.1	51.4	6.4	6.4	-53.1	74.4	39.4	-8.3	2.5
% 1980-1983	-1.7	0.0	0.0	-6.7	-6.7	-5.6	5.6	0.0	-3.8	0.0	0.0	-1.2
% 1970-1983	0.6	12.4	0.5	-46.0	41.3	0.5	12.4	-53.1	67.7	39.4	-8.3	1.3
Austria												
1970	179	19	18	21	16	13	21	13	16	13	29	83
1980	197	19	21	16	17	18	21	11	26	19	28	90
1983	195	19	20	16	16	18	21	11	25	19	28	90
% 1970-1980	10.1	0.5	17.3	-23.5	6.9	39.4	0.4	-14.8	63.4	47.2	-3.1	8.4
% 1980-1983	-1.0	0.0	-4.8	0.0	-5.9	0.0	0.0	0.0	-3.8	0.0	0.0	0.0
% 1970-1983	8.9	0.5	11.7	-23.5	0.6	39.4	0.4	-14.8	57.1	47.2	-3.1	8.4
Belgium												
1970	173	20	19	18	12	16	21	14	19	8	26	81
1980	190	19	24	19	13	19	21	14	26	9	27	89
1983	184	19	21	18	13	17	21	14	25	9	27	85
% 1970-1980	9.8	-4.6	26.9	6.1	9.2	19.4	0.4	0.6	37.5	13.8	4.2	9.9
% 1980-1983	-3.2	0.0	-12.5	-5.3	0.0	-10.5	0.0	0.0	-3.8	0.0	0.0	-4.5
% 1970-1983	6.4	-4.6	11.1	0.5	9.2	6.9	0.4	0.6	32.2	13.8	4.2	4.9
Canada												
1970	157	24	19	18	13	19	18	6	17	6	17	76
1980	166	21	20	15	16	17	20	7	26	6	18	78
1983	168	23	20	14	15	20	19	7	25	6	18	80
% 1970-1980	5.7	-12.2	5.8	-16.2	23.9	-10.1	11.7	18.4	53.8	1.5	6.4	2.6
% 1980-1983	1.2	9.5	0.0	-6.7	-6.3	17.6	-5.0	0.0	-3.8	0.0	0.0	2.6
% 1970-1983	7.0	-3.8	5.8	-21.8	16.2	5.8	6.1	18.4	47.8	1.5	6.4	5.3
Denmark												
1970	196	23	20	22	13	15	22	17	15	20	29	91
1980	208	20	21	15	15	19	21	23	26	20	29	92
1983	207	20	23	13	14	19	21	23	25	20	29	92
% 1970-1980	6.1	-13.0	5.5	-31.5	16.2	27.4	-4.2	36.0	74.4	0.5	0.3	1.1
% 1980-1983	-0.5	0.0	9.5	-13.3	-6.7	0.0	0.0	0.0	-3.8	0.0	0.0	0.0
% 1970-1983	5.6	-13.0	15.5	-40.7	8.4	27.4	-4.2	36.0	67.7	0.5	0.3	1.1
Finland												
1970	167	21	18	23	16	11	22	6	13	18	19	80
1980	178	19	19	15	16	17	21	10	22	19	20	81
1983	175	19	17	14	16	17	21	10	22	19	20	80
% 1970-1980	6.6	-9.1	6.1	-34.5	0.6	55.8	-4.2	69.2	70.4	6.1	5.8	1.3
% 1980-1983	-1.7	0.0	-10.5	-6.7	0.0	0.0	0.0	0.0	0.0	0.0	0.0	-1.2
% 1970-1983	4.8	-9.1	-5.1	-38.9	0.6	55.8	-4.2	69.2	70.4	6.1	5.8	0.0

Table A.1 (cont.)

COUNTRY		INDEX OF SOCIAL PROGRESS (ISP)	Education	Health	Women	Defense	Economic	Demographic	Geographic	Participation	Cultural	Welfare	WEIGHTED INDEX OF SOCIAL PROGRESS
France	1970	175	19	19	16	9	17	19	15	19	15	27	81
	1980	193	18	21	22	12	19	19	14	24	16	27	90
	1983	190	17	22	22	12	18	19	14	24	16	27	88
% 1970-1980		10.3	-4.8	11.1	38.3	33.3	12.4	0.5	-6.1	26.9	7.3	0.3	11.1
% 1980-1983		-1.6	-5.6	4.8	0.0	0.0	-5.3	0.0	0.0	0.0	0.0	0.0	-2.2
% 1970-1983		8.6	-10.1	16.3	38.3	33.3	6.4	0.5	-6.1	26.9	7.3	0.3	8.6
Germany, FDR													
	1970	183	18	19	21	10	15	19	14	17	20	30	85
	1980	201	24	21	18	13	20	22	13	24	18	29	94
	1983	199	25	20	17	13	20	21	13	24	18	29	93
% 1970-1980		9.8	34.0	11.1	-13.9	31.2	34.1	16.3	-6.5	41.9	-9.6	-3.0	10.6
% 1980-1983		-1.0	4.2	-4.8	-5.6	0.0	0.0	-4.5	0.0	0.0	0.0	0.0	-1.1
% 1970-1983		8.7	39.6	5.8	-18.7	31.2	34.1	11.1	-6.5	41.9	-9.6	-3.0	9.4
Greece													
	1970	136	11	19	15	7	12	21	13	1	20	17	64
	1980	164	12	22	15	9	16	20	10	22	20	18	76
	1983	160	11	22	15	9	12	19	10	24	20	18	75
% 1970-1980		20.6	10.0	16.3	0.6	30.2	34.3	-4.4	-22.5	2317.6	0.5	6.4	18.8
% 1980-1983		-2.4	-8.3	0.0	0.0	0.0	-25.0	-5.0	0.0	9.1	0.0	0.0	-1.3
% 1970-1983		17.6	0.8	16.3	0.6	30.2	0.8	-9.1	-22.5	2537.4	0.5	6.4	17.2
Ireland													
	1970	184	17	19	21	16	12	22	17	14	20	26	84
	1980	187	18	22	15	16	16	17	12	26	20	27	85
	1983	185	18	24	15	15	13	16	12	25	20	27	85
% 1970-1980		1.6	6.4	16.3	-28.3	0.6	34.3	-22.4	-29.0	86.9	0.5	4.2	1.2
% 1980-1983		-1.1	0.0	9.1	0.0	-6.3	-18.8	-5.9	0.0	-3.8	0.0	0.0	0.0
% 1970-1983		0.5	6.4	26.9	-28.3	-5.7	9.2	-27.0	-29.0	79.7	0.5	4.2	1.2
Israel													
	1970	84	19	19	14	-49	19	14	15	13	12	8	55
	1980	104	21	19	25	-37	6	14	13	22	9	11	63
	1983	111	21	18	24	-34	2	14	13	22	9	11	62
% 1970-1980		23.8	11.1	0.5	79.7	24.6	-68.3	0.6	-12.8	70.4	-24.4	39.1	14.5
% 1980-1983		6.7	0.0	-5.3	-4.0	8.1	-66.7	0.0	0.0	0.0	0.0	0.0	-1.6
% 1970-1983		32.1	11.1	-4.8	72.5	30.7	-89.4	0.6	-12.8	70.4	-24.4	39.1	12.7
Italy													
	1970	176	18	19	15	12	13	20	16	15	21	27	81
	1980	203	18	23	28	15	15	20	16	22	20	26	93
	1983	202	19	21	27	14	15	20	16	24	20	26	93
% 1970-1980		15.3	0.5	21.6	87.8	25.9	16.2	0.5	0.6	47.6	-4.4	-3.4	14.8
% 1980-1983		-0.5	5.6	-8.7	-3.6	-6.7	0.0	0.0	0.0	9.1	0.0	0.0	0.0
% 1970-1983		14.8	6.1	11.1	81.1	17.5	16.2	0.5	0.6	61.0	-4.4	-3.4	14.8
Japan													
	1970	155	16	19	15	17	17	18	2	17	21	13	73
	1980	178	18	20	29	18	19	19	-3	24	20	16	86
	1983	174	17	20	27	16	17	19	-3	25	20	16	85

167

Table A.1 (cont.)

COUNTRY	INDEX OF SOCIAL PROGRESS (ISP)	Educa-tion	Health	Women	Defense	Economic	Demo-graphic	Geo-graphic	Partici-pation	Cultural	Welfare	WEIGHTED INDEX OF SOCIAL PROGRESS
% 1970-1980	14.8	13.1	5.8	94.5	6.4	12.4	6.1	-257.1	41.9	-4.4	23.9	17.8
% 1980-1983	-2.2	-5.6	0.0	-6.9	-11.1	-10.5	0.0	0.0	4.2	0.0	0.0	-1.2
% 1970-1983	12.3	6.9	5.8	81.1	-5.4	0.5	6.1	-257.1	47.8	-4.4	23.9	16.4
Netherlands												
1970	185	21	20	22	10	15	20	14	21	16	26	87
1980	188	21	21	15	14	20	21	13	26	14	26	87
1983	184	21	21	13	13	18	21	13	25	14	26	85
% 1970-1980	1.6	0.4	5.5	-31.5	41.3	34.1	5.5	-6.5	24.3	-12.0	0.3	0.0
% 1980-1983	-2.1	0.0	0.0	-13.3	-7.1	-10.0	0.0	0.0	-3.8	0.0	0.0	-2.3
% 1970-1983	-0.5	0.4	5.5	-40.7	31.2	20.7	5.5	-6.5	19.6	-12.0	0.3	-2.3
New Zealand												
1970	176	17	19	28	14	10	17	14	17	14	26	82
1980	176	18	19	16	16	14	18	9	26	15	25	81
1983	176	17	20	16	15	15	19	9	25	15	25	82
% 1970-1980	0.0	6.4	0.5	-42.7	15.0	41.3	6.4	-35.3	53.8	7.8	-3.5	-1.2
% 1980-1983	0.0	-5.6	5.3	0.0	-6.3	7.1	5.6	0.0	-3.8	0.0	0.0	1.2
% 1970-1983	0.0	0.5	5.8	-42.7	7.8	51.4	12.4	-35.3	47.8	7.8	-3.5	0.0
Norway												
1970	184	22	20	24	10	16	21	7	19	20	25	89
1980	192	23	20	15	14	19	21	9	26	20	25	90
1983	186	20	19	13	13	21	21	9	25	20	25	86
% 1970-1980	4.3	5.0	0.5	-37.3	41.3	19.4	0.4	30.2	37.5	0.5	0.4	1.1
% 1980-1983	-3.1	-13.0	-5.0	-13.3	-7.1	10.5	0.0	0.0	-3.8	0.0	0.0	-4.4
% 1970-1983	1.1	-8.7	-4.6	-45.6	31.2	32.0	0.4	30.2	32.2	0.5	0.4	-3.4
Portugal												
1970	133	8	17	11	2	11	20	14	15	21	14	62
1980	158	16	18	11	13	8	18	17	22	20	16	70
1983	163	17	18	13	13	7	18	17	24	20	16	73
% 1970-1980	18.8	102.3	6.4	0.8	580.6	-26.7	-9.6	22.2	47.6	-4.4	15.0	12.9
% 1980-1983	3.2	6.3	0.0	18.2	0.0	-12.5	0.0	0.0	9.1	0.0	0.0	4.3
% 1970-1983	22.6	114.9	6.4	19.2	580.6	-35.8	-9.6	22.2	61.0	-4.4	15.0	17.7
South Africa												
1970	120	10	8	21	14	13	8	19	13	-5	19	51
1980	100	7	12	10	13	11	9	12	7	3	16	43
1983	94	5	12	8	12	11	9	12	7	3	16	41
% 1970-1980	-16.7	-29.4	51.7	-52.2	-6.5	-14.8	13.8	-36.5	-45.8	158.9	-15.4	-15.7
% 1980-1983	-6.0	-28.6	0.0	-20.0	-7.7	0.0	0.0	0.0	0.0	0.0	0.0	-4.7
% 1970-1983	-21.7	-49.5	51.7	-61.7	-13.7	-14.8	13.8	-36.5	-45.8	158.9	-15.4	-19.6
Spain												
1970	158	11	19	20	14	10	19	16	14	13	22	72
1980	176	13	21	15	15	17	19	17	22	13	22	78
1983	171	12	21	15	15	13	19	17	24	13	22	76
% 1970-1980	11.4	19.2	11.1	-24.7	7.8	71.5	0.5	6.9	58.2	0.7	0.4	8.3
% 1980-1983	-2.8	-7.7	0.0	0.0	0.0	-23.5	0.0	0.0	9.1	0.0	0.0	-2.6
% 1970-1983	8.2	10.0	11.1	-24.7	7.8	31.2	0.5	6.9	72.5	0.7	0.4	5.6

168

Table A.1 (cont.)

COUNTRY	! INDEX OF! SOCIAL ! PROGRESS! (ISP) !	Educa- tion	Health	Women	Defense	Economic	Demo- graphic	Geo- graphic	Partici- pation	Cultural	Welfare	! WEIGHTED ! INDEX OF ! SOCIAL ! PROGRESS
Sweden	!										!	
1970 !	195 !	24	20	27	10	20	22	7	21	20	24 !	95
1980 !	194 !	23	20	17	14	19	22	10	26	19	25 !	91
1983 !	192 !	23	20	16	13	18	21	10	25	19	25 !	90
% 1970-1980 !	-0.5 !	-3.8	0.5	-36.8	41.3	-4.6	0.4	44.7	24.3	-4.6	4.6 !	-4.2
% 1980-1983 !	-1.0 !	0.0	0.0	-5.9	-7.1	-5.3	-4.5	0.0	-3.8	0.0	0.0 !	-1.1
% 1970-1983 !	-1.5 !	-3.8	0.5	-40.5	31.2	-9.6	-4.2	44.7	19.6	-4.6	4.6 !	-5.3
Switzerland !	!										!	
1970 !	164 !	17	20	10	13	16	21	15	20	12	20 !	75
1980 !	180 !	18	21	15	16	20	22	11	26	10	21 !	83
1983 !	178 !	17	21	14	15	21	22	11	25	10	21 !	82
% 1970-1980 !	9.8 !	6.4	5.5	51.4	23.9	25.7	5.2	-26.2	30.6	-16.0	5.5 !	10.7
% 1980-1983 !	-1.1 !	-5.6	0.0	-6.7	-6.3	5.0	0.0	0.0	-3.8	0.0	0.0 !	-1.2
% 1970-1983 !	8.5 !	0.5	5.5	41.3	16.2	32.0	5.2	-26.2	25.6	-16.0	5.5 !	9.3
United Kingdom!	!										!	
1970 !	186 !	19	19	21	7	12	20	16	33	13	26 !	87
1980 !	177 !	18	20	17	10	16	20	10	26	14	27 !	84
1983 !	177 !	18	20	17	10	18	20	10	25	14	26 !	83
% 1970-1980 !	-4.8 !	-4.8	5.8	-18.7	44.7	34.3	0.5	-37.1	-21.0	8.4	4.2 !	-3.4
% 1980-1983 !	0.0 !	0.0	0.0	0.0	0.0	12.5	0.0	0.0	-3.8	0.0	-3.7 !	-1.2
% 1970-1983 !	-4.8 !	-4.8	5.8	-18.7	44.7	51.1	0.5	-37.1	-24.0	8.4	0.3 !	-4.6
United States !	!										!	
1970 !	124 !	21	20	21	-3	23	13	-20	22	13	14 !	72
1980 !	147 !	20	21	20	9	18	16	-12	26	16	13 !	77
1983 !	145 !	19	21	19	8	19	15	-12	25	16	13 !	76
% 1970-1980 !	18.5 !	-4.4	5.5	-4.4	391.3	-21.4	23.9	40.3	18.7	23.9	-6.5 !	6.9
% 1980-1983 !	-1.4 !	-5.0	0.0	-5.0	-11.1	5.6	-6.3	0.0	-3.8	0.0	0.0 !	-1.3
% 1970-1983 !	16.9 !	-9.1	5.5	-9.1	358.9	-17.1	16.2	40.3	14.1	23.9	-6.5 !	5.6
Yugoslavia !	!										!	
1970 !	138 !	17	16	14	6	15	19	15	11	6	20 !	65
1980 !	137 !	15	19	15	11	14	19	15	3	5	20 !	64
1983 !	134 !	14	19	14	13	12	18	15	3	5	20 !	62
% 1970-1980 !	-0.8 !	-11.3	19.4	7.8	86.1	-6.1	0.5	0.6	-72.5	-15.4	0.5 !	-1.5
% 1980-1983 !	-2.2 !	-6.7	0.0	-6.7	18.2	-14.3	-5.3	0.0	0.0	0.0	0.0 !	-3.1
% 1970-1983 !	-3.0 !	-17.2	19.4	0.6	120.0	-19.5	-4.8	0.6	-72.5	-15.4	0.5 !	-4.6
EASTERN TRADING AREA NATIONS (n=8)												!
Albania !	!											!
1970 !	136 !	16	15	12	11	19	15	13	10	15	10 !	61
1980 !	116 !	16	15	12	5	13	16	14	-2	14	12 !	54
1983 !	122 !	14	17	11	11	14	16	14	-2	14	13 !	55
% 1970-1980 !	-14.7 !	0.6	0.6	0.8	-54.2	-31.3	7.3	8.4	-120.2	-6.1	21.1 !	-11.5
% 1980-1983 !	5.2 !	-12.5	13.3	-8.3	120.0	7.7	0.0	0.0	0.0	0.0	8.3 !	1.9
% 1970-1983 !	-10.3 !	-12.0	14.0	-7.6	0.8	-26.0	7.3	8.4	-120.2	-6.1	31.2 !	-9.8

169

Table A.1 (cont.)

COUNTRY	INDEX OF SOCIAL PROGRESS (ISP)	Education	Health	Women	Defense	Economic	Demographic	Geographic	Participation	Cultural	Welfare	WEIGHTED INDEX OF SOCIAL PROGRESS
Bulgaria												
1970	166	18	19	14	11	22	24	15	10	12	21	77
1980	151	19	22	18	6	18	20	17	-2	12	22	72
1983	150	19	21	17	6	17	20	17	-2	12	22	71
% 1970-1980	-9.0	6.1	16.3	29.4	-45.0	-17.8	-16.4	14.0	-120.2	0.8	5.2	-6.5
% 1980-1983	-0.7	0.0	-4.5	-5.6	0.0	-5.6	0.0	0.0	0.0	0.0	0.0	-1.4
% 1970-1983	-9.6	6.1	11.1	22.2	-45.0	-22.4	-16.4	14.0	-120.2	0.8	5.2	-7.8
Czechoslovakia												
1970	165	18	18	21	7	20	22	15	8	11	25	79
1980	154	16	21	22	9	17	19	18	-2	10	23	72
1983	152	16	20	21	9	16	18	18	0	10	23	71
% 1970-1980	-6.7	-10.7	17.3	5.2	30.2	-14.6	-13.3	20.7	-125.3	-8.3	-7.7	-8.9
% 1980-1983	-1.3	0.0	-4.8	-4.5	0.0	-5.9	-5.3	0.0	100.0	0.0	0.0	-1.4
% 1970-1983	-7.9	-10.7	11.7	0.4	30.2	-19.6	-17.8	20.7	-100.0	-8.3	-7.7	-10.1
Germany, Dem. (E)												
1970	NA	NA	NA	NA	NA	NA	NA	NA	NA	NA	NA	NA
1980	161	15	22	17	9	20	21	17	-2	17	25	75
1983	156	15	21	16	9	18	20	17	-2	17	24	73
% 1970-1980	NA	NA	NA	NA	NA	NA	NA	NA	NA	NA	NA	NA
% 1980-1983	-3.1	0.0	-4.5	-5.9	0.0	-10.0	-4.8	0.0	0.0	0.0	-4.0	-2.7
% 1970-1983	NA	NA	NA	NA	NA	NA	NA	NA	NA	NA	NA	NA
Hungary												
1970	173	19	17	17	12	17	23	18	10	17	23	79
1980	165	17	19	18	11	17	20	21	3	15	23	75
1983	162	18	19	18	12	16	19	21	3	15	23	74
% 1970-1980	-4.6	-10.1	12.4	6.4	-7.6	0.5	-12.7	17.3	-69.7	-11.3	0.4	-5.1
% 1980-1983	-1.8	5.9	0.0	0.0	9.1	-5.9	-5.0	0.0	0.0	0.0	0.0	-1.3
% 1970-1983	-6.4	-4.8	12.4	6.4	0.8	-5.4	-17.1	17.3	-69.7	-11.3	0.4	-6.3
Poland												
1970	167	19	18	21	7	18	20	16	11	18	19	78
1980	157	15	20	17	9	16	18	19	7	18	19	71
1983	151	14	18	16	10	13	17	19	7	18	19	68
% 1970-1980	-6.0	-20.7	11.7	-18.7	30.2	-10.7	-9.6	19.4	-35.8	0.5	0.5	-9.0
% 1980-1983	-3.8	-6.7	-10.0	-5.9	11.1	-18.8	-5.6	0.0	0.0	0.0	0.0	-4.2
% 1970-1983	-9.6	-26.0	0.5	-23.5	44.7	-27.4	-14.6	19.4	-35.8	0.5	0.5	-12.8
Romania												
1970	162	18	17	18	11	19	19	16	11	15	18	74
1980	155	14	18	47	11	23	18	18	0	16	19	70
1983	148	13	18	16	11	18	18	18	0	16	19	67
% 1970-1980	-4.3	-21.8	6.4	162.4	0.8	21.6	-4.8	13.1	-100.0	7.3	6.1	-5.4
% 1980-1983	-4.5	-7.1	0.0	-66.0	0.0	-21.7	0.0	0.0	0.0	0.0	0.0	-4.3
% 1970-1983	-8.6	-27.4	6.4	-10.7	0.8	-4.8	-4.8	13.1	-100.0	7.3	6.1	-9.5
USSR												
1970	134	24	18	22	2	19	10	10	16	-4	17	67

Table A.1 (cont.)

COUNTRY	INDEX OF SOCIAL PROGRESS (ISP)	Education	Health	Women	Defense	Economic	Demographic	Geographic	Participation	Cultural	Welfare	WEIGHTED INDEX OF SOCIAL PROGRESS
1980	101	21	18	17	-7	18	12	7	1	-6	18	56
1983	96	20	18	16	-2	13	11	7	0	-6	18	52
% 1970-1980	-24.6	-12.2	0.5	-22.4	-466.5	-4.8	21.1	-29.4	-93.7	-46.7	6.4	-16.4
% 1980-1983	-5.0	-4.8	0.0	-5.9	71.4	-27.8	-8.3	0.0	-100.0	0.0	0.0	-7.1
% 1970-1983	-28.4	-16.4	0.5	-27.0	-204.7	-31.3	11.0	-29.4	-100.0	-46.7	6.4	-22.4

DEVELOPING COUNTRIES

Algeria

1970	85	10	8	4	13	8	4	8	1	15	14	36
1980	86	12	6	5	14	6	5	9	1	15	13	36
1983	88	9	8	5	14	9	4	9	1	15	13	36
% 1970-1980	1.2	21.1	-24.1	27.9	8.4	-24.1	27.9	13.8	9.9	0.6	-6.5	0.0
% 1980-1983	2.3	-25.0	33.3	0.0	0.0	50.0	-20.0	0.0	0.0	0.0	0.0	0.0
% 1970-1983	3.5	-9.2	1.1	27.9	8.4	13.8	2.3	13.8	9.9	0.6	-6.5	0.0

Angola

1970	NA	NA	NA	NA	NA	NA	NA	NA	NA	NA	NA	NA
1980	15	6	-2	3	1	1	3	10	-2	-4	-2	5
1983	-5	5	-2	1	-15	1	3	10	-2	-4	-2	0
% 1970-1980	NA	NA	NA	NA	NA	NA	NA	NA	NA	NA	NA	NA
% 1980-1983	-133.3	-16.7	0.0	-66.7	-1600.0	0.0	0.0	0.0	0.0	0.0	0.0	-100.0
% 1970-1983	NA	NA	NA	NA	NA	NA	NA	NA	NA	NA	NA	NA

Argentina

1970	136	15	15	18	14	7	18	15	6	15	13	61
1980	128	16	17	19	13	1	16	10	3	18	14	60
1983	132	16	17	22	14	-5	15	10	11	18	15	62
% 1970-1980	-5.9	7.3	14.0	6.1	-6.5	-85.5	-10.7	-32.9	-49.2	20.7	8.4	-1.6
% 1980-1983	3.1	0.0	0.0	15.8	7.7	-600.0	-6.3	0.0	266.7	0.0	7.1	3.3
% 1970-1983	-2.9	7.3	14.0	22.8	0.6	-172.4	-16.2	-32.9	86.1	20.7	16.2	1.6

Bolivia

1970	81	12	12	7	16	4	6	8	2	5	9	35
1980	91	11	4	12	14	8	6	10	15	2	7	37
1983	82	10	4	12	14	1	5	10	16	2	7	34
% 1970-1980	12.3	-7.6	-66.4	73.7	-12.0	104.6	1.5	26.4	685.3	-59.3	-21.4	5.7
% 1980-1983	-9.9	-9.1	0.0	0.0	0.0	-87.5	-16.7	0.0	6.7	0.0	0.0	-8.1
% 1970-1983	1.2	-16.0	-66.4	73.7	-12.0	-74.4	-15.4	26.4	737.7	-59.3	-21.4	-2.9

Brazil

1970	123	14	14	18	13	3	7	7	10	20	17	56
1980	131	12	12	10	18	11	10	6	14	20	19	57
1983	128	12	12	10	17	8	10	6	15	20	19	56
% 1970-1980	6.5	-13.7	-13.7	-44.2	39.4	278.0	44.7	-13.2	41.3	0.5	12.4	1.8
% 1980-1983	-2.3	0.0	0.0	0.0	-5.6	-27.3	0.0	0.0	7.1	0.0	0.0	-1.8
% 1970-1983	4.1	-13.7	-13.7	-44.2	31.7	174.9	44.7	-13.2	51.4	0.5	12.4	0.0

Burma

1970	78	6	9	15	5	12	10	8	-1	10	4	36

171

COUNTRY	INDEX OF SOCIAL PROGRESS (ISP)	Education	Health	Women	Defense	Economic	Demographic	Geographic	Participation	Cultural	Welfare	WEIGHTED INDEX OF SOCIAL PROGRESS
1980	66	3	10	7	13	5	8	10	0	6	5	27
1983	72	2	9	8	13	12	9	10	-2	6	5	29
% 1970-1980	-15.4	-49.2	12.2	-53.1	164.8	-58.0	-19.3	26.4	-100.0	-39.5	27.9	-25.0
% 1980-1983	9.1	-33.3	-10.0	14.3	0.0	140.0	12.5	0.0	-200.0	0.0	0.0	7.4
% 1970-1983	-7.7	-66.2	1.0	-46.3	164.8	0.8	-9.2	26.4	-83.5	-39.5	27.9	-19.4
Cameroon												
1970	60	5	-1	10	14	7	7	10	11	-8	5	23
1980	59	5	4	6	16	9	6	12	1	-8	7	22
1983	57	6	3	9	15	8	4	12	1	-8	7	21
% 1970-1980	-1.7	1.8	467.0	-39.5	15.0	30.2	-13.2	21.1	-90.8	-1.1	42.6	-4.3
% 1980-1983	-3.4	20.0	-25.0	50.0	-6.3	-11.1	-33.3	0.0	0.0	0.0	0.0	-4.5
% 1970-1983	-5.0	22.2	-375.2	-9.2	7.8	15.8	-42.1	21.1	-90.8	-1.1	42.6	-8.7
Chile												
1970	135	13	14	16	14	5	13	5	16	18	21	62
1980	112	15	14	14	13	-9	16	6	7	14	22	54
1983	121	16	15	13	11	1	16	6	7	14	21	58
% 1970-1980	-17.0	16.2	0.6	-12.0	-6.5	-283.3	23.9	22.2	-56.0	-21.8	5.2	-12.9
% 1980-1983	8.0	6.7	7.1	-7.1	-15.4	111.1	0.0	0.0	0.0	0.0	-4.5	7.4
% 1970-1983	-10.4	23.9	7.8	-18.3	-20.9	-79.6	23.9	22.2	-56.0	-21.8	0.4	-6.5
China												
1970	NA	NA	NA	NA	NA	NA	NA	NA	NA	NA	NA	NA
1980	69	12	13	10	0	14	-2	-3	3	16	6	36
1983	74	12	14	9	5	16	-1	-3	1	16	6	37
% 1970-1980	NA	NA	NA	NA	NA	NA	NA	NA	NA	NA	NA	NA
% 1980-1983	7.2	0.0	7.7	-10.0	500.0	14.3	50.0	0.0	-66.7	0.0	0.0	2.8
% 1970-1983	NA	NA	NA	NA	NA	NA	NA	NA	NA	NA	NA	NA
Colombia												
1970	118	9	12	12	16	9	6	8	14	20	12	50
1980	131	12	13	13	17	11	10	7	21	14	11	57
1983	132	13	13	15	16	10	11	7	21	14	11	59
% 1970-1980	11.0	34.7	9.2	9.2	6.9	23.5	69.2	-11.5	51.0	-29.7	-7.6	14.0
% 1980-1983	0.8	8.3	0.0	15.4	-5.9	-9.1	10.0	0.0	0.0	0.0	0.0	3.5
% 1970-1983	11.9	45.9	9.2	25.9	0.6	12.2	86.1	-11.5	51.0	-29.7	-7.6	18.0
Congo, PR												
1970	NA	NA	NA	NA	NA	NA	NA	NA	NA	NA	NA	NA
1980	54	8	3	8	12	0	7	10	-2	-3	10	22
1983	69	7	11	8	13	7	7	10	0	-3	10	30
% 1970-1980	NA	NA	NA	NA	NA	NA	NA	NA	NA	NA	NA	NA
% 1980-1983	27.8	-12.5	266.7	0.0	8.3	700.0	0.0	0.0	100.0	0.0	0.0	36.4
% 1970-1983	NA	NA	NA	NA	NA	NA	NA	NA	NA	NA	NA	NA
Costa Rica												
1970	137	20	15	14	16	10	7	11	17	20	7	60
1980	155	19	17	14	18	10	14	11	26	16	10	69
1983	142	15	18	15	17	0	14	11	25	16	10	63
% 1970-1980	13.1	-4.6	14.0	0.6	13.1	0.9	102.6	0.8	53.8	-19.6	44.7	15.0

Table A.1 (cont.)

COUNTRY	INDEX OF SOCIAL PROGRESS (ISP)	Education	Health	Women	Defense	Economic	Demographic	Geographic	Participation	Cultural	Welfare	WEIGHTED INDEX OF SOCIAL PROGRESS
% 1980-1983	-8.4	-21.1	5.9	7.1	-5.6	-100.0	0.0	0.0	-3.8	0.0	0.0	-8.7
% 1970-1983	3.6	-24.7	20.7	7.8	6.9	-100.0	102.6	0.8	47.8	-19.6	44.7	5.0
Cuba												
1970	139	22	17	19	4	12	14	13	6	20	12	67
1980	122	21	19	16	7	11	18	13	1	7	9	59
1983	126	20	20	16	9	13	19	13	1	7	9	61
% 1970-1980	-12.2	-4.2	12.4	-15.4	79.0	-7.6	29.4	0.7	-83.1	-64.8	-24.4	-11.9
% 1980-1983	3.3	-4.8	5.3	0.0	28.6	18.2	5.6	0.0	0.0	0.0	0.0	3.4
% 1970-1983	-9.4	-8.7	18.3	-15.4	130.2	9.2	36.6	0.7	-83.1	-64.8	-24.4	-9.0
Dominican Rep												
1970	112	6	15	14	13	10	4	11	13	20	6	47
1980	129	6	11	18	17	10	8	15	21	16	8	53
1983	132	6	10	17	16	10	9	15	24	16	8	55
% 1970-1980	15.2	1.5	-26.2	29.4	31.7	0.9	104.6	37.5	62.7	-19.6	35.4	12.8
% 1980-1983	2.3	0.0	-9.1	-5.6	-5.9	0.0	12.5	0.0	14.3	0.0	0.0	3.8
% 1970-1983	17.9	1.5	-32.9	22.2	23.9	0.9	130.2	37.5	85.9	-19.6	35.4	17.0
Ecuador												
1970	108	11	11	16	14	11	6	2	12	14	11	49
1980	121	15	9	11	15	10	8	5	22	12	13	53
1983	122	14	9	14	16	7	10	5	22	12	13	54
% 1970-1980	12.0	37.5	-17.5	-30.9	7.8	-8.3	35.4	161.8	84.7	-13.7	19.2	8.2
% 1980-1983	0.8	-6.7	0.0	27.3	6.7	-30.0	25.0	0.0	0.0	0.0	0.0	1.9
% 1970-1983	13.0	28.3	-17.5	-12.0	15.0	-35.8	69.2	161.8	84.7	-13.7	19.2	10.2
Egypt, UAR												
1970	70	9	9	4	-10	8	7	7	10	20	6	35
1980	81	8	11	4	0	6	9	9	9	17	8	37
1983	89	8	12	3	6	8	9	9	9	17	8	39
% 1970-1980	15.7	-10.2	23.5	2.3	100.0	-24.1	30.2	30.2	-9.2	-14.6	35.4	5.7
% 1980-1983	9.9	0.0	9.1	-25.0	600.0	33.3	0.0	0.0	0.0	0.0	0.0	5.4
% 1970-1983	27.1	-10.2	34.7	-23.3	160.5	1.1	30.2	30.2	-9.2	-14.6	35.4	11.4
El Salvador												
1970	115	9	14	11	12	9	7	15	14	17	7	48
1980	109	5	10	6	14	11	8	16	12	17	9	73
1983	97	5	9	5	12	7	8	16	10	17	9	38
% 1970-1980	-5.2	-43.9	-28.1	-45.0	17.5	23.5	15.8	7.3	-13.7	0.5	30.2	52.1
% 1980-1983	-11.0	0.0	-10.0	-16.7	-14.3	-36.4	0.0	0.0	-16.7	0.0	0.0	-47.9
% 1970-1983	-15.7	-43.9	-35.3	-54.2	0.8	-21.4	15.8	7.3	-28.1	0.5	30.2	-20.8
Ghana												
1970	57	6	8	6	13	9	6	14	-1	-6	2	22
1980	56	4	4	2	19	2	3	12	12	-6	5	18
1983	48	5	2	1	17	-2	5	12	7	-6	5	14
% 1970-1980	-1.8	-32.3	-49.4	-66.2	47.2	-77.6	-49.2	-13.7	1200.9	-1.5	161.8	-18.2
% 1980-1983	-14.3	25.0	-50.0	-50.0	-10.5	-200.0	66.7	0.0	-41.7	0.0	0.0	-22.2
% 1970-1983	-15.8	-15.4	-74.7	-83.1	31.7	-122.4	-15.4	-13.7	742.2	-1.5	161.8	-36.4

Table A.1 (cont.)

COUNTRY	INDEX OF SOCIAL PROGRESS (ISP)	Educa-tion	Health	Women	Defense	Economic	Demo-graphic	Geo-graphic	Partici-pation	Cultural	Welfare	WEIGHTED INDEX OF SOCIAL PROGRESS
Guatemala												
1970	64	4	9	8	17	9	5	-12	14	7	3	30
1980	67	3	8	3	17	12	7	-6	12	7	5	30
1983	59	3	8	4	14	11	8	-6	6	7	5	27
% 1970-1980	4.7	-23.3	-10.2	-62.1	0.5	34.7	42.6	50.4	-13.7	1.3	71.8	0.0
% 1980-1983	-11.9	0.0	0.0	33.3	-17.6	-8.3	14.3	0.0	-50.0	0.0	0.0	-10.0
% 1970-1983	-7.8	-23.3	-10.2	-49.4	-17.2	23.5	62.9	50.4	-56.9	1.3	71.8	-10.0
Honduras												
1970	88	9	12	10	14	9	4	-1	11	18	2	40
1980	80	8	8	8	12	4	5	1	10	18	5	35
1983	92	10	8	9	12	8	5	1	15	18	5	41
% 1970-1980	-9.1	-10.2	-32.8	-19.3	-13.7	-55.1	27.9	191.7	-8.3	0.5	161.8	-12.5
% 1980-1983	15.0	25.0	0.0	12.5	0.0	100.0	0.0	0.0	50.0	0.0	0.0	17.1
% 1970-1983	4.5	12.2	-32.8	-9.2	-13.7	-10.2	27.9	191.7	37.5	0.5	161.8	2.5
Hong Kong												
1970	NA	NA	NA	NA	NA	NA	NA	NA	NA	NA	NA	NA
1980	129	12	19	11	17	11	18	6	15	17	6	59
1983	132	12	19	10	16	16	17	6	15	17	6	60
% 1970-1980	NA	NA	NA	NA	NA	NA	NA	NA	NA	NA	NA	NA
% 1980-1983	2.3	0.0	0.0	-9.1	-5.9	45.5	-5.6	0.0	0.0	0.0	0.0	1.7
% 1970-1983	NA	NA	NA	NA	NA	NA	NA	NA	NA	NA	NA	NA
India												
1970	54	4	5	8	12	5	-10	7	15	1	7	19
1980	70	3	4	3	14	9	-2	3	22	6	8	27
1983	72	3	7	3	13	11	-3	3	21	6	8	28
% 1970-1980	29.6	-23.3	-18.5	-62.1	17.5	83.3	80.2	-56.6	47.6	559.3	15.8	42.1
% 1980-1983	2.9	0.0	75.0	0.0	-7.1	22.2	-50.0	0.0	-4.5	0.0	0.0	3.7
% 1970-1983	33.3	-23.3	42.6	-62.1	9.2	124.0	70.3	-56.6	40.8	559.3	15.8	47.4
Indonesia												
1970	26	5	2	10	11	-23	0	6	8	4	3	9
1980	95	9	7	23	13	10	7	9	9	4	6	42
1983	101	11	6	24	12	13	6	9	9	4	6	45
% 1970-1980	265.4	83.3	266.5	132.1	19.2	5600.0	700.0	52.3	13.8	2.3	106.2	366.7
% 1980-1983	6.3	22.2	-14.3	4.3	-7.7	30.0	-14.3	0.0	0.0	0.0	0.0	7.1
% 1970-1983	288.5	124.0	214.1	142.2	10.0	5900.0	676.0	52.3	13.8	2.3	106.2	400.0
Iran												
1970	65	5	8	2	5	14	5	-5	13	8	10	32
1980	76	15	6	6	6	12	6	-5	7	11	12	38
1983	90	12	10	5	11	21	7	-5	6	11	12	43
% 1970-1980	16.9	205.5	-24.1	214.1	22.2	-13.7	22.2	-1.8	-45.8	39.1	21.1	18.8
% 1980-1983	18.4	-20.0	66.7	-16.7	83.3	75.0	16.7	0.0	-14.3	0.0	0.0	13.2
% 1970-1983	38.5	144.4	26.4	161.8	124.0	51.0	42.6	-1.8	-53.5	39.1	21.1	34.4
Iraq												
1970	62	13	14	-3	-10	11	6	10	1	14	6	32
1980	61	11	11	12	-21	13	4	12	-2	14	7	35

Table A.1 (cont.)

COUNTRY	INDEX OF SOCIAL PROGRESS (ISP)	Education	Health	Women	Defense	Economic	Demographic	Geographic	Participation	Cultural	Welfare	WEIGHTED INDEX OF SOCIAL PROGRESS
1983	49	10	12	12	-50	28	4	12	0	14	8	37
% 1970-1980	-1.6	-14.8	-20.9	488.3	-108.1	19.2	-32.3	21.1	-319.8	0.6	18.4	9.4
% 1980-1983	-19.7	-9.1	9.1	0.0	-138.1	115.4	0.0	0.0	100.0	0.0	14.3	5.7
% 1970-1983	-21.0	-22.5	-13.7	488.3	-395.5	156.6	-32.3	21.1	-100.0	0.6	35.4	15.6
Ivory Coast												
1970	68	5	1	4	16	11	6	14	9	-4	6	24
1980	65	11	2	5	17	8	0	11	7	-6	9	24
1983	63	6	5	4	16	7	2	11	9	-6	9	23
% 1970-1980	-4.4	124.0	119.8	27.9	6.9	-26.7	-100.0	-20.9	-21.4	-46.7	52.3	0.0
% 1980-1983	-3.1	-45.5	150.0	-20.0	-5.9	-12.5	200.0	0.0	28.6	0.0	0.0	-4.2
% 1970-1983	-7.4	22.2	449.5	2.3	0.6	-35.8	-66.2	-20.9	1.0	-46.7	52.3	-4.2
Jamaica												
1970	129	11	17	14	18	12	11	12	11	19	4	55
1980	141	16	18	22	17	3	12	13	21	16	4	62
1983	137	15	15	21	16	5	12	13	21	16	4	60
% 1970-1980	9.3	46.7	6.4	58.2	-5.1	-74.8	10.0	9.2	92.5	-15.4	2.3	12.7
% 1980-1983	-2.8	-6.3	-16.7	-4.5	-5.9	66.7	0.0	0.0	0.0	0.0	0.0	-3.2
% 1970-1983	6.2	37.5	-11.3	51.0	-10.7	-58.0	10.0	9.2	92.5	-15.4	2.3	9.1
Jordan												
1970	41	5	15	5	-33	8	4	8	5	20	4	29
1980	62	13	11	21	-31	10	5	10	1	19	2	39
1983	95	12	14	21	-4	12	6	10	1	19	3	47
% 1970-1980	51.2	164.8	-26.2	327.7	6.3	26.4	27.9	26.4	-79.6	-4.6	-48.8	34.5
% 1980-1983	53.2	-7.7	27.3	0.0	87.1	20.0	20.0	0.0	0.0	0.0	50.0	20.5
% 1970-1983	131.7	144.4	-6.1	327.7	87.9	51.7	53.5	26.4	-79.6	-4.6	-23.3	62.1
Kampuchea												
1970	48	10	4	3	5	-15	13	4	3	14	7	23
1980	41	-4	-3	6	12	2	8	8	-2	16	-2	12
1983	41	-6	-6	4	12	8	8	8	-2	16	-2	11
% 1970-1980	-14.6	-140.4	-176.7	106.2	144.4	3200.0	-38.0	104.6	-168.7	15.0	-128.9	-47.8
% 1980-1983	0.0	-50.0	-100.0	-33.3	0.0	300.0	0.0	0.0	0.0	0.0	0.0	-8.3
% 1970-1983	-14.6	-160.5	-253.5	37.5	144.4	3800.0	-38.0	104.6	-168.7	15.0	-128.9	-52.2
Kenya												
1970	68	7	11	2	16	13	5	8	9	-4	2	27
1980	63	13	6	5	11	7	2	10	10	-5	4	26
1983	65	12	6	8	15	6	1	10	9	-5	4	26
% 1970-1980	-7.4	88.1	-45.0	161.8	-30.9	-45.8	-59.3	26.4	12.2	-22.2	109.4	-3.7
% 1980-1983	3.2	-7.7	0.0	60.0	36.4	-14.3	-50.0	0.0	-10.0	0.0	0.0	0.0
% 1970-1983	-4.4	73.7	-45.0	318.8	-5.7	-53.5	-79.6	26.4	1.0	-22.2	109.4	-3.7
Korea, Dem. (N)												
1970	NA	NA	NA	NA	NA	NA	NA	NA	NA	NA	NA	NA
1980	70	6	17	17	-17	13	12	7	-2	18	-2	40
1983	78	5	17	18	-6	11	12	7	-2	18	-2	41
% 1970-1980	NA	NA	NA	NA	NA	NA	NA	NA	NA	NA	NA	NA
% 1980-1983	11.4	-16.7	0.0	5.9	64.7	-15.4	0.0	0.0	0.0	0.0	0.0	2.5

Table A.1 (cont.)

COUNTRY	INDEX OF SOCIAL PROGRESS (ISP)	Educa-tion	Health	Women	Defense	Economic	Demo-graphic	Geo-graphic	Partici-pation	Cultural	Welfare	WEIGHTED INDEX OF SOCIAL PROGRESS
% 1970-1983	NA	NA	NA	NA	NA	NA	NA	NA	NA	NA	NA	NA
Korea, Rep. (S)												
1970	103	9	17	15	9	12	10	2	14	14	1	49
1980	117	11	17	13	8	15	15	5	10	18	4	55
1983	112	12	16	13	10	13	16	5	7	18	4	53
% 1970-1980	13.6	23.5	0.5	-12.8	-10.2	25.9	51.4	161.8	-28.1	29.4	339.6	12.2
% 1980-1983	-4.3	9.1	-5.9	0.0	25.0	-13.3	6.7	0.0	-30.0	0.0	0.0	-3.6
% 1970-1983	8.7	34.7	-5.4	-12.8	12.2	9.2	61.5	161.8	-49.7	29.4	339.6	8.2
Lebanon												
1970	117	15	16	10	12	10	14	10	13	11	6	53
1980	137	16	14	27	9	12	14	14	12	11	9	64
1983	136	16	15	27	6	12	15	14	10	11	9	64
% 1970-1980	17.1	7.3	-12.0	172.5	-24.4	21.1	0.6	41.3	-7.0	0.8	52.3	20.8
% 1980-1983	-0.7	0.0	7.1	0.0	-33.3	0.0	7.1	0.0	-16.7	0.0	0.0	0.0
% 1970-1983	16.2	7.3	-5.7	172.5	-49.6	21.1	7.8	41.3	-22.5	0.8	52.3	20.8
Liberia												
1970	68	-1	5	2	17	11	9	10	16	-1	0	24
1980	53	6	4	1	16	6	5	6	7	1	2	20
1983	48	6	4	-1	14	5	3	6	9	1	2	17
% 1970-1980	-22.1	650.5	-18.5	-47.6	-5.4	-45.0	-43.9	-39.5	-56.0	191.7	200.0	-16.7
% 1980-1983	-9.4	0.0	0.0	-200.0	-12.5	-16.7	-40.0	0.0	28.6	0.0	0.0	-15.0
% 1970-1983	-29.4	650.5	-18.5	-152.4	-17.2	-54.2	-66.3	-39.5	-43.4	191.7	200.0	-29.2
Libya	-											
1970	47	12	-3	-1	-4	14	5	6	-1	17	2	21
1980	90	10	15	5	4	21	3	9	1	18	4	40
1983	70	11	15	3	-7	11	3	9	1	18	5	35
% 1970-1980	91.5	-16.0	585.4	558.7	197.8	51.0	-38.9	52.3	191.7	6.4	109.4	90.5
% 1980-1983	-22.2	10.0	0.0	-40.0	-275.0	-47.6	0.0	0.0	0.0	0.0	25.0	-12.5
% 1970-1983	48.9	-7.6	585.4	375.2	-71.1	-20.9	-38.9	52.3	191.7	6.4	161.8	66.7
Madagascar												
1970	81	-1	6	10	15	8	4	15	9	8	7	30
1980	76	6	5	11	12	4	5	10	1	12	9	31
1983	83	7	8	10	15	4	4	10	3	12	9	34
% 1970-1980	-6.2	650.5	-15.4	11.0	-19.5	-49.4	27.9	-32.9	-88.8	51.7	30.2	3.3
% 1980-1983	9.2	16.7	60.0	-9.1	25.0	0.0	-20.0	0.0	200.0	0.0	0.0	9.7
% 1970-1983	2.5	742.2	35.4	0.9	0.6	-49.4	2.3	-32.9	-66.3	51.7	30.2	13.3
Malaysia												
1970	80	10	13	8	11	10	7	8	12	-4	5	36
1980	102	14	16	9	11	13	12	12	13	-3	5	46
1983	102	16	16	8	10	13	12	12	13	-3	5	46
% 1970-1980	27.5	41.3	23.9	13.8	0.8	31.2	73.7	51.7	9.2	26.7	1.8	27.8
% 1980-1983	0.0	14.3	0.0	-11.1	-9.1	0.0	0.0	0.0	0.0	0.0	0.0	0.0
% 1970-1983	27.5	61.5	23.9	1.1	-8.3	31.2	73.7	51.7	9.2	26.7	1.8	27.8
Mauritania												

176

Table A.1 (cont.)

COUNTRY	INDEX OF SOCIAL PROGRESS (ISP)	Educa-tion	Health	Women	Defense	Economic	Demo-graphic	Geo-graphic	Partici-pation	Cultural	Welfare	WEIGHTED INDEX OF SOCIAL PROGRESS
1970	63	6	-2	-1	16	4	7	3	9	15	6	23
1980	21	0	0	1	-2	-5	3	1	1	15	9	10
1983	38	-1	1	-1	10	1	5	1	0	15	9	14
% 1970-1980	-66.7	-100.0	100.0	191.7	-112.6	-227.9	-56.6	-65.6	-88.8	0.6	52.3	-56.5
% 1980-1983	81.0	-100.0	100.0	-200.0	600.0	120.0	66.7	0.0	-100.0	0.0	0.0	40.0
% 1970-1983	-39.7	-116.9	147.8	0.0	-37.1	-74.4	-27.6	-65.6	-100.0	0.6	52.3	-39.1
Mauritius												
1970	NA	NA	NA	NA	NA	NA	NA	NA	NA	NA	NA	NA
1980	133	16	16	14	19	12	10	21	15	1	8	56
1983	136	15	15	14	18	10	16	21	18	1	8	58
% 1970-1980	NA	NA	NA	NA	NA	NA	NA	NA	NA	NA	NA	NA
% 1980-1983	2.3	-6.3	-6.3	0.0	-5.3	-16.7	60.0	0.0	20.0	0.0	0.0	3.6
% 1970-1983	NA	NA	NA	NA	NA	NA	NA	NA	NA	NA	NA	NA
Mexico												
1970	119	8	14	15	17	12	6	12	14	15	6	50
1980	116	12	15	13	19	9	7	6	15	12	8	51
1983	114	12	16	14	17	8	8	6	13	12	8	51
% 1970-1980	-2.5	51.7	7.8	-12.8	12.4	-24.4	18.4	-49.6	7.8	-19.5	35.4	2.0
% 1980-1983	-1.7	0.0	6.7	7.7	-10.5	-11.1	14.3	0.0	-13.3	0.0	0.0	0.0
% 1970-1983	-4.2	51.7	15.0	-6.1	0.5	-32.8	35.4	-49.6	-6.5	-19.5	35.4	2.0
Mongolia												
1970	NA	NA	NA	NA	NA	NA	NA	NA	NA	NA	NA	NA
1980	71	10	14	10	1	7	12	4	-2	14	-2	37
1983	75	9	14	12	4	7	13	4	-2	14	-2	38
% 1970-1980	NA	NA	NA	NA	NA	NA	NA	NA	NA	NA	NA	NA
% 1980-1983	5.6	-10.0	0.0	20.0	300.0	0.0	8.3	0.0	0.0	0.0	0.0	2.7
% 1970-1983	NA	NA	NA	NA	NA	NA	NA	NA	NA	NA	NA	NA
Morocco												
1970	73	7	4	-1	12	10	4	8	8	11	10	29
1980	88	7	8	3	6	6	5	13	13	16	11	36
1983	87	9	6	4	6	6	6	13	10	16	11	36
% 1970-1980	20.5	1.3	104.6	375.2	-49.6	-39.5	27.9	64.3	64.3	46.7	11.0	24.1
% 1980-1983	-1.1	28.6	-25.0	33.3	0.0	0.0	20.0	0.0	-23.1	0.0	0.0	0.0
% 1970-1983	19.2	30.2	53.5	467.0	-49.6	-39.5	53.5	64.3	26.4	46.7	11.0	24.1
Mozambique												
1970	NA	NA	NA	NA	NA	NA	NA	NA	NA	NA	NA	NA
1980	22	-5	-6	2	13	3	1	9	-2	7	-2	2
1983	34	1	-3	6	13	0	3	9	0	7	-2	9
% 1970-1980	NA	NA	NA	NA	NA	NA	NA	NA	NA	NA	NA	NA
% 1980-1983	54.5	120.0	-50.0	200.0	0.0	-100.0	200.0	0.0	100.0	0.0	0.0	350.0
% 1970-1983	NA	NA	NA	NA	NA	NA	NA	NA	NA	NA	NA	NA
Nicaragua												
1970	81	7	12	10	16	8	3	-8	11	18	4	38
1980	68	9	9	9	9	1	5	-3	9	15	7	33
1983	63	12	9	11	3	-3	4	-3	7	15	7	33

Table A.1 (cont.)

COUNTRY	INDEX OF SOCIAL PROGRESS (ISP)	Educa- tion	Health	Women	Defense	Economic	Demo- graphic	Geo- graphic	Partici- pation	Cultural	Welfare	WEIGHTED INDEX OF SOCIAL PROGRESS
X 1970-1980	-16.0	30.2	-24.4	-9.2	-43.4	-87.4	71.8	62.9	-17.5	-16.2	79.0	-13.2
X 1980-1983	-7.4	33.3	0.0	22.2	-66.7	-400.0	-20.0	0.0	-22.2	0.0	0.0	0.0
X 1970-1983	-22.2	73.7	-24.4	11.0	-81.1	-137.9	37.5	62.9	-35.8	-16.2	79.0	-13.2
Nigeria												
1970	19	2	6	1	0	2	2	14	-2	-8	2	6
1980	72	8	2	4	14	9	3	16	21	-10	5	26
1983	72	7	4	2	14	10	2	16	21	-10	5	25
X 1970-1980	278.9	318.8	-66.2	339.6	1400.0	371.2	57.1	15.0	1104.8	-23.6	161.8	333.3
X 1980-1983	0.0	-12.5	100.0	-50.0	0.0	11.1	-33.3	0.0	0.0	0.0	0.0	-3.8
X 1970-1983	278.9	266.5	-32.3	119.8	1400.0	423.6	4.7	15.0	1104.8	-23.6	161.8	316.7
Pakistan												
1970	53	-3	10		10	9	3	9	3	8	4	20
1980	50	-2	8	-2	10	7	3	9	1	10	5	18
1983	50	-2	5	-3	10	10	3	9	2	10	5	17
X 1970-1980	-5.7	35.3	-19.3	-200.0	0.9	-21.4	3.1	1.0	-65.6	26.4	27.9	-10.0
X 1980-1983	0.0	0.0	-37.5	-50.0	0.0	42.9	0.0	0.0	100.0	0.0	0.0	-5.6
X 1970-1983	-5.7	35.3	-49.5	-300.0	0.9	12.2	3.1	1.0	-31.3	26.4	27.9	-15.0
Panama												
1970	125	16	16	14	17	9	8	7	13	17	8	56
1980	125	16	15	14	17	6	13	10	9	15	10	56
1983	129	16	16	15	16	8	13	10	10	15	10	58
X 1970-1980	0.0	0.6	-5.7	0.6	0.5	-32.7	64.3	44.7	-30.3	-11.3	26.4	0.0
X 1980-1983	3.2	0.0	6.7	7.1	-5.9	33.3	0.0	0.0	11.1	0.0	0.0	3.6
X 1970-1983	3.2	0.6	0.6	7.8	-5.4	-10.2	64.3	44.7	-22.5	-11.3	26.4	3.6
Papua-New Guinea												
1970	NA	NA	NA	NA	NA	NA	NA	NA	NA	NA	NA	NA
1980	71	6	4	4	16	10	8	2	22	0	0	29
1983	71	9	3	6	16	8	8	2	22	0	0	29
X 1970-1980	NA	NA	NA	NA	NA	NA	NA	NA	NA	NA	NA	NA
X 1980-1983	0.0	50.0	-25.0	50.0	0.0	-20.0	0.0	0.0	0.0	0.0	0.0	0.0
X 1970-1983	NA	NA	NA	NA	NA	NA	NA	NA	NA	NA	NA	NA
Paraguay												
1970	113	11	15	10	14	9	7	10	10	18	9	49
1980	123	9	17	12	16	11	9	10	9	18	11	54
1983	123	9	15	13	15	12	11	10	9	18	11	54
X 1970-1980	8.8	-17.5	14.0	21.1	15.0	23.5	30.2	0.9	-9.2	0.5	23.5	10.2
X 1980-1983	0.0	0.0	-11.8	8.3	-6.3	9.1	22.2	0.0	0.0	0.0	0.0	0.0
X 1970-1983	8.8	-17.5	0.6	31.2	7.8	34.7	59.2	0.9	-9.2	0.5	23.5	10.2
Peru												
1970	79	11	11	12	11	2	7	1	7	7	10	38
1980	77	11	9	9	9	3	9	0	10	5	11	37
1983	82	11	7	12	10	1	9	0	16	5	11	39
X 1970-1980	-2.5	0.8	-17.5	-24.4	-17.5	57.1	30.2	-100.0	44.7	-27.6	11.0	-2.6
X 1980-1983	6.5	0.0	-22.2	33.3	11.1	-66.7	0.0	0.0	60.0	0.0	0.0	5.4
X 1970-1983	3.8	0.8	-35.8	0.8	-8.3	-47.6	30.2	-100.0	131.5	-27.6	11.0	2.6

Table A.1 (cont.)

COUNTRY	INDEX OF SOCIAL PROGRESS (ISP)	Educa-tion	Health	Women	Defense	Economic	Demo-graphic	Geo-graphic	Partici-pation	Cultural	Welfare	WEIGHTED INDEX OF SOCIAL PROGRESS
Philippines												
1970	97	14	10	15	16	9	5	8	13	2	5	42
1980	93	11	12	9	16	11	10	8	9	-1	7	41
1983	92	10	12	7	15	11	10	8	9	-1	7	41
% 1970-1980	-4.1	-20.9	21.1	-39.6	0.6	23.5	103.7	1.1	-30.3	-152.4	42.6	-2.4
% 1980-1983	-1.1	-9.1	0.0	-22.2	-6.3	0.0	0.0	0.0	0.0	0.0	0.0	0.0
% 1970-1983	-5.2	-28.1	21.1	-53.1	-5.7	23.5	103.7	1.1	-30.3	-152.4	42.6	-2.4
Saudi Arabia												
1970	NA	NA	NA	NA	NA	NA	NA	NA	NA	NA	NA	NA
1980	62	9	9	-1	-7	16	3	9	1	20	4	29
1983	48	9	11	-1	-17	10	3	9	0	20	4	26
% 1970-1980	NA	NA	NA	NA	NA	NA	NA	NA	NA	NA	NA	NA
% 1980-1983	-22.6	0.0	22.2	0.0	-142.9	-37.5	0.0	0.0	-100.0	0.0	0.0	-10.3
% 1970-1983	NA	NA	NA	NA	NA	NA	NA	NA	NA	NA	NA	NA
Senegal												
1970	76	1	6	3	15	10	6	15	9	4	7	27
1980	57	1	1	-2	15	4	3	11	14	3	8	18
1983	54	1	1	-2	15	2	4	11	12	3	8	18
% 1970-1980	-25.0	9.9	-83.1	-168.7	0.6	-59.6	-49.2	-26.2	57.1	-23.3	15.8	-33.3
% 1980-1983	-5.3	0.0	0.0	0.0	0.0	-50.0	33.3	0.0	-14.3	0.0	0.0	0.0
% 1970-1983	-28.9	9.9	-83.1	-168.7	0.6	-79.8	-32.3	-26.2	34.7	-23.3	15.8	-33.3
Singapore												
1970	105	14	19	7	7	13	16	10	8	6	5	50
1980	127	12	20	12	9	22	20	11	9	7	5	60
1983	126	14	19	13	10	18	19	11	10	7	5	59
% 1970-1980	21.0	-13.7	5.8	73.7	30.2	70.4	25.7	11.0	13.8	18.4	1.8	20.0
% 1980-1983	-0.8	16.7	-5.0	8.3	11.1	-18.2	-5.0	0.0	11.1	0.0	0.0	-1.7
% 1970-1983	20.0	0.6	0.5	88.1	44.7	39.4	19.4	11.0	26.4	18.4	1.8	18.0
Sri Lanka												
1970	118	11	15	16	17	11	12	12	12	6	6	51
1980	129	12	12	14	16	10	15	16	21	7	7	55
1983	128	11	13	14	16	12	15	16	17	7	7	55
% 1970-1980	9.3	10.0	-19.5	-12.0	-5.4	-8.3	25.9	34.3	76.3	18.4	18.4	7.8
% 1980-1983	-0.8	-8.3	8.3	0.0	0.0	20.0	0.0	0.0	-19.0	0.0	0.0	0.0
% 1970-1983	8.5	0.8	-12.8	-12.0	-5.4	10.0	25.9	34.3	42.7	18.4	18.4	7.8
Syria												
1970	70	9	14	2	-6	13	5	15	1	15	2	32
1980	81	10	15	8	-11	16	6	15	7	12	3	40
1983	93	13	15	8	-1	16	6	15	4	12	3	43
% 1970-1980	15.7	12.2	7.8	318.8	-80.6	23.9	22.2	0.6	669.2	-19.5	57.1	25.0
% 1980-1983	14.8	30.0	0.0	0.0	90.9	0.0	0.0	0.0	-42.9	0.0	0.0	7.5
% 1970-1983	32.9	45.9	7.8	318.8	83.6	23.9	22.2	0.6	339.6	-19.5	57.1	34.4
Taiwan												
1970	NA	NA	NA	NA	NA	NA	NA	NA	NA	NA	NA	NA

179

Table A.1 (cont.)

COUNTRY	! INDEX OF! SOCIAL PROGRESS! (ISP)	Education	Health	Women	Defense	Economic	Demographic	Geographic	Participation	Cultural	Welfare	! WEIGHTED INDEX OF SOCIAL PROGRESS
1980 !	96 !	11	18	27	-32	13	15	11	9	17	7 !	58
1983 !	87 !	10	17	26	-40	15	14	11	9	17	8 !	55
% 1970-1980 !	NA !	NA	NA	NA	NA	NA	NA	NA	NA	NA	NA !	NA
% 1980-1983 !	-9.4 !	-9.1	-5.6	-3.7	-25.0	15.4	-6.7	0.0	0.0	0.0	14.3 !	-5.2
% 1970-1983 !	NA !	NA	NA	NA	NA	NA	NA	NA	NA	NA	NA !	NA
Thailand												
1970 !	102 !	10	13	15	12	13	7	9	9	12	2 !	45
1980 !	123 !	12	11	12	12	15	11	17	14	15	4 !	52
1983 !	122 !	13	11	12	12	13	12	17	13	15	4 !	52
% 1970-1980 !	20.6 !	21.1	-14.8	-19.5	0.8	16.2	59.2	90.8	57.1	25.9	109.4 !	15.6
% 1980-1983 !	-0.8 !	8.3	0.0	0.0	0.0	-13.3	9.1	0.0	-7.1	0.0	0.0 !	0.0
% 1970-1983 !	19.6 !	31.2	-14.8	-19.5	0.8	0.7	73.7	90.8	45.9	25.9	109.4 !	15.6
Trinidad/Tobago												
1970 !	122 !	14	16	15	18	9	15	11	11	9	4 !	54
1980 !	134 !	12	16	12	18	10	17	16	22	4	7 !	57
1983 !	134 !	15	17	12	13	10	16	16	24	4	7 !	59
% 1970-1980 !	9.8 !	-13.7	0.6	-19.5	0.5	12.2	14.0	46.7	101.6	-55.1	79.0 !	5.6
% 1980-1983 !	0.0 !	25.0	6.3	0.0	-27.8	0.0	-5.9	0.0	9.1	0.0	0.0 !	3.5
% 1970-1983 !	9.8 !	7.8	6.9	-19.5	-27.4	12.2	7.3	46.7	120.0	-55.1	79.0 !	9.3
Tunisia												
1970 !	108 !	14	9	4	15	9	7	13	10	19	8 !	44
1980 !	114 !	9	11	6	12	13	11	15	7	19	11 !	48
1983 !	117 !	11	11	8	14	9	10	15	9	19	11 !	49
% 1970-1980 !	5.6 !	-35.3	23.5	53.5	-19.5	45.9	59.2	16.2	-29.4	0.5	39.1 !	9.1
% 1980-1983 !	2.6 !	22.2	0.0	33.3	16.7	-30.8	-9.1	0.0	28.6	0.0	0.0 !	2.1
% 1970-1983 !	8.3 !	-20.9	23.5	104.6	-6.1	1.0	44.7	16.2	-9.2	0.5	39.1 !	11.4
Turkey												
1970 !	102 !	10	6	13	8	8	8	12	14	17	6 !	44
1980 !	114 !	11	12	10	6	9	10	10	21	17	3 !	49
1983 !	105 !	10	13	9	5	7	11	10	14	17	3 !	46
% 1970-1980 !	11.8 !	11.0	103.0	-22.5	-24.1	13.8	26.4	-16.0	51.0	0.5	-49.2 !	11.4
% 1980-1983 !	-7.9 !	-9.1	8.3	-10.0	-16.7	-22.2	10.0	0.0	-33.3	0.0	0.0 !	-6.1
% 1970-1983 !	2.9 !	0.9	120.0	-30.3	-36.8	-11.5	39.1	-16.0	0.6	0.5	-49.2 !	4.5
Uruguay												
1970 !	147 !	17	17	18	15	-2	19	19	14	13	17 !	66
1980 !	135 !	13	16	21	14	4	19	11	1	12	25 !	63
1983 !	142 !	14	15	22	13	6	19	11	6	12	25 !	66
% 1970-1980 !	-8.2 !	-23.1	-5.4	17.3	-6.1	291.4	0.5	-41.8	-92.8	-7.0	47.8 !	-4.5
% 1980-1983 !	5.2 !	7.7	-6.3	4.8	-7.1	50.0	0.0	0.0	500.0	0.0	0.0 !	4.8
% 1970-1983 !	-3.4 !	-17.2	-11.3	22.8	-12.8	387.1	0.5	-41.8	-56.9	-7.0	47.8 !	0.0
Venezuela												
1970 !	125 !	14	17	13	14	13	7	9	14	19	5 !	55
1980 !	142 !	15	15	18	17	11	10	9	24	15	7 !	63
1983 !	140 !	16	14	20	16	10	9	9	24	15	8 !	62
% 1970-1980 !	13.6 !	7.8	-11.3	39.4	22.2	-14.8	44.7	1.0	72.5	-20.7	42.6 !	14.5

Table A.1 (cont.)

COUNTRY	INDEX OF SOCIAL PROGRESS (ISP)	Education	Health	Women	Defense	Economic	Demographic	Geographic	Participation	Cultural	Welfare	WEIGHTED INDEX OF SOCIAL PROGRESS
% 1980-1983	-1.4	6.7	-6.7	11.1	-5.9	-9.1	-10.0	0.0	0.0	0.0	14.3	-1.6
% 1970-1983	12.0	15.0	-17.2	54.9	15.0	-22.5	30.2	1.0	72.5	-20.7	62.9	12.7
Vietnam												
1970	41	2	10	12	-25	3	11	8	3	10	7	28
1980	79	11	7	13	12	9	8	9	-2	13	-2	33
1983	84	10	10	13	12	10	8	9	0	13	-2	36
% 1970-1980	92.7	475.9	-29.4	9.2	147.8	209.3	-26.7	13.8	-168.7	31.2	-128.9	17.9
% 1980-1983	6.3	-9.1	42.9	0.0	0.0	11.1	0.0	0.0	-100.0	0.0	0.0	9.1
% 1970-1983	104.9	423.6	0.9	9.2	147.8	243.6	-26.7	13.8	-100.0	31.2	-128.9	28.6
Zaire												
1970	43	9	-4	3	11	6	5	11	3	-6	5	15
1980	55	10	2	7	14	-2	3	10	1	2	8	21
1983	57	10	3	6	16	-1	4	10	0	2	8	22
% 1970-1980	27.9	12.2	148.9	140.5	28.3	-133.8	-38.9	-8.3	-65.6	132.8	62.9	40.0
% 1980-1983	3.6	0.0	50.0	-14.3	14.3	-50.0	33.3	0.0	-100.0	0.0	0.0	4.8
% 1970-1983	32.6	12.2	173.3	106.2	46.7	-116.9	-18.5	-8.3	-100.0	132.8	62.9	46.7
Zambia												
1970	72	8	9	2	17	7	3	12	11	0	3	27
1980	51	9	4	9	-9	4	3	9	9	8	5	25
1983	51	9	4	10	-4	1	3	9	7	8	5	24
% 1970-1980	-29.2	13.8	-55.1	371.2	-153.2	-42.1	3.1	-24.4	-17.5	898.0	71.8	-7.4
% 1980-1983	0.0	0.0	0.0	11.1	55.6	-75.0	0.0	0.0	-22.2	0.0	0.0	-4.0
% 1970-1983	-29.2	13.8	-55.1	423.6	-123.7	-85.5	3.1	-24.4	-35.8	898.0	71.8	-11.1
Zimbabwe												
1970	78	10	12	4	15	9	5	8	11	7	-3	32
1980	67	9	6	12	3	8	2	10	10	9	-2	29
1983	84	19	6	14	9	6	2	10	10	9	-2	37
% 1970-1980	-14.1	-9.2	-49.6	206.9	-79.9	-10.2	-59.3	26.4	-8.3	30.2	35.3	-9.4
% 1980-1983	25.4	111.1	0.0	16.7	200.0	-25.0	0.0	0.0	0.0	0.0	0.0	27.6
% 1970-1983	7.7	91.7	-49.6	258.1	-39.6	-32.7	-59.3	26.4	-8.3	30.2	35.3	15.6

LEAST DEVELOPING COUNTRIES (N=25)

COUNTRY	ISP	Education	Health	Women	Defense	Economic	Demographic	Geographic	Participation	Cultural	Welfare	Weighted ISP
Afghanistan*												
1970	NA	NA	NA	NA	NA	NA	NA	NA	NA	NA	NA	NA
1980	24	-2	-6	-4	8	7	1	10	-2	7	4	4
1983	26	-3	-6	-4	11	9	-2	10	-2	7	4	3
% 1970-1980	NA	NA	NA	NA	NA	NA	NA	NA	NA	NA	NA	NA
% 1980-1983	8.3	-50.0	0.0	0.0	37.5	28.6	-300.0	0.0	0.0	0.0	0.0	-25.0
% 1970-1983	NA	NA	NA	NA	NA	NA	NA	NA	NA	NA	NA	NA
Bangladesh*												
1970	NA	NA	NA	NA	NA	NA	NA	NA	NA	NA	NA	NA
1980	49	-1	1	0	16	4	3	-6	15	18	-2	18
1983	42	-1	1	-1	15	8	4	-6	7	18	-2	16
% 1970-1980	NA	NA	NA	NA	NA	NA	NA	NA	NA	NA	NA	NA

181

Table A.1 (cont.)

COUNTRY	INDEX OF SOCIAL PROGRESS (ISP)	Education	Health	Women	Defense	Economic	Demographic	Geographic	Participation	Cultural	Welfare	WEIGHTED INDEX OF SOCIAL PROGRESS
% 1980-1983	-14.3	0.0	0.0	-100.0	-6.3	100.0	33.3	0.0	-53.3	0.0	0.0	-11.1
% 1970-1983	NA	NA	NA	NA	NA	NA	NA	NA	NA	NA	NA	NA
Benin*												
1970	43	2	0	1	14	7	5	7	-1	3	5	14
1980	52	3	1	0	16	6	3	11	0	3	9	17
1983	50	4	0	0	14	6	2	11	0	3	9	16
% 1970-1980	20.9	57.1	-1211.1	-100.0	15.0	-13.2	-38.9	59.2	100.0	3.1	83.3	21.4
% 1980-1983	-3.8	33.3	-100.0	-100.0	-12.5	0.0	-33.3	0.0	0.0	0.0	0.0	-5.9
% 1970-1983	16.3	109.4	-100.0	-100.0	0.6	-13.2	-59.3	59.2	0.0	3.1	83.3	14.3
Burkina-Faso*												
1970	35	-2	-17	1	16	6	4	19	-2	4	6	3
1980	46	-7	-10	-1	14	6	3	11	21	0	9	11
1983	45	-8	-9	4	14	8	4	11	11	0	9	11
% 1970-1980	31.4	-234.9	41.5	-209.9	-12.0	1.5	-23.3	-41.8	1104.8	-100.0	52.3	266.7
% 1980-1983	-2.2	-14.3	10.0	500.0	0.0	33.3	33.3	0.0	-47.6	0.0	0.0	0.0
% 1970-1983	28.6	-282.8	47.3	339.6	-12.0	35.4	2.3	-41.8	626.3	-100.0	52.3	266.7
Burundi*												
1970	35	1	-10	-2	16	7	2	14	0	5	2	5
1980	41	-1	-5	-4	13	9	4	19	-2	3	5	8
1983	45	-2	-5	-3	13	9	5	19	1	3	6	10
% 1970-1980	17.1	-209.9	50.4	-91.4	-18.3	30.2	109.4	36.6	-212.2	-38.9	161.8	60.0
% 1980-1983	9.8	-100.0	0.0	25.0	0.0	0.0	25.0	0.0	150.0	0.0	20.0	25.0
% 1970-1983	28.6	-319.8	50.4	-43.5	-18.3	30.2	161.8	36.6	100.0	-38.9	214.1	100.0
Central African Republic*												
1970	34	-1	-6	3	12	10	5	5	-1	1	6	10
1980	40	0	-2	0	15	7	7	8	0	-4	9	12
1983	44	1	-2	0	15	7	8	8	2	-4	9	14
% 1970-1980	17.6	100.0	67.2	-100.0	25.9	-29.4	42.6	62.9	100.0	-539.6	52.3	20.0
% 1980-1983	10.0	100.0	0.0	0.0	0.0	0.0	14.3	0.0	200.0	0.0	0.0	16.7
% 1970-1983	29.4	191.7	67.2	-100.0	25.9	-29.4	62.9	62.9	283.5	-539.6	52.3	40.0
Chad*												
1970	25	-7	-10	-1	9	5	6	13	11	-7	6	3
1980	7	-8	-9	-4	10	3	6	10	0	-7	8	-4
1983	13	-10	-10	-6	14	8	6	10	0	-7	8	-3
% 1970-1980	-72.0	-12.8	10.8	-267.0	12.2	-38.9	1.5	-22.5	-100.0	-1.3	35.4	-233.3
% 1980-1983	85.7	-25.0	-11.1	-50.0	40.0	166.7	0.0	0.0	0.0	0.0	0.0	-25.0
% 1970-1983	-48.0	-41.0	-0.9	-450.5	57.1	62.9	1.5	-22.5	-100.0	-1.3	35.4	-200.0
Ethiopia*												
1970	35	-6	-7	-2	14	8	4	17	11	-4	0	4
1980	-8	-6	-12	-3	2	6	2	11	-2	-6	1	-10
1983	3	-5	-10	-4	5	10	3	11	-2	-6	1	-6
% 1970-1980	-122.9	-1.5	-69.3	-43.5	-85.6	-24.1	-48.8	-34.9	-118.3	-46.7	100.0	-350.0
% 1980-1983	-137.5	16.7	16.7	-33.3	150.0	66.7	50.0	0.0	0.0	0.0	0.0	-40.0
% 1970-1983	-91.4	17.9	-41.0	-91.4	-64.1	26.4	-23.3	-34.9	-118.3	-46.7	100.0	-250.0

Table A.1 (cont.)

COUNTRY	INDEX OF SOCIAL PROGRESS (ISP)	Education	Health	Women	Defense	Economic	Demographic	Geographic	Participation	Cultural	Welfare	WEIGHTED INDEX OF SOCIAL PROGRESS
Guinea*												
1970	42	1	-2	1	8	7	4	11	5	0	7	14
1980	22	0	-3	-3	10	2	3	6	-2	0	9	5
1983	21	-1	-4	-4	10	5	1	6	-2	0	10	4
% 1970-1980	-47.6	-100.0	-43.5	-429.7	26.4	-71.1	-23.3	-45.0	-140.7	-100.0	30.2	-64.3
% 1980-1983	-4.5	-100.0	-33.3	-33.3	0.0	150.0	-66.7	0.0	0.0	0.0	11.1	-20.0
% 1970-1983	-50.0	-209.9	-91.4	-539.6	26.4	-27.6	-74.4	-45.0	-140.7	-100.0	44.7	-71.4
Haiti*												
1970	72	4	1	5	14	5	8	3	11	20	1	28
1980	68	-1	5	-1	16	6	10	8	3	18	3	25
1983	67	-2	4	1	16	8	10	8	0	18	3	24
% 1970-1980	-5.6	-125.6	449.5	-120.4	15.0	22.2	26.4	174.9	-72.5	-9.6	229.7	-10.7
% 1980-1983	-1.5	-100.0	-20.0	200.0	0.0	33.3	0.0	0.0	-100.0	0.0	0.0	-4.0
% 1970-1983	-6.9	-151.2	339.6	-79.6	15.0	62.9	26.4	174.9	-100.0	-9.6	229.7	-14.3
Lao PDR*												
1970	NA	NA	NA	NA	NA	NA	NA	NA	NA	NA	NA	NA
1980	53	10	0	8	12	8	6	10	-2	2	-2	20
1983	41	9	-12	6	12	12	6	10	-2	2	-2	12
% 1970-1980	NA	NA	NA	NA	NA	NA	NA	NA	NA	NA	NA	NA
% 1980-1983	-22.6	-10.0	-1200.0	-25.0	0.0	50.0	0.0	0.0	0.0	0.0	0.0	-40.0
% 1970-1983	NA	NA	NA	NA	NA	NA	NA	NA	NA	NA	NA	NA
Lesotho*												
1970	NA	NA	NA	NA	NA	NA	NA	NA	NA	NA	NA	NA
1980	93	9	4	11	16	11	7	11	9	15	-2	36
1983	88	8	3	15	13	8	7	11	9	15	-2	35
% 1970-1980	NA	NA	NA	NA	NA	NA	NA	NA	NA	NA	NA	NA
% 1980-1983	-5.4	-11.1	-25.0	36.4	-18.8	-27.3	0.0	0.0	0.0	0.0	0.0	-2.8
% 1970-1983	NA	NA	NA	NA	NA	NA	NA	NA	NA	NA	NA	NA
Malawi*												
1970	42	2	-4	0	18	7	3	9	8	-3	2	11
1980	28	-3	-7	0	11	7	1	12	0	7	1	4
1983	34	-3	-6	0	15	8	0	12	0	7	1	6
% 1970-1980	-33.3	-257.1	-71.1	-100.0	-38.6	1.3	-65.6	34.7	-100.0	326.5	-47.6	-63.6
% 1980-1983	21.4	0.0	14.3	0.0	36.4	14.3	-100.0	0.0	0.0	0.0	0.0	50.0
% 1970-1983	-19.0	-257.1	-46.7	-100.0	-16.2	15.8	-100.0	34.7	-100.0	326.5	-47.6	-45.5
Mali*												
1970	45	2	-4	2	14	9	3	11	-1	3	6	13
1980	35	-1	-3	-4	14	4	3	9	0	4	9	8
1983	33	-2	-5	-5	14	6	3	9	0	4	9	7
% 1970-1980	-22.2	-152.4	26.7	-309.4	0.6	-55.1	3.1	-17.5	100.0	37.5	52.3	-38.5
% 1980-1983	-5.7	-100.0	-66.7	-25.0	0.0	50.0	0.0	0.0	0.0	0.0	0.0	-12.5
% 1970-1983	-26.7	-204.7	-22.2	-361.8	0.6	-32.7	3.1	-17.5	-100.0	37.5	52.3	-46.2
Nepal*												
1970	49	0	-3	-5	18	6	7	10	11	5	0	13
1980	57	2	-4	1	18	6	5	11	10	5	2	17

Table A.1 (cont.)

COUNTRY	INDEX OF SOCIAL PROGRESS (ISP)	Education	Health	Women	Defense	Economic	Demographic	Geographic	Participation	Cultural	Welfare	WEIGHTED INDEX OF SOCIAL PROGRESS
1983	56	-1	-3	-1	16	8	5	11	13	5	2	16
% 1970-1980	16.3	200.0	-29.4	119.6	0.5	1.5	-27.6	11.0	-8.3	1.8	200.0	30.8
% 1980-1983	-1.8	-150.0	25.0	-200.0	-11.1	33.3	0.0	0.0	30.0	0.0	0.0	-5.9
% 1970-1983	14.3	-100.0	-2.9	80.4	-10.7	35.4	-27.6	11.0	19.2	1.8	200.0	23.1
Niger‡												
1970	34	-4	-10	-1	17	7	3	7	9	3	3	6
1980	39	-2	-4	-4	17	4	2	9	4	6	7	8
1983	41	-3	-3	-6	17	9	2	9	4	6	7	10
% 1970-1980	14.7	51.1	60.4	-267.0	0.5	-42.1	-31.3	30.2	-55.1	106.2	140.5	33.3
% 1980-1983	5.1	-50.0	25.0	-50.0	0.0	125.0	0.0	0.0	0.0	0.0	0.0	25.0
% 1970-1983	20.6	26.7	70.3	-450.5	0.5	30.2	-31.3	30.2	-55.1	106.2	140.5	66.7
Rwanda‡												
1970	62	1	-7	4	15	5	3	17	11	10	3	17
1980	62	1	-3	6	16	8	1	18	1	11	4	18
1983	70	3	-2	5	16	12	1	18	1	11	4	22
% 1970-1980	0.0	9.9	57.7	53.5	7.3	62.9	-65.6	6.4	-90.8	11.0	37.5	5.9
% 1980-1983	12.9	200.0	33.3	-16.7	0.0	50.0	0.0	0.0	0.0	0.0	0.0	22.2
% 1970-1983	12.9	229.7	71.8	27.9	7.3	144.4	-65.6	6.4	-90.8	11.0	37.5	29.4
Sierra Leone‡												
1970	77	1	1	0	17	8	9	18	20	1	2	25
1980	46	2	-3	-1	17	4	5	13	9	-2	2	12
1983	39	1	-6	-1	15	8	2	13	9	-2	2	8
% 1970-1980	-40.3	119.8	-429.7	-100.0	0.5	-49.4	-43.9	-27.4	-54.8	-319.8	4.7	-52.0
% 1980-1983	-15.2	-50.0	100.0	0.0	-11.8	100.0	-60.0	0.0	0.0	0.0	0.0	-33.3
% 1970-1983	-49.4	9.9	-759.3	-100.0	-11.3	1.1	-77.6	-27.4	-54.8	-319.8	4.7	-68.0
Somalia‡												
1970	59	5	0	-4	14	6	5	11	0	20	2	19
1980	36	-3	1	-4	8	2	4	9	-2	19	3	10
1983	28	-5	-1	-4	5	1	2	9	-2	19	3	6
% 1970-1980	-39.0	-161.1	100.0	-2.2	-42.5	-66.2	-18.5	-17.5	-200.0	-4.6	57.1	-47.4
% 1980-1983	-22.2	-66.7	-200.0	0.0	-37.5	-50.0	-50.0	0.0	0.0	0.0	0.0	-40.0
% 1970-1983	-52.5	-201.8	-200.0	-2.2	-64.1	-83.1	-59.3	-17.5	-200.0	-4.6	57.1	-68.4
Sudan‡												
1970	48	0	6	0	10	13	5	8	-1	2	5	18
1980	53	4	4	3	13	4	3	10	9	5	-1	18
1983	52	3	3	2	15	4	3	10	9	5	-1	17
% 1970-1980	10.4	-4000.0	-32.3	-3000.0	31.2	-69.0	-38.9	26.4	925.7	161.8	-120.4	0.0
% 1980-1983	-1.9	-25.0	-25.0	-33.3	15.4	0.0	0.0	0.0	0.0	0.0	0.0	-5.6
% 1970-1983	8.3	-3000.0	-49.2	-2000.0	51.4	-69.0	-38.9	26.4	925.7	161.8	-120.4	-5.6
Tanzania‡												
1970	41	1	0	1	12	9	4	15	8	-12	3	12
1980	52	13	2	10	14	6	3	10	1	-11	2	20
1983	53	10	4	12	14	7	2	10	1	-11	2	21
% 1970-1980	26.8	1328.6	-200.0	998.9	17.5	-32.7	-23.3	-32.9	-87.4	9.0	-31.3	66.7
% 1980-1983	1.9	-23.1	100.0	20.0	0.0	16.7	-33.3	0.0	0.0	0.0	0.0	5.0

Table A.1 (cont.)

COUNTRY	INDEX OF SOCIAL PROGRESS (ISP)	Education	Health	Women	Defense	Economic	Demographic	Geographic	Participation	Cultural	Welfare	WEIGHTED INDEX OF SOCIAL PROGRESS
% 1970-1983	29.3	998.9	-400.0	1218.7	17.5	-21.4	-48.8	-32.9	-87.4	9.0	-31.3	75.0
Togo*												
1970	38	-2	-2	2	16	9	2	10	-1	1	3	9
1980	44	7	2	4	15	1	3	12	0	-5	6	15
1983	49	8	1	6	14	3	3	12	0	-5	6	17
% 1970-1980	15.8	434.9	195.7	109.4	-5.7	-88.8	57.1	21.1	100.0	-649.5	106.2	66.7
% 1980-1983	11.4	14.3	-50.0	50.0	-6.7	200.0	0.0	0.0	0.0	0.0	0.0	13.3
% 1970-1983	28.9	482.8	147.8	214.1	-12.0	-66.3	57.1	21.1	100.0	-649.5	106.2	88.9
Uganda*												
1970	43	7	3	0	14	6	7	13	-2	-7	2	14
1980	49	1	1	7	18	4	6	15	1	-5	2	14
1983	44	1	-3	8	16	0	3	15	6	-5	2	12
% 1970-1980	14.0	-85.5	-65.6	-700.0	29.4	-32.3	-13.2	16.2	147.8	29.5	4.7	0.0
% 1980-1983	-10.2	0.0	-400.0	14.3	-11.1	-100.0	-50.0	0.0	500.0	0.0	0.0	-14.3
% 1970-1983	2.3	-85.5	-203.1	-800.0	15.0	-100.0	-56.6	16.2	147.8	29.5	4.7	-14.3
Yemen, Arab Republic (N)*												
1970	NA	NA	NA	NA	NA	NA	NA	NA	NA	NA	NA	NA
1980	26	0	-4	-1	-10	9	1	9	3	20	-2	10
1983	48	5	0	11	-7	8	1	9	3	20	-2	21
% 1970-1980	NA	NA	NA	NA	NA	NA	NA	NA	NA	NA	NA	NA
% 1980-1983	84.6	500.0	100.0	1200.0	30.0	-11.1	0.0	0.0	0.0	0.0	0.0	110.0
% 1970-1983	NA	NA	NA	NA	NA	NA	NA	NA	NA	NA	NA	NA
Yemen, PDR (S)*												
1970	37	5	6	-6	-11	9	4	11	4	18	-3	17
1980	52	9	1	2	0	14	3	9	0	16	-2	22
1983	39	10	2	2	-4	3	3	9	0	16	-2	17
% 1970-1980	40.5	83.3	-83.1	132.8	100.0	57.1	-23.3	-17.5	-100.0	-10.7	35.3	29.4
% 1980-1983	-25.0	11.1	100.0	0.0	-400.0	-78.6	0.0	0.0	0.0	0.0	0.0	-22.7
% 1970-1983	5.4	103.7	-66.2	132.8	63.9	-66.3	-23.3	-17.5	-100.0	-10.7	35.3	0.0

NOTES:

1. Readers familiar with the Index of Social Progress (ISP) and Index of Net Social Progress (INSP) country scores that were reported in earlier versions of this research (Estes, 1984a) should not confuse those indexes with the current ISP83 or the WISP. Earlier versions of the ISP, for example, made use of 11 subindexes whereas the ISP83 is formed out of only 10. Similarly, WISP scores reflect separately weighted and summed scores for all countries. Refer to Appendix B of the present volume for a fuller explanation of the differences between the various indexes.

2. Index scores do not always add up evenly because of subindex rounding.

3. In computing WISP scores factor loadings obtained in 1983 were applied to all three of the weighted indexes.

Asterisks indicate LDCs.

Table A.2
Country Rankings on the Index and Subindexes of Social Progress, 1983 Only
($n = 124$)

COUNTRY	INDEX OF SOCIAL PROGRESS (ISP)	Education	Health	Women	Defense	Economic	Demographic	Geographic	Participation	Cultural	Welfare	WEIGHTED INDEX OF SOCIAL PROGRESS
Afghanistan*	120.00	117.33	117.25	118.25	82.20	65.20	123.00	56.04	112.08	78.14	92.14	121.00
Albania	46.33	38.17	34.17	63.33	82.20	30.00	31.17	24.25	112.08	53.14	34.25	45.25
Algeria	66.50	74.13	75.25	88.25	41.06	65.20	87.11	78.05	86.11	44.11	34.25	73.33
Angola	124.00	92.17	107.33	103.33	120.00	111.14	96.08	56.04	112.08	112.50	113.08	122.00
Argentina	36.25	26.14	34.17	7.33	41.06	124.00	37.25	56.04	46.50	17.09	33.00	31.25
Australia	16.00	10.13	22.17	37.10	41.06	17.20	14.09	99.20	1.07	17.09	19.33	15.00
Austria	4.00	10.13	13.11	22.13	7.05	9.13	2.13	43.08	1.07	11.17	3.00	4.50
Bangladesh*	109.00	109.25	100.25	109.17	25.06	70.05	87.11	122.50	66.13	17.09	113.08	103.33
Belgium	9.50	10.13	5.13	15.33	57.07	17.20	2.13	24.25	1.07	74.33	4.33	8.25
Benin*	97.50	98.00	104.50	106.33	41.06	96.17	109.13	43.08	95.05	96.25	49.10	103.33
Bolivia	73.50	64.10	87.17	56.14	41.06	111.14	81.17	56.04	35.50	100.33	70.14	78.50
Brazil	41.50	48.10	59.20	66.25	2.20	70.05	54.20	104.17	37.33	1.10	24.33	44.00
Bulgaria	25.00	10.13	5.13	18.25	102.25	17.20	10.25	9.14	112.08	62.08	17.50	24.50
Burkina-Faso*	105.50	123.00	121.00	92.20	41.06	70.05	87.11	43.08	46.50	105.33	49.10	111.50
Burma	78.33	103.00	71.25	74.13	57.07	40.11	59.11	56.04	112.08	85.25	82.10	82.50
Burundi*	105.50	113.25	115.50	116.50	57.07	65.20	81.17	4.50	86.11	96.25	77.20	113.50
Cameroon	90.50	88.25	93.20	70.25	25.06	70.05	87.11	35.13	86.11	122.00	70.14	94.33
Canada	18.00	2.50	13.11	37.10	25.06	5.50	14.09	99.20	1.07	85.25	27.33	16.50
Cen African Rep!	107.50	104.20	107.33	106.33	25.06	87.11	65.14	95.25	84.50	112.50	49.10	106.33
Chad*	122.00	124.00	122.50	123.50	41.06	70.05	75.17	56.04	95.05	121.00	59.09	123.00
Chile	49.00	26.14	44.13	47.11	82.20	111.14	31.17	104.17	66.13	53.14	19.33	41.33
China	77.00	48.10	52.25	70.25	106.25	22.20	122.00	118.33	86.11	34.10	77.20	70.33
Colombia	36.25	44.25	56.33	30.14	7.05	55.10	50.25	99.20	29.25	53.14	39.17	38.33
Congo, PR	84.00	85.33	64.25	74.13	57.07	87.11	72.33	56.04	95.05	110.50	45.25	81.00
Costa Rica	28.50	33.20	28.17	30.14	2.20	118.33	41.33	43.08	1.07	34.10	45.25	30.00
Cuba	43.50	6.20	13.11	22.13	96.20	31.11	14.09	28.14	86.11	78.14	49.10	35.00
Czechoslovakia	23.00	26.14	13.11	10.33	96.20	22.20	25.25	6.33	95.05	71.33	15.50	24.50
Denmark	1.00	6.20	2.00	47.11	41.06	7.50	2.13	1.00	1.07	1.10	1.50	3.00
Dominican Rep.	36.25	88.25	68.33	18.25	7.05	55.10	59.11	19.20	16.11	34.10	59.09	45.25
Ecuador	46.33	38.17	71.25	37.10	7.05	87.11	54.20	110.50	25.25	62.08	34.25	49.50
Egypt, UAR	65.00	82.33	59.20	97.33	102.25	70.05	59.11	78.05	54.11	28.17	59.09	66.50
El Salvador	57.00	92.17	71.25	88.25	72.10	87.11	65.14	14.20	48.10	28.17	49.10	68.50
Ethiopia*	123.00	120.50	122.50	118.25	106.25	55.10	96.08	43.08	112.08	117.25	109.50	124.00
Finland	14.00	10.13	34.17	37.10	7.05	17.20	2.13	56.04	25.25	11.17	22.50	16.50
France	6.00	21.20	3.50	7.33	72.10	9.13	14.09	24.25	16.11	34.10	4.33	6.00
Germany, Dem.	22.00	33.20	5.13	22.13	96.20	9.13	10.25	9.14	112.08	28.17	14.00	22.50
Germany, FDR	3.00	1.00	13.11	18.25	57.07	5.50	2.13	28.14	16.11	17.09	1.50	1.50
Ghana	101.25	92.17	98.50	103.33	2.20	122.00	81.17	35.13	66.13	117.25	82.10	106.33
Greece	21.00	58.17	3.50	30.14	96.20	40.11	14.09	56.04	16.11	1.10	27.33	20.00
Guatemala	89.00	99.25	75.25	92.20	41.06	49.17	65.14	122.50	74.25	78.14	82.10	85.00
Guinea*	121.00	109.25	114.00	118.25	87.11	102.33	117.25	104.17	112.08	105.33	45.25	120.00
Haiti*	85.00	113.25	87.17	103.33	7.05	70.05	54.20	95.25	95.05	17.09	99.20	89.50
Honduras	62.50	64.10	75.25	70.25	72.10	70.05	81.17	115.50	37.33	17.09	82.10	62.25

Table A.2 (cont.)

COUNTRY	INDEX OF SOCIAL PROGRESS (ISP)	Education	Health	Women	Defense	Economic	Demographic	Geographic	Participation	Cultural	Welfare	WEIGHTED INDEX OF SOCIAL PROGRESS
Hong Kong	36.25	48.10	22.17	66.25	7.05	22.20	29.50	104.17	37.33	28.17	77.20	36.50
Hungary	20.00	18.33	22.17	15.33	72.10	22.20	14.09	2.50	80.25	44.11	15.50	21.00
India	78.33	99.25	79.50	97.33	57.07	49.17	124.00	113.00	29.25	85.25	59.09	84.00
Indonesia	56.00	58.17	81.25	5.50	72.10	31.11	75.17	78.05	54.11	93.33	77.20	59.00
Iran	64.00	48.10	68.33	88.25	82.20	2.33	72.33	121.00	74.25	68.33	38.00	60.50
Iraq	99.50	64.10	59.20	56.14	124.00	1.00	87.11	35.13	95.05	53.14	59.09	70.33
Ireland	8.00	18.33	1.00	30.14	25.06	31.11	31.17	35.13	1.07	1.10	4.33	8.25
Israel	53.00	4.50	28.17	5.50	122.00	109.50	41.33	28.14	25.25	74.33	39.17	31.25
Italy	2.00	10.13	5.13	1.33	41.06	27.33	10.25	14.20	16.11	1.10	7.33	1.50
Ivory Coast	87.50	88.25	85.50	92.20	7.05	87.11	109.13	43.08	54.11	117.25	49.10	91.00
Jamaica	31.00	33.20	44.13	10.33	7.05	102.33	46.25	28.14	29.25	34.10	92.14	36.50
Japan	15.00	21.20	13.11	1.33	7.05	17.20	14.09	118.33	1.07	1.10	30.33	8.25
Jordan	59.00	48.10	52.25	10.33	114.33	40.11	75.17	56.04	86.11	11.17	99.20	56.00
Kampuchea	110.33	122.00	117.25	92.20	72.10	70.05	65.14	95.25	112.08	34.10	113.08	111.50
Kenya	86.00	48.10	81.25	74.13	25.06	96.17	117.25	56.04	54.11	114.33	92.14	86.50
Korea, Dem. (N)	75.00	92.17	34.17	15.33	117.00	49.17	46.25	99.20	112.08	17.09	113.08	62.25
Korea, Rep. (S)	52.00	48.10	40.25	47.11	87.11	31.11	31.17	110.50	66.13	17.09	92.14	51.00
Laos PDR*	110.33	74.13	124.00	83.20	72.10	40.11	75.17	56.04	112.08	100.33	113.08	109.50
Lebanon	101.25	88.25	87.17	109.17	41.06	102.33	96.08	104.17	54.11	103.50	104.20	98.20
Lesotho*	66.50	82.33	93.20	30.14	57.07	70.05	72.33	43.08	54.11	44.11	113.08	76.50
Liberia	32.50	26.14	44.13	1.33	102.25	40.11	37.25	24.25	48.10	68.33	49.10	29.00
Libya	82.50	58.17	44.13	97.33	118.50	49.17	96.08	78.05	86.11	17.09	82.10	76.50
Madagascar	72.00	85.33	75.25	66.25	25.06	105.50	87.11	56.04	80.25	62.08	49.10	78.50
Malawi*	116.50	117.33	117.25	106.33	25.06	70.05	121.00	35.13	95.05	78.14	109.50	118.50
Malaysia	55.00	26.14	40.25	74.13	87.11	31.11	46.25	35.13	41.25	110.50	82.10	57.50
Mali*	118.00	113.25	115.50	122.00	41.06	96.17	96.08	78.05	95.05	93.33	49.10	117.00
Mauritania	115.00	109.25	100.25	109.17	87.11	111.14	81.17	115.50	95.05	44.11	49.10	106.33
Mauritius	32.50	33.20	44.13	37.10	1.00	55.10	31.17	2.50	33.00	103.50	59.09	41.33
Mexico	51.00	48.10	40.25	37.10	2.20	70.05	65.14	104.17	41.25	62.08	59.09	54.00
Mongolia	76.00	74.13	52.25	56.14	110.00	87.11	44.50	112.00	112.08	53.14	113.08	68.50
Morocco	68.50	74.13	81.25	92.20	102.25	96.17	75.17	28.14	48.10	34.10	39.17	73.33
Mozambique	116.50	104.20	110.25	83.20	57.07	118.33	96.08	78.05	95.05	78.14	113.08	115.00
Nepal*	92.00	109.25	110.25	109.17	7.05	70.05	81.17	43.08	41.25	89.25	104.20	103.33
Netherlands	9.50	4.50	5.13	47.11	57.07	9.13	2.13	28.14	1.07	53.14	7.33	8.25
New Zealand	13.00	21.20	13.11	22.13	25.06	27.33	14.09	78.05	1.07	44.11	10.25	13.50
Nicaragua	87.50	48.10	71.25	63.33	111.00	123.00	87.11	118.33	66.13	44.11	70.14	80.00
Niger*	110.33	117.33	110.25	123.50	2.20	65.20	109.13	78.05	78.50	85.25	70.14	113.50
Nigeria	78.33	85.33	87.17	100.33	41.06	55.10	109.13	14.20	29.25	123.00	82.10	88.00
Norway	7.00	6.20	22.17	47.11	57.07	2.33	2.13	78.05	1.07	1.10	10.25	7.00
Pakistan	97.50	113.25	85.50	116.50	87.11	55.10	96.08	78.05	84.50	71.33	82.10	98.20
Panama	40.00	26.14	40.25	30.14	7.05	70.05	44.50	56.04	48.10	44.11	45.25	41.33
Papua-New Guin.	81.00	74.13	93.20	83.20	7.05	70.05	65.14	114.00	25.25	105.33	111.00	82.50
Paraguay	45.00	74.13	44.13	47.11	25.06	40.11	50.25	56.04	54.11	17.09	39.17	49.50

187

Table A.2 (cont.)

COUNTRY	INDEX OF SOCIAL PROGRESS (ISP)	Education	Health	Women	Defense	Economic	Demographic	Geographic	Participation	Cultural	Welfare	WEIGHTED INDEX OF SOCIAL PROGRESS
Peru	73.50	58.17	79.50	56.14	87.11	111.14	59.11	117.00	35.50	89.25	39.17	66.50
Philippines	62.50	64.10	59.20	82.00	25.06	49.17	54.20	95.25	54.11	108.00	70.14	62.25
Poland	24.00	38.17	28.17	22.13	87.11	31.11	29.50	4.50	66.13	17.09	24.33	26.00
Portugal	19.00	21.20	28.17	47.11	57.07	87.11	25.25	9.14	16.11	1.10	30.33	22.50
Romania	26.00	44.25	28.17	22.13	82.20	9.13	25.25	6.33	95.05	34.10	24.33	27.00
Rwanda‡	82.50	99.25	107.33	88.25	7.05	40.11	117.25	6.33	86.11	68.33	92.14	92.50
Saudi Arabia	101.25	74.13	64.25	109.17	121.00	55.10	96.08	78.05	95.05	1.10	92.14	86.50
Senegal	93.00	104.20	100.25	115.00	25.06	109.50	87.11	43.08	45.00	96.25	59.09	97.00
Sierra Leone‡	113.50	104.20	117.25	109.17	25.06	70.05	109.13	28.14	54.11	109.00	104.20	116.00
Singapore	43.50	38.17	22.17	47.11	87.11	9.13	14.09	43.08	48.10	78.14	82.10	38.33
Somalia‡	119.00	120.50	106.00	118.25	106.25	111.14	109.13	78.05	112.08	11.17	99.20	118.50
South Africa	60.00	92.17	59.20	74.13	72.10	49.17	59.11	35.13	66.13	96.25	30.33	62.25
Spain	17.00	48.10	5.13	30.14	25.06	31.11	14.09	9.14	16.11	60.50	17.50	18.50
Sri Lanka	41.50	58.17	56.33	37.10	7.05	40.11	37.25	14.20	34.00	78.14	70.14	45.25
Sudan‡	95.00	99.25	93.20	100.33	25.06	105.50	96.08	56.04	54.11	89.25	112.00	98.20
Sweden	5.00	2.50	13.11	22.13	57.07	9.13	2.13	56.04	1.07	11.17	10.25	4.50
Switzerland	11.00	21.20	5.13	37.10	25.06	2.33	1.00	43.08	1.07	71.33	19.33	13.50
Syria	61.00	44.25	44.13	74.13	112.00	22.20	75.17	19.20	78.50	62.08	99.20	60.50
Taiwan	68.50	64.10	34.17	4.00	123.00	27.33	41.33	43.08	54.11	28.17	59.09	45.25
Tanzania‡	94.00	64.10	87.17	56.14	41.06	87.11	109.13	56.04	86.11	124.00	104.20	94.33
Thailand	46.33	44.25	64.25	56.14	72.10	31.11	46.25	9.14	41.25	44.11	92.14	52.50
Togo‡	99.50	82.33	100.25	83.20	41.06	107.50	96.08	35.13	95.05	114.33	77.20	98.20
Trinidad/Tobago!	34.50	33.20	34.17	56.14	57.07	55.10	31.17	14.20	16.11	93.33	70.14	38.33
Tunisia	50.00	58.17	64.25	74.13	41.06	65.20	54.20	19.20	54.11	11.17	39.17	55.00
Turkey	54.00	64.10	56.33	70.25	106.25	87.11	50.25	56.04	40.00	28.17	99.20	57.50
USSR	58.00	6.20	28.17	22.13	113.00	31.11	50.25	99.20	95.05	117.25	27.33	52.50
Uganda‡	107.50	104.20	110.25	74.13	7.05	118.33	96.08	19.20	74.25	114.33	104.20	109.50
United Kingdom	12.00	18.33	13.11	18.25	87.11	9.13	10.25	56.04	1.07	53.14	7.33	12.00
United States	27.00	10.13	5.13	14.00	101.00	7.50	37.25	124.00	1.07	34.10	34.25	18.50
Uruguay	28.50	38.17	44.13	7.33	57.07	96.17	14.09	43.08	74.25	62.08	10.25	28.00
Venezuela	30.00	26.14	52.25	13.00	7.05	55.10	59.11	78.05	16.11	44.11	59.09	31.25
Vietnam	70.50	64.10	68.33	47.11	72.10	55.10	65.14	78.05	95.05	60.50	113.08	73.33
Yemen, Arab	101.25	92.17	104.50	63.33	118.50	70.05	117.25	78.05	80.25	1.10	113.08	94.33
Yemen, PDR (S)	113.50	64.10	98.50	100.33	114.33	107.50	96.08	78.05	95.05	34.10	113.08	98.20
Yugoslavia	34.50	38.17	22.17	37.10	57.07	40.11	25.25	19.20	80.25	89.25	22.50	31.25
Zaire	90.50	64.10	93.20	83.20	7.05	121.00	87.11	56.04	95.05	100.33	59.09	92.50
Zambia	96.00	74.13	87.17	66.25	114.33	111.14	96.08	78.05	66.13	77.00	82.10	89.50
Zimbabwe	70.50	10.13	81.25	37.10	96.20	96.17	109.13	56.04	48.10	74.33	113.08	70.33

NOTE: See Table A.1 Notes.

APPENDIX B:

INDICATOR SOURCES AND OPERATIONAL DEFINITIONS

This appendix contains information concerning the sources and operational definitions of the 36 indicators that form the revised Index of Social Progress (ISP83). Readers interested in obtaining more detailed information concerning one or another set of these indicators should consult the primary data sources identified for the indicators.

EDUCATION SUBINDEX

Gross School Enrollment Ratio, First Level (+)

All ratios are expressed as percentages. The gross enrollment ratio is the total enrollment of all ages divided by the population of the specific age groups that correspond to the age groups of primary schooling. These statistics include both males and females, children aged 6 to 11 years and adults receiving education at the primary-school level.
Sources: UNESCO (1983), Table 3.2, pp. III–19 to III–70; UNESCO (1984), Table 3.2, pp. III–20 to III–70.

Pupil/Teacher Ratio, First Level (−)

The pupil/teacher ratio is based on UNESCO estimates that take into account the number of trained educators relative to the number of students enrolled in primary school programs.
Sources: UNESCO (1983), Table 3.4, pp. III–83 to III–106; UNESCO (1984), Table 3.4, pp. III–86 to III–107.

Percentage Adult Illiteracy (−)

Adult illiteracy is the percentage of persons aged 15 years and over who can neither read nor write.

Sources: UNESCO (1983), Table 1.3, pp. I–16 to I–23. UNICEF (1984), Table 4, pp. 118–19; Sivard (1985a), Table 3, pp. 39–41; Sivard (1985b), Table 3, pp. 38–43.

Percentage of Total GNP in Education (+)

The education estimate takes into account public and private expenditures at all levels of education—primary, secondary, and post-secondary, including vocational education.

Sources: UNESCO (1982), Table 4.1, pp. IV–5 to IV–21; UNESCO (1984), Table 4.1, pp. IV–5 to IV–21; Sivard (1985b), Table 3, pp. 38–43.

HEALTH STATUS SUBINDEX

Male Life Expectancy at Birth (+)

Life expectation at birth indicates the number of years a newborn infant would live if patterns of mortality prevailing for all people at the time of its birth were to stay the same throughout its life. Data are from the UN Population Division, supplemented by World Bank estimates (World Bank, 1985:231).

Sources: World Bank (1984), Table 23, pp. 262–63; World Bank (1985), Table 23, pp. 218–19; United Nations (1983), Table 20, pp. 71–77; United Nations (1984), Table 21, pp. 438–65; UNICEF (1985), Table 1, pp. 112–13.

Rate of Infant Mortality Per 1,000 Live-Born (−)

The infant mortality rate is the number of infants who die before reaching one year of age, per thousand live births in a given year.

Sources: World Bank (1982), Table 21, pp. 150–51; UNICEF (1984), Table 5, pp. 120–21; World Bank (1984), Table 23, pp. 262–63; World Bank (1985), Table 23, pp. 218–19; Sivard (1985b), Table 3, pp. 38–43.

Population in Thousands Per Physician (−)

These estimates were derived from World Health Organization (WHO) data, some of which have been revised to reflect new information. They also take into account revised estimates of population (World Bank, 1985:239).

Sources: World Bank (1983), Table 24, pp. 194–95; World Bank (1984), Table 24, pp. 264–65; World Bank (1985), Table 24, pp. 220–21; Sivard (1985b), Table 3, pp. 38–43.

Per Capita Daily Calorie Supply as a Percentage of Requirement (+)

The daily calorie supply per capita was calculated by dividing the calorie equivalent of the food supplies in an economy by the population.

The daily calorie requirement per capita refers to the calories needed to sustain a person at normal levels of activity and health, taking into account age and sex distributions, average body weights, and environmental temperatures. Both sets of estimates are from the Food and Agricultural Organization (World Bank, 1985:240).

Sources: World Bank (1983), Table 24, pp. 194–95; World Bank (1984), Table 24, pp. 264–65; World Bank (1985), Table 24, pp. 220–21; Sivard (1985b), Table 3, pp. 38–43.

WOMEN'S STATUS SUBINDEX

Percentage Age-Eligible Girls Attending First-Level Schools (+)

Indicates the percentage of girls aged 6 to 11 that are enrolled in primary schools. When not otherwise available , estimates of age-eligible girls are based on the percentage of all females, including women, enrolled in programs of primary education within the particular country.

Sources: UNESCO (1983), Table 3.2, pp. III–19 to III–70; UNESCO (1984), Table 3.2, pp. III–20 to III–70; World Bank (1985), Table 25, pp. 222–23.

Percentage Adult Female Illiteracy (−)

The percentage of females aged 15 years and older who can neither read nor write.

Sources: UNESCO (1983), Table 1.3, pp. I–16 to I–23; UNESCO (1984), Table 1.3, pp. I–16 to I–23; UNICEF (1984), Table 1, pp. 112–13; Sivard (1985a), Table 1, pp. 35–37.

Age of Constitutional Document or Most Recent Amendment Affecting the Legal Rights of Women (+)

The constitutional documents used are those available as of December, 1984 in the compendium *Constitutions of the Countries of the World* [A. P. Blaustein and

G. H. Flanz, eds. (Dobbs Ferry, NY: Oceania Publications, 1984)]. In some cases, however, this compendium does not reflect the most recent amendments, suspensions, and so on. More recent constitutions were used when available. Countries not listed . . . are those whose constitutions do not have provisions relevant to this indicator, those whose constitutions are suspended or unavailable, and countries in which there is conflict as to which constitution is legitimate (IPPF, 1985).

"Age of document" for the two time periods of this study was computed by subtracting document date provided by IPPF et al. from 1983 to 1980, respectively.

Sources: International Planned Parenthood Federation, (1985); Cairns (1985).

DEFENSE EFFORT SUBINDEX

Military Expenditures as a Percentage of GNP (−)

The meaning of the ratio of military expenditures to GNP differs somewhat between most communist countries and non-communist countries. For non-communist countries, both military expenditures and GNP are converted from the national currency unit to dollars at the same exchange rate. . . . For communist countries, however, military expenditures and GNP are computed differently (USACDA, 1985:141–42).

Sources: World Bank (1983), Table 26, pp. 198–99; U.S. Arms Control and Disarmament Agency (1985), Table 1, pp. 47–88; Sivard (1985b), Table 2, pp. 35–36.

ECONOMIC SUBINDEX

Per Capita Gross National Product in Dollars (+)

Gross national product (GNP) measures the total domestic and foreign output claimed by residents. It comprises gross domestic product (GNP) adjusted by net factor income from abroad. That income comprises the income residents receive from abroad for factor services (labor, investment, and interest) less similar payments made to nonresidents who contributed to the domestic economy. It is calculated without making deductions for depreciation. . . . The GNP *per capita* figures were calculated according to the newly revised *World Bank Atlas* method (World Bank, 1985:230).

Sources: World Bank (1981), Table 1, pp. 134–35; World Bank (1982), Table 1, pp. 110–11; UNICEF (1984), Table 6, pp. 122–23; UNICEF (1985), Table 1, pp. 112–13; World Bank (1985), Table 1, pp. 174–75.

GNP Per Capita Average Growth Rate (Percent) (+)

The formula used in calculating these statistics takes into account current GNP (local currency) for the years indicated; GNP deflator for the years shown; annual average exchange rate (local currency/U.S. dollars) for the period; mid-year population size for the period; and U.S. GNP deflator for the base year. For a more detailed explanation of the methods used in calculating these statistics see World Bank (1985:231).

Sources: World Bank (1981), Table 1, pp. 134–35; World Bank (1982), Table 1, pp. 110–11; UNICEF (1984), Table 6, pp. 122–23; UNICEF (1985), Table 6, pp. 123–24; World Bank (1985), Table 1, pp. 1974–75.

Average Annual Rate of Inflation (−)

The *average annual rate of inflation* is the least squares growth rate of the implicit gross domestic product (GDP) deflator, for each of the periods shown. . . . This measure of inflation, like any other measure of inflation, has limitations. For some purposes, however, it is used as an indicator of inflation because it is the most broadly based deflator, showing annual price movements for all goods and services produced in the economy" (World Bank, 1985:231).

Sources: World Bank (1982), Table 1, pp. 110–11; UNICEF (1984), Table 6, pp. 122–23; World Bank (1985), Table 1, pp. 174–75.

Average Index of Per Capita Food Production (+)

This indicator shows the average annual quantity of food produced *per capita* for the base years in relation to that produced using an earlier base period as a statistical constant.

The estimates were derived from those of the Food and Agricultural Organization (FAO), which are calculated by dividing indices of the quantity of food production by indices of total population. For this index, food is defined as comprising cereals, starchy roots, sugar cane, sugar beet, pulses, edible oils, nuts, fruits, vegetables, livestock, and livestock products. Quantities of food production are measured net of animal feed, seeds for use in agriculture, and food lost in processing and distribution (World Bank, 1985:233).

Sources: World Bank (1982), Table 1, pp. 110–11; UNICEF (1984), Table 2, pp. 114–15; World Bank (1985), Table 6, pp. 184–85.

External Public Debt as a Percentage of GNP (−)

External public debt outstanding and disbursed represents the amount of public and publicly guaranteed loans that has been disbursed, net of repayments of principal and write-offs at year-end. For estimating external public debt as a percentage of GNP, the debt figures were converted into U.S. dollars from currencies of repayment at end-of-year official exchange rates. . . . The summary measures are weighted by GNP in current dollars (World Bank, 1985:236).

Sources: World Bank (1982), Table 15, pp. 138–39; World Bank (1985), Table 16, pp. 204–5.

DEMOGRAPHIC SUBINDEX

Total Population (Millions) (−)

Based on mid-year estimates, sample surveys, and, in some cases, complete censuses undertaken by nations and reported to the United Nations and other international demographic data-collecting organizations.

Sources: World Bank (1982), Table 1, pp. 110–11; United Nations (1984), Table 5, pp. 151–55; World Bank (1985), Table 19, pp. 210–11; UNICEF (1985), Table 5, pp. 120–21.

Crude Birth Rate Per 1,000 Population (−)

Indicates the number of live births per 1,000 population in a year.

Sources: World Bank (1982), Table 18, pp. 144–45; World Bank (1985), Table 20, pp. 212–13; United Nations (1985), Table 20, pp. 71–77; UNICEF (1985), Table 5, pp. 120–21.

Crude Death Rate Per 1,000 Population (−)

Indicates the number of deaths per 1,000 population in a year.

Sources: World Bank (1982), 18, pp. 144–45; World Bank (1985), Table 20, pp. 212–13; United Nations (1985), 20, pp. 71–77; UNICEF (1985), Table 5, pp. 120–21.

Rate of Population Increase (−)

The number of persons added to a population per 1,000 persons already in that population, ignoring immigration.

Sources: World Bank (1982), Table 17, pp. 142–43; World Bank (1985), Table 19, pp. 210–11; UNICEF (1985), Table 5, pp. 129–31.

Percentage of Population Under 15 Years (−)

Computed by dividing total number of persons in a country 15 years of age and younger by total population of that country.

Sources: United Nations (1982), Table 7, pp. 208–36; United Nations (1985), Table 7, pp. 188–253; Lane, (1984).

GEOGRAPHY SUBINDEX

Percentage Arable Land Mass (+)

Includes arable land and land permanently planted in crops, plus permanent meadows and pastures, divided by total country area.
Sources: Sivard (1985b), Table 2, 135–37.

Natural Disasters Vulnerability Index, 1947–1979 (−)

A major disaster is defined as "one that meets at least one of the following criteria: (1) a minimum of $1 million property damage; (2) a minimum of 100 persons dead; (3) a minimum of 100 persons injured" (Regulska, 1980:1). Natural disasters include floods, *tsunamis*, earthquakes, hurricanes, landslides, and so on.

In constructing this index, the total number of natural disasters occurring over the period 1947–1979 was divided by 32, the number of years for which observations were made. The Vulnerability Index score that results from this calculation relfects a national average annual number of natural disaster impacts.

Note: Raw score values for this indicator are reported in Estes (1984a), Appendix C.

Sources: Regulska (1980). Missing data estimated for selected countries on the basis of subregional analyses undertaken by Reed (1981:17–21).

Average Annual Fatalities from Major Natural Disasters Per Million Population (−)

Reports loss of life from disaster impacts by country and by deaths divided by million persons in the population during year of event occurrence.

Note: Raw score values for this indicator are reported in Estes (1984a), Appendix C.

Sources: Regulska (1980). Missing data estimated for selected countries computed on the basis of subregional analyses undertaken by Reed (1981:17–21).

POLITICAL PARTICIPATION SUBINDEX

Violations of Political Rights Index (−)

Political rights are primarily the rights to participate directly or through freely elected representatives in the determination of the nature of law and its administration in a society. In a large modern state this apparently requires competing political parties and ideally several tiers of elected government. The effectiveness of the political equality promised by the system varies from society to society and can never be perfect. But if reasonably extended by experience and law, and judicially protected, a multiparty democracy provides the nearest approximation to political equality that is attainable—and only political equality respects the dignity of each individual (Gastil, 1984:4).

The scale uses the numbers 1 to 7, with 1 representing the highest level of political rights and 7 the lowest.

Sources: Gastil (1984), Table 1, pp. 12–15; Table 9, pp. 457–65.

Violations of Civil Liberties Index (−)

Civil liberties include in the first place those freedoms that make possible the organization and mobilization of new, alternative, or non-official opinions. They include freedom of the news media, and of political, professional, worker, peasant, and other organizations. Civil liberties imply that there should be no prisoners of conscience, and certainly no execution and torture for the expression of beliefs or the organization of opposition where these are not directly related to violence against the system.... Civil liberties extend beyond these more political domains to questions such as religious freedom and freedom of residence. It can be argued that without the autonomous individuality such freedoms imply, the other civil liberties cannot be fully developed (Gastil, 1984:4–5).

The scale uses the numbers 1 to 7, with 1 representing the highest level of civil rights and 7 the lowest.

Source: Gastil (1984), Table 9, pp. 457–65; Table 1, pp. 12–15.

Composite Violations of Human Freedoms Index (−)

This index reflects a composite rating based on national averages attained on the civil liberties and political rights indexes. States are rated as either "free" (1), "partly free" (2), or "not free" (3). For a discussion of how this index was developed, see Gastil (1984: 19, 22).

Source: Gastil (1984), Table 9, pp. 457–65; Table 1, pp. 12–15.

CULTURAL DIVERSITY SUBINDEX

Largest Percentage Sharing Same Mother Tongue (+)

Percentages calculated from absolute figures.... Where censuses ... list bilinguals separately, these have been added to the speakers of the non-official languages.... (Rustow, 1967: 284).

Sources: Rustow (1967), pp. 284–86; Lane (1984), pp. 515–600; U.S. Department of State (1981–85).

Largest Percentage Sharing Same Basic Religious Beliefs (+)

These data are estimates only. Percentages are based on the number of persons in a country affiliated with a particular religious tradition, divided by the size of that country's population.

Sources: Delury (1979), pp. 513–98; Bacheller (1980), pp. 504–710; Lane (1984), pp. 515–600; U.S. Department of State (1981–85).

Largest Percentage Sharing Same or Similar Racial/Ethnic Group Origins (+)

Indicates largest proportion of the population that share the same or similar ethnic or racial group origins as measured by racial and/or ethnic group stock, tribal affiliations, cultural traditions, and the like. These data are estimates only. Percentages are based on the number of persons in country divided by the size of that country's population.

Sources: Bacheller (1980), pp. 504–710; Lane (1984), pp. 515–600; U.S. Department of State (1981–85).

WELFARE EFFORT SUBINDEX

"First Law" is usually the first consolidated compulsory legislation extending protection against a specific risk to a substantial segment of the salaried labor force on an industrywide or nationwide basis, rather than to a particular occupational group such as seamen, miners, bank employees, and so on (USDHHS, 1984, p. viii).

Years Since First Law—Old Age, Invalidity, Death (+)

Includes programs that provide pensions or lump-sum payments to help replace the income loss resulting from old age, from permanent retirement, from a permanent or continuing and more or less total disablement, or from the death of a working provider.

Source: United States Department of Health and Human Services (1984, 1986).

Years Since First Law—Sickness and Maternity (+)

Includes: (1) cash benefits to replace wages lost as a result of relatively short-term sickness of non-occupational origin; (2) cash benefits to replace wages lost during maternity leave; and (3) medical benefits in the event of either of these contingencies.

Source: United States Department of Health and Human Services (1984, 1986).

Years Since First Law—Work Injury (+)

Includes social security programs that provide cash payments and medical care during periods of temporary disability resulting from a work injury or occupational disease or illness.

Source: United States Department of Health and Human Services (1984, 1986).

Years Since First Law—Unemployment (+)

Often structured independently of other social security measures, these programs provide cash benefits and reemployment services to claimants and beneficiaries. Such programs are typically linked with other employment services (e.g., career assessment, jobs location, training and retraining, and so on).

Source: United States Department of Health and Human Services (1984, 1986).

Years Since First Law—Family Allowance (+)

Family allowances are primarily regular cash payments to families with children. In some countries, these programs also include school grants, birth grants, maternal and child health services, and sometimes allowances for adult dependents. These programs are closely integrated with other social security measures in some countries; in others, they are entirely separate.

Source: United States Department of Health and Human Services (1984, 1986).

APPENDIX C:

INDEX AND SUBINDEX COMPUTATIONAL NOTES

INDEX COMPUTATIONAL NOTES

Index and subindex scores were computed in six steps: (1) computation of measures of central tendency and dispersion; (2) transformation of indicator raw scores into standardized units of measurement; (3) alteration of the directionality of indicators so as to correctly reflect indicator positive and negative effects on changes in adequacy of social provision; (4) computation of unweighted subindex scores; (5) computation of aggregated Index of Social Progress (ISP83) scores; and (6) computation of the Weighted Index of Social Progress (WISP) scores. All statistical work was completed using SYSTAT, a statistical package designed for use on personal computers, and LOTUS 1–2–3.

Step 1. Computation of Measures of Central Tendency and Dispersion

Raw score means, standard derivations, variance and other measures of central tendency and dispersion were computed for all 108 indicator observations (three observations for each of 36 indicators—1970, 1980, and 1983). The results of these computations are summarized in Table C–6.

Step 2. Raw Score Transformation into Standardized Units of Measurement

Indicator raw score values were transformed from variable units of measurement (e.g., rates per 1,000, dollars, grams, percentages, ratios,

Table C.1
Illustration of Raw Score Transformation into Standardized Z-Scores, China, 1983

Indicator	Raw Score (X_i)	Country-group Mean Score (X_i-M)	Standard Deviation (SD)	Z-Score
Rate of Infant Mortality per 1,000 Live-Born	38.0	71.6	51.1	−0.655
Population in Thousands per Physician	1.7	8.5	13.0	−0.524
Life Expectancy at 1 Year, Males	65.0	58.8	10.8	0.578
Per Capita Daily Calorie Supply as % of Requirement	109.0	110.8	19.7	−0.092

and so on), into standardized units of measurement (Z-scores) using the following formula: $(x_i - M/SD)$, where x_i is the original value of the ith case; M is the mean of the variable; and SD is the standard deviation. Z-scores generate a new variable with a group means of O and a group standard deviation of 1 (see Blalock, 1979). Inasmuch as Z-scores are premised on the mathematical assumptions of the normal distribution, Z-scores for an individual nation reflect the relative position of that nation along the horizontal of the normal curve, that is, in units of standard deviations from the group mean of 0 (−3, −2, −1, 0, +1, +2, +3, etc.).

Table C.1 illustrates the Z-score data standardization procedure as applied to the health subindex for China (1983).

Table 3.1 reports raw score values for all ISP indicators by year and by development grouping. The percentage of change in these indicators over the study period's 14 years is summarized in Table 3.2.

Step. 3. Directionality of Indicators

The directional signs of many ISP variables had to be altered so that social progress "gains" and "losses" along these indicators could be properly aggregated into overall ISP and subindex scores. In the above health subindex Z-scores illustration for China, for example, both "rate of infant mortality (−)" and "population in thousands per physician (−)" are stated so that decreases in the numbers reported for these indicators actually reflect *increases* in overall level of national social provision; that is, lower rates of infant mortality and lower patient caseloads for physicians are assessed more favorably than are higher rates of infant mortality or higher patient–physician caseloads. By design, approximately half ($n = 18$) of the 38 ISP indicators reflect gains in social progress by decreasing numerically rather than increasing (see Table 2.1 for the directional signs of all ISP and subindex indicators).

So as to accurately reflect gains and losses in social progress over time, however, Z-score values obtained for inversely stated indicators were multiplied by a constant value of -1. In effect, this procedure altered only the mathematical sign of these indicators and not their numerical value. In the data transformation illustration for China, for example, the signs of the first two indicators were reversed so that the Z-score values of these indicators could be properly subtracted from and added to composite ISP scores (e.g., from -0.655 to $+0.655$, -0.524 to $+0.524$). The mathematical sign of the Z-score for "life expectancy" remained unchanged since increases in this indicator correctly reflect positive increases in level of social progress. This procedure was repeated for all inversely stated ISP indicators as part of the statistical procedures required to compute subindex scores (see Step 4 for subindex formulae).

Step 4. Computation of Subindex Scores

Three arithmetic steps were required to compute subindex scores:

a. The mathematical signs of negatively stated directional indicators were reversed for the reasons and in the manner described in Step 3 above;
b. The unweighted Z-score values of all subindex indicators were totaled; and then
c. The sum of the Z-scores was divided by the number of indicators contained in the subindex (three for the health subindex, five for the women's status subindex, etc.).

The formula used to compute the scores for the health subindex illustrates the procedures used in the computation of all ten subindexes of the ISP83:

ZHLTH83 = (((ZMALE83 + (-1 * ZINFAN83) + (-1 * ZPHYS83) + (ZCALO83))/4)

In the SYSTAT statistical program, an asterisk (*) is used to indicate multiplication and a slash (/) is used to indicate division. Thus, in the above formula the program was instructed to multiply ZINF80 (infant mortality rate) and ZPHYS80 (population in thousands per physician) by a constant value of -1 (i.e., to reverse the directionality sign of the indicator), then to sum the total of the four indicators and then to divide the sum of the Z-score values of the four subindex indicators by 4, that is, the number of indicators contained in the subindex.

These formulae provided summed subindex scores that are really statistical averages of the various indicators—ranging in number from one to five—that make up the various ISP83 subindexes. For example, the 1983 health subindex score for China equals 0.416: $(((+0.655) + (+0.524) + (+0.578) + (-0.092))/4) = +0.416$. In this way, each of the ten ISP83 subindexes contributes exactly 10.0 percent to a given nation's composite ISP83 scores (i.e., 100% / 10 subindexes = 10.0%).

The size and numbers resulting from the various Z-score transformations and summations of steps (a) through (c) proved to be too small for them to be conveniently handled, even within a computer. Also, addition of the subindex Z-score averages resulted in negative subindex scores for approximately one-half of the 124 nations included in the study (e.g., health subindex range = -1.180 to $+0.350$; mean = 0.000).

In order to solve the dual problems of number size and awkwardness, and to eliminate negative mathematical signs from ISP83 subindex scores, two additional computational steps were performed:

d. composite subindex scores were multiplied by a constant value of +10, thereby reducing the awkwardness of the numbers to be handled by increasing their size; and

e. a constant of +10 was *added* to each subindex score, which for the majority of countries with negative subindex scores, converted their score from a negative to a positive value.

Again, health subindex scores for China (1983) illustrate the computational effect of these procedures. Where

$$HLSUB83 = ((ZHLTH83 * 10) + 10)$$

then for China (1983)

$$STNHL83 = ((+0.416 * 10) + 10)$$
$$= ((4.160) + 10)$$
$$= +14.160$$

The subindex transformations that resulted from these procedures resulted in subindex scores that could be more readily understood and handled mathematically. Table 4.1 reports subindex scores for all nations for each of the three time periods of the study. The scores reported in that table were obtained using the statistical procedures just described.

Table C.2
Index of Social Progress (ISP83) Score for China by Subindex, 1983

Subindex	Unstandardized Subindex Scores	Standardized Subindex Scores
1. Education	0.21	12.1
2. Health status	0.42	14.2
3. Women's status	-0.11	8.9
4. Defense effort	-0.45	5.5
5. Economic	0.57	15.7
6. Demography	-1.13	-1.3
7. Geography	-1.33	-3.3
8. Political participation	-0.85	1.5
9. Cultural diversity	0.58	15.8
10. Welfare effort	-0.44	5.6
Total ISP83 Score		74.7

Step 5. Computation of Composite Index of Social Progress (ISP83) Scores

Index of Social Progress (ISP83) scores were computed through simple addition of the ten unweighted, but standardized, subindex scores. Thus, ISP83 scores for 1983 equal

ISP83 = (health subindex score for 1983 + education subindex score for 1983 + welfare subindex score for 1983 + ... etc.)

Two of the ten ISP83 subindexes were used as statistical constants for both 1980 and 1983, that is, the geographic and the cultural diversity subindexes. Consequently, the subindex scores on these subindexes are identical for both 1980 and 1983. Readers interested in examining country raw score values for the indicators included in the geographic subindex are referred to Table C.1 reprinted in Estes (1984a: 198–209).

The results of these calculations are illustrated in Table C.2, which reports 1983 subindex and composite ISP83 scores for China (1983).

Step 6. Weighted Index of Social Progress (WISP) Scores

Standardization of the ISP83 into the *Weighted* Index of Social Progress (WISP) occurred in four steps: (1) a factor analysis was conducted for the purpose of identifying the principal ISP83 components (i.e., "factors"); (2) the standardized subindex scores of each nation were then multiplied by the factor loading with which each subindex was most associated; (3) the weighted standardized subindexes were then summed and subsequently multiplied by the percentage of variance that each factor contributed to the explanation of total ISP83 variance; finally (4) the statistically weighted subindexes were summed to obtain total Weighted Index of Social Progress (WISP) scores. The following sections contain more complete descriptions of these computational steps.

6a. The Derivation of Index Statistical Weights Through Factor Analysis

Factor analysis was used to identify the appropriate system of statistical weights that best reflected the influence of each subindex on the study's unifying construct of "adequacy of national social provision." In carrying out the factor analysis a principal component analysis with varimax rotation was undertaken (see Bailey, 1982: 373–79; and Dunteman, 1984: 156–204, for an explanation of the methodology of factor analysis; and Adelman and Morris, 1967, for an example of factor analysis applied to scale construction in comparative political and economic analysis). As seen in the rotated factor loadings reported in Table C.3, this analysis confirmed the multidimensional nature of the ISP83 and identified the index's principal components (i.e., those factors with eigenvalues of at least 1.0 and which, separately, explained at least 10 percent of the total variance contained in the ISP83 but which, together, account for at least 65 percent of the total variance).

As expected, the three principal ISP83 components are associated with changes over time in the adequacy of human services provided by nations (Factor 1), patterns of national defense expenditures (Factor 2), and national patterns of natural disasters and the loss of human life associated with those disasters (Factor 3). Together, these three factors account for 73.3 percent of the total variance of the ISP83.

6b. Weighting the Subindexes

The subindex factor "loadings" obtained from the analysis reported above were used to weight each of the ISP83 subindexes:

WISP 1 = (.94 * HEALTH SUB + .88 * DEMOGRAPHIC SUB + .88 *
         EDUCATION SUB + .75 * WELFARE SUB + .83 * WOMAN

Table C.3
Varimax Factor Loading Matrix for ISP83 Subindexes, 1983

Subindex	Factor 1	Factor 2	Factor 3
Health	0.94	0.01	-0.00
Demographic	0.88	-0.19	0.19
Education	0.88	-0.05	0.03
Welfare effort	0.75	-0.31	0.23
Women's status	0.83	0.06	0.02
Political participation	0.62	-0.52	-0.16
Economic	0.65	0.14	0.12
Cultural diversity	0.60	0.21	-0.36
Defense effort	-0.09	-0.92	0.04
Geographic	0.15	0.02	0.93
Latent roots (eigenvalues)	4.89	1.32	1.12
Percentage of total variance explained by the factor	48.88	13.23	11.20

$$\text{SUB} + .62 * \text{PARTICIPATION SUB} + .65 * \text{ECONOMICS SUB} + .60 * \text{CULTURAL SUB})$$
$$\text{WISP 2} = (.92 * \text{DEFENSE SUB})$$
$$\text{WISP 3} = (.93 * \text{GEOGRAPHIC SUB})$$

The values that resulted from these formulae resulted in adjusted raw score subindex values that better reflected the differential contribution of each subindex to an explanation of the total variance associated with the "adequacy of social provision" concept. The use of these weighted subindex scores also provided a more accurate basis for the inclusion of each subindex into the overall ISP83 measure. Table C.4 illustrates the impact of this weighting procedure on ISP83 adjusted subindex scores for China (1983).

6c. Computing Weighted Index of Social Progress Scores

The final step in arriving at Weighted Index of Social Progress (WISP) scores was to combine the weighted scores of subindexes associated with a particular factor into a composite index. Inasmuch as each factor accounts for a different portion of the total variance of the ISP83, however, a new formula was constructed. Thus, inasmuch as Factor 1 explained 48.8 percent of ISP83 variance, it was assigned a weight of .667 (i.e., Factor 1 explains 66.7 percent of all of the variance explained by the three factors taken together), Factor 2 was assigned a weight of .180 and Factor 3 was assigned a weight of .153. The use of factor weights in this way has the effect of lowering the proportional impact of the defense effort and geographic subindexes on the overall Weighted Index of Social Progress scores. Consequently, the following formula was used in constructing final scores on the WISP for each of the three time periods studied:

$$WISP83 = ((.667 * WISP1) + (.180 * WISP2) + (.153 * WISP\,3))$$

For China, application of the formula resulted in the following WISP score for 1983:

$$WISP83 = ((.667 * 54.4) + (.18 * 5.1) + (.153 * -3.1))$$
$$WISP = 36.7 = 37$$

Table C.5 shows the percentage relative contribution of each subindex to the aggregated WISP scores.

OTHER COMPUTATIONAL NOTES

Table C.6 reports measures of central tendency and dispersion for all indexes and subindexes; Table C.7 is a correlation matrix of Pearson correlation coefficients for the study's various indexes and subindexes.

Table C.4
Impact of Statistical Weighting on Subindex Scores, China, 1983

Subindex	Unweighted Standardized Scores	Factor Analysis Weight	Weighted Standardized Score
Factor 1			
Health	14.2	.94	13.3
Demographic	-1.3	.88	-1.1
Education	12.1	.88	10.6
Welfare effort	5.6	.75	4.2
Women's status	8.9	.83	7.4
Participation	1.5	.62	0.9
Economic	15.7	.65	10.2
Cultural diversity	15.8	.60	9.5
Factor 2			
Defense effort	5.5	.92	5.1
Factor 3			
Geographic	-3.3	.93	-3.1

Table C.5
Percentage Contribution of ISP83 Subindex Scores to Weighted Index of Social Progress (WISP) Scores

Subindex	Factor Loading	Factor Weight	Percent of Subindex Contributed to WISP Scores
Health	.94	.667	.63
Demographic	.88	.667	.59
Education	.88	.667	.59
Welfare effort	.75	.667	.50
Women's status	.83	.667	.55
Participation	.62	.667	.41
Economic	.65	.667	.43
Cultural	.60	.667	.40
Defense effort	.92	.180	.17
Geographic	.93	.153	.14
Average Contribution of Each Subindex (%)			44.1

Table C.6
Measures of Central Tendency and Dispersion on the Standardized Indexes and Subindexes of Social Progress by Year ($n = 124$)

Subindex	Modal year	Measures of central tendency	SD	Minimum	Maximum
				Measures of dispersion	
Education	1970	10.0	8.0	− 7.0	24.0
	1980	10.0	7.0	− 8.0	24.0
	1983	10.0	7.0	−10.0	25.0
Health	1970	10.0	9.0	−17.0	20.0
	1980	10.0	9.0	−12.0	24.0
	1983	10.0	9.0	−12.0	24.0
Women's Status	1970	10.0	8.0	− 6.0	28.0
	1980	10.0	7.9	− 4.2	28.8
	1983	10.0	7.9	− 5.8	27.1
Defense effort	1970	10.0	10.0	−49.0	18.0
	1980	10.0	9.0	−37.0	19.0
	1983	10.0	9.0	−50.0	18.0
Economics	1970	10.0	6.0	−23.0	23.0
	1980	10.0	6.1	− 8.9	22.7
	1983	10.0	6.0	− 4.7	27.8
Demography	1970	10.0	7.0	−10.0	24.0
	1980	10.0	6.9	− 2.5	22.3
	1983	10.0	6.9	− 3.2	22.1
Geographic	1970	10.0	6.0	−20.0	19.0
	1980	10.0	5.6	−12.1	23.0
	1983	10.0	5.6	−12.1	23.0
Participation	1970	10.0	6.0	− 2.0	33.0
	1980	10.0	9.7	− 1.9	25.5
	1983	10.0	9.8	− 1.7	25.4
Cultural	1970	10.0	9.0	−12.0	21.0
	1980	10.0	8.3	−10.5	20.2
	1983	10.0	8.3	−10.5	20.2
Welfare effort	1970	10.0	9.0	− 3.0	30.0
	1980	10.0	9.0	− 1.5	28.9
	1983	10.0	8.0	− 2.0	28.8
ISP83	1970	100.0	49.9	19.0	196.0
	1980	100.0	53.0	− 8.0	208.0
	1983	100.0	52.0	− 5.0	207.0
WISP83	1970	44.5	25.6	2.8	94.5
	1980	44.1	26.5	−10.0	93.8
	1983	44.1	26.0	− 5.7	93.1

Table C.7
Pearson Correlation Matrix of Standardized Index and Subindex Scores, 1983 Only ($n = 124$)

Subindex	EDUC	HLTH	WOMEN	DEF	ECON	DEMO	GEO	PART	CULT	WELF	ISP83	WISP83
Education	1.00											
Health	0.86	1.00										
Women's Status	0.78	0.77	1.00									
Defense Effort	-0.05	-0.07	-0.11	1.00								
Economics	0.46	0.55	0.38	-0.12	1.00							
Demography	0.73	0.82	0.70	0.11	0.56	1.00						
Geographic	0.14	0.13	0.15	0.02	0.11	0.27	1.00					
Participation	0.56	0.53	0.46	0.26	0.30	0.55	0.01	1.00				
Cultural	0.37	0.53	0.41	-0.15	0.31	0.44	-0.06	0.28	1.00			
Welfare Effort	0.62	0.67	0.49	0.17	0.49	0.75	0.25	0.51	0.32	1.00		
ISP83	0.82	0.88	0.76	0.23	0.59	0.90	0.26	0.71	0.53	0.82	1.00	
WISP83	0.87	0.93	0.81	0.09	0.62	0.91	0.19	0.68	0.56	0.81	0.99	1.00

Note: Correlation coefficients greater than .17 are significant at the $p < .05$ level of confidence with 124 degrees of freedom.

BIBLIOGRAPHY

Abelson, Philip. 1987. "World Food." *Science* (April 3) 231: 9.

Adelman, I., and C. T. Morris. 1967. *Society, Politics, and Economic Development: A Quantitative Approach.* Baltimore, MD: Johns Hopkins University Press.

American Public Health Association. 1985. "The Health Effects of U.S. Militarism." *The Nation's Health*, September, pp. 23–25.

Bacheller, Martin A., ed. 1980. *The Hammond Almanac, 1981.* Maplewood, NJ: Hammond Almanac.

Bailey, Kenneth D. 1982. *Methods of Social Research.* New York: The Free Press.

Barclay, William, et al. 1976. *Racial Conflict, Discrimination, and Power: Historical and Contemporary Studies.* New York: AMS Press.

Blalock, Hubert M. 1979. *Social Statistics*, 2d ed. New York: McGraw-Hill.

Brandt, Willy. 1984. "The North–South Challenge." *World Press Review*, June, p. 21.

Brown, Lester R. 1985. "Stopping Population Growth." In *State of the World, 1985*, edited by Lester R. Brown. New York: W. W. Norton.

Burstein, P. 1985. *Discrimination, Jobs, and Politics: The Struggle for Equal Employment.* Chicago, IL: University of Chicago Press.

Cairns, Gail, et al. 1985. *Women: Progress Toward Equality.* London: International Planned Parenthood Foundation.

Camp, Sharon L., and Joseph Speidel. 1987. *The International Human Suffering Index.* Washington, D.C.: Population Crisis Committee.

Center for Defense Information. 1983. *The World at War.* Washington, D.C: Center for Defense Information.

Claudon, P. 1985. *World Debt Crisis.* New York: Ballinger.

Cloward, Richard, and Frances Fox Piven. 1971. *Regulating the Poor: The Functions of Public Welfare.* New York: Pantheon.

Cuny, Frederick C. 1983. *Disasters and Development.* Oxford: Oxford University Press.

Delamaide, D. 1985. *Debt Shock: The Full Story of the World Debt Crisis*. New York: Doubleday.

Delury, George E., ed. 1979. *The World Almanac and Book of Facts. 1980*. New York: Newspaper Enterprise Association.

Dickenson, J. P., et al. 1983. *A Geography of the Third World*. New York: Methuen.

Dixon, John. 1986. *Social Security Traditions and Their Global Applications*. Belconnen, Australia: International Fellowship for Social and Economic Development.

Dornbusch, Rudiger, and Stanley Fischer. 1986. "Third World Debt." *Science* 234:836–41.

Dunteman, George H. 1984. *Introduction to Multivariate Analysis*. Beverly Hills, CA: Sage Publications.

Duodu, Cameron. 1985. "The IMF's African Nightmare." *South* (July):31–38.

Eckholm, Erik. 1984. "Fatal Disasters on the Rise: Increased Peril Attributed to Unwise Land Use and Poverty." *New York Times*, July 31, pp. C2-C3.

Ehrlich, Paul, and Anne Ehrlich. 1972. *Ecoscience: Population, Resources, and Environment*. San Francisco, CA: W. H. Freeman.

Erikson, Robert, et al., eds. 1987. *The Scandinavian Model: Welfare States and Welfare Research*. Armonk, NY: M. E. Sharpe.

Estes, Richard J. 1983. "Education for Comparative Social Welfare Research." In *Education for International Social Welfare*, edited by Daniel S. Sanders. Honolulu, HI: A Joint Publication of the Council on Social Work Education and the University of Hawaii School of Social Work.

———. 1984a. *The Social Progress of Nations*. New York: Praeger.

———. 1984b. "World Social Progress: 1968–1978." *Social Development Issues* 8:54–63.

———. 1986. "Trends in European Social Development," *Europe* (November).

———. 1987a. "Beyond Famine Relief: The Continuing Crisis in Development." *International Journal of Contemporary Sociology*, 24:27–42.

———. 1987b. "Toward a Quality of Life Index." In *The Third World: States of Mind and Being*, edited by James Norwine and Alfonso Gonzalez. London: George Allen & Unwin.

Fidel, Kenneth, ed. 1975. *Militarism in Developing Nations*. New Brunswick, NJ: Transaction Books.

Flora, Peter, and Arnold J. Heidenheimer, eds. 1981. *The Development of Welfare States in Europe and America*. New Brunswick, NJ: Transaction Books.

Foreign Affairs Committee of the House of Commons. 1985. *Famine in Africa*. London: Her Majesty's Stationery Office.

Forrester, Jay W. 1973. *World Dynamics*, 2d ed. Cambridge: Wright-Allen Press.

Fuchs, Victor R. 1986. "Sex Differences in Economic Well-Being." *Science* 232:459–64.

Gastil, Raymond D. 1984. *Freedom in the World: Political Rights and Civil Liberties*. Westport, CT: Greenwood Press.

———, ed. 1986. *Freedom in the World: Political Rights and Civil Liberties, 1983–1984*. Westport, CT: Greenwood Press.

Gauhar, Altaf. 1982. "The Hidden Costs of the Arms Race." *South* (July):7–14.

———. 1985. *The Rich and the Poor: Development, Negotiations, and Cooperation*. Boulder, CO: Westview.

Giliomee, H., and L. Schlemmer. 1985. *Up Against the Fences: Poverty, Passes, and Privilege in South Africa.* New York: St. Martin's.

Gilliam, Dorothy. 1987. "Third World Strategies." *Washington Post*, April 6, p. D3.

Grant, James P. 1984. *State of the World's Children, 1985.* New York: Oxford University Press, for the United Nations Children's Fund.

Hadler, Sandra. 1976. *Developing Country Food Grain Projections for 1985.* Washington, D.C.: World Bank, Staff Working Paper no. 247.

Harden, Blaine. 1986. "Severe Famine Forecast in Africa's Future." *Washington Post*, September 7, pp. A21, A24.

———. 1987. "AIDS Seen as Threat to Africa's Future." *Washington Post*, May 31, pp. A1, A18.

Hardiman, Margaret, and James Midgley. 1982. *The Social Dimensions of Development: Social Policy and Planning in the Third World.* Chichester: John Wiley and Sons.

Heckler, Margaret M. 1985. *Report of the Secretary's Task Force on Black and Minority Health*, vol. 1. Washington, D.C.: Department of Health and Human Services.

Horowitz, Louis Irving. 1966. *Three Worlds of Development: The Theory and Practice of International Stratification.* New York: Oxford University Press.

Humana, Charles. 1986. *World Human Rights Guide.* New York: Facts on File Publications.

Hunger Project. 1985. *Ending Hunger: An Idea Whose Time Has Come.* New York: Praeger.

Independent Commission on International Development Issues (Willy Brandt, Chair). 1980. *North–South: A Program for Survival.* Cambridge, MA: MIT Press.

International Food Policy Research Institute. 1977. *Food Needs of Developing Countries: Projections of Production and Consumption to 1990.* Washington, D.C.

International Labour Office. 1983. *The Cost of Social Security*, 11th ed. Geneva.

International Planned Parenthood Federation. 1985. *Women: Progress toward Equality.* London: IPPF.

International Women's Tribune, 1983. *Rights of Women: A Workbook of International Conventions Relating to Women's Issues and Concerns.* Santo Domingo, Dominican Republic: International Women's Tribune.

Jimenez, Emmanuel. 1987. *Pricing Policy in the Social Sectors: Cost Recovery for Education and Health in Developing Countries.* Baltimore, MD: Johns Hopkins University Press, for the World Bank.

Katz, Michael. 1986. *In the Shadow of the Poorhouse: A Social History of Welfare in America.* New York: Harper & Row.

Kittle, Robert A., and Robert F. Black. 1984. "U.S. Again World's No. 1 Arms Merchant." *U.S. News and World Report*, May 28, p. 59.

Krugman, P. 1985. "International Debt Strategies in an Uncertain World." In *International Debt and the Developing Countries*, edited by G. Smith and J. Cuddington. Washington, D.C.: World Bank, pp. 79–100.

Landskron, William A., ed. 1983. *Annual Review of United Nations Affairs, 1982.* Dobbs Ferry, NY: Oceana Publications.

Lane, Hana U., ed. 1984. *The World Almanac and Book of Facts, 1985*. New York: Newspaper Enterprise Association.

MacFarlane, S. 1985. *Superpower Rivalry and Third World Radicalism*. Baltimore, MD: Johns Hopkins University Press.

"Malaysia: Moving Into the Big League." 1985 *South* (September):215–28.

Mayson, C. 1985. *A Certain Sound: The Struggle for Liberation in Southern Africa*. New York: Orbis.

Mellor, John W., and Sarah Gavian. 1987. "Famine: Causes, Prevention, and Relief." *Science* (January 30):539–45.

Morawetz, David. 1977. *Twenty-Five Years of Economic Development: 1950–1975*. Baltimore, MD: Johns Hopkins University Press, for the World Bank.

Morris, A. 1986. *The Origins of the Civil Rights Movement: Black Communities Organizing*. New York: The Free Press.

Morris, Morris D. 1979. *Measuring the Conditions of the World's Poor*. New York: Pergamon.

"Natural Disasters: The Human Connection." 1986. Cox Newspaper Special Report.

Netter, Thomas. 1986. "Food Outlook Poor in 6 African Nations." *New York Times*, April 21, p. A3.

Organization for Economic Cooperation and Development. 1981. *The Welfare State in Crisis: An Account of the Conference on Social Policies in the 1980s*. Paris.

———. 1985. *Social Expenditures, 1960–1990: Problems of Growth and Control*. Paris.

Owens, Edgar, and Robert Shaw. 1974. *Development Reconsidered: Bridging the Gap Between Government and People*. Lexington, MA: Lexington Books.

Perrin, Jacques. 1984. "The Production of Know-How and Obstacles to its Transfer." *Prospects* 14:479–85.

Perrow, Charles. 1984. *Normal Accidents: Living With High-Risk Technologies*. New York: Basic Books.

Persaud, Wilberne H. 1981. "Technology Transfer: Conceptual and Development Issues." *Social and Economic Studies* 3:1–17.

Poats, Rutherford M., chair. 1985. *Twenty-Five Years of Development Cooperation: A Review*. Organization for Economic Cooperation and Development.

Podesta, Don. 1987. "Ethnic Conflicts: Toll Mounts." *Washington Post*, May 26, pp. A1, A17.

Reed, John L. 1981. "A Comparative Analysis of Natural Disasters." Masters of Social Work Thesis. Philadelphia: University of Pennsylvania School of Social Work.

Regulska, Joanna. 1980. *Global Trends in Natural Disasters*. Denver, CO: Natural Hazard Research Institute, University of Colorado.

Rein, Martin, and Lee Rainwater. 1986. *Public/Private Interplay in Social Protection: A Comparative Study*. Armonk, NY: M. E. Sharpe.

Rimlinger, Gaston. 1971. *Welfare Policy and Industrialization in Europe, America, and Russia*. New York: John Wiley.

Rudov, Melvin, and Nancy Santangelo. 1979. *Health Status of Minorities and Low Income Groups*. Washington, D.C.: Department of Health, Education, and Welfare.

Ruggie, Mary. 1984. *The State of Working Women: A Comparative Study of Britain and Sweden*. Princeton: NJ: Princeton University Press.

Rustow, Dankwart A. 1967. *A World of Nations: Problems of Political Modernization*. Washington, D.C.: Brookings Institution.

Schaefer, Richard T. 1984. *Racial and Ethnic Groups*, 2d ed. Boston, MA: Little, Brown & Co.

Schneider, Keith. 1986. "Scientific Advances Lead to Era of Food Surplus Around the World." *New York Times*, September 9, pp. C1, C10.

Schuler, Margaret. 1987. *Empowerment and the Law: Strategies of Third World Women*. Washington, D.C.: OEF International, 1986.

Sivard, Ruth L. 1985. *Women. A World Survey*. Washington, D.C.: World Priorities.

———. 1985b. *World Military and Social Expenditures, 1985*. Washington, D.C.: World Priorities.

Stockholm International Peace Research Institute. 1986. *World Armaments and Disarmament, 1986*. Stockholm.

Stockwell, Edward G., and Karen A. Laidlow. 1981. *Third World Development: Problems and Prospects*. Chicago, IL: Nelson-Hall.

Thompson, Leonard. 1986. *The Political Mythology of Apartheid*. New Haven, CT: Yale University Press.

Tinbergen, Jan. 1976. *Reshaping the International Order: A Report to the Club of Rome*. New York: E. P. Dutton.

UNESCO (United Nations Educational, Scientific, and Cultural Organization). 1982. *Statistical Yearbook, 1982*. Paris.

———. 1983. *Statistical Yearbook, 1983*. Paris.

———. 1984. *Statistical Yearbook, 1984*. Paris.

UNICEF (United Nation's Children's Fund). 1984. *The State of the World's Children, 1984*. New York: Oxford University Press.

———. 1985. *Statistical Yearbook, 1985*. Paris.

———. 1987. *The State of the World's Children, 1987*. New York: Oxford University Press, for UNICEF.

United Nations. 1977. *World Economic Survey, 1976*. New York. Sales no. E/5995/Rev.1.

———. 1978a. *Human Rights: A Compilation of International Instruments*. New York. Sales no. E.78.XIV.2.

———. 1978b. *Economic and Social Consequences of the Arms Race and of Military Expenditures: Updated Report of the Secretary-General*. New York. Sales no. E.78.IX.1.

———. 1979. *1978 Report on the World Social Situation*. New York. Sales nos. E.79.IV.1 and E.79.IV.3.

———. 1982. *Demographic Yearbook, 1981*. New York. Sales no. E/F82.XIII.1.

———. 1983. *Statistical Yearbook, 1981*. New York.

———. 1984. *Demographic Yearbook, 1982*. New York.

———. 1985a. *Demographic Yearbook, 1982*. New York.

———. 1985b. *Statistical Yearbook, 1983*. New York.

———. 1987a. *Demographic Yearbook, 1986*. New York.

———. 1987b. *The State of the World's Population*. New York.

———. 1987c. *Yearbook of Human Rights*. New York.

United Nations International Research and Training Institute for the Advancement of Women. 1984. *Compiling Social Indicators on the Situation of Women.*
New York. Sales no. E.84.XVII.2.

United States Arms Control and Disarmament Agency (USACDA). 1983. *World
Military Expenditures and Arms Transfers, 1971–1980.* Washington, D.C.

———. 1985. *World Military Expenditures and Arms Transfers, 1972–1983.* Washington, D.C. Publication no. 59.

United States Department of Commerce. 1987. *Statistical Abstracts of the United
States, 1987.* Washington, D.C.: Government Printing Office.

United States Department of Health and Human Services (USDHHS). 1984. *Social
Security Programs Throughout the World, 1983.* Washington, D.C.: Social
Security Administration. Research report no. 59.

———. 1986. *Social Security Programs Throughout the World, 1985.* Washington,
D.C.: Social Security Administration.

United States Department of State. 1981–85. *Background Notes.* Washington, D.C.:
Bureau of Public Affairs Series.

Van Oudenaren, John. 1984. *The Soviet Union and Eastern Europe: Options for the
1980s and Beyond.* Santa Monica, CA: Rand Corporation.

Vennhoven, Ruut. 1984. *Conditions of Happiness.* Hingham, MA: Kluwer Boston
Academic Publishers.

Wallender, Harvey W. 1979. *Technology Transfer and Management in Developing
Countries: Company Cases and Policy Analyses in Brazil, Kenya, Korea, Peru,
and Tanzania.* Cambridge, MA: Ballinger.

Ward, Barbara, ed. 1971. *The Widening Gap: Development in the 70s.* New York:
Columbia University Press.

Wijkman, Anders, and Lloyd Timberlake. 1984. *Natural Disasters: Acts of God or
Acts of Man?* Washington, D.C.: Earthscan.

Wilensky, Harold. L. 1975. *The Welfare State and Equality.* Berkeley, CA: University of California Press.

Wolf, Charles Jr., 1985. "The Costs of the Soviet Empire." *Science* (November
29): 997–1002.

Women: A World Report. 1985. Oxford: Oxford University Press.

World Bank. 1981. *World Development Report, 1981.* New York: Oxford University
Press.

———. 1982. *World Development Report, 1982.* New York: Oxford University
Press.

———. 1983. *World Development Report, 1983.* New York: Oxford University
Press.

———. 1984. *World Development Report, 1984.* New York: Oxford University
Press.

———. 1985. *World Development Report, 1985.* New York: Oxford University
Press.

———. 1986. *World Development Report, 1986.* Washington, D.C.: World Bank.

———. 1987a. *Financing Health Services in Developing Countries: An Agenda for
Reform.* Washington, D.C.: World Bank.

———. 1987b. *World Development Report, 1987.* Washington, D.C.: Oxford University Press, for the World Bank.

World Resources Institute. 1987. *World Resources, 1987.* New York: Basic Books.

Young, Harry F. 1983. *Atlas of U.S. Foreign Relations.* Washington, D.C.: U.S.
Department of State.

ABOUT THE AUTHOR

RICHARD J. ESTES, D.S.W., is Professor of Social Work and Director of Doctoral Education at the University of Pennsylvania in Philadelphia. He holds graduate degrees in social work from the University of Pennsylvania and the University of California at Berkeley. He also holds a post-master's Certificate in Psychiatric Social Work from the Menninger Foundation in Topeka, Kansas.

Dr. Estes' international activities have been extensive. He is president of the Philadelphia Area Chapter of the Society for International Development, a member of the International Committee of the Council on Social Work Education, and a board member of the North American Region of the International Council on Social Welfare, and currently serves as the North American representative on the International Program Planning Committees of the International Association of Schools of Social Work (Austria) and the Inter-University Consortium for International Social Development (Finland). Dr. Estes is also a Senior Fellow of the International Fellowship for Social and Economic Development (Australia).

Dr. Estes also has been the recipient of numerous awards and grants for his research on comparative social welfare, including two Fulbright-Hays Awards—as senior lecturer in fall 1978 to the Teheran, Iran, School of Social Work and, during spring 1979, as a senior researcher to the Institute for Advanced Social Work Education in Trondheim, Norway. He recently returned from two months of research field visits to the People's Republic of China, where he was appointed Honorary Research Professor to the Institute for Economic, Technical and Social Development Research of the State Council, China's most important policymaking body.

Dr. Estes' publications in comparative social development have been extensive. They include more than a dozen articles and research monographs on various aspects of international social development, as well as his 1984 volume entitled *The Social Progress of Nations* (New York: Praeger). His other books include *Health Care and the Social Services* and *Directory of Social Welfare Research Capabilities*. Dr. Estes consults broadly on international development topics in all areas of the world. He makes his home with his three daughters in Narberth, Pennsylvania.